Reminiscences

of

Vice Admiral Kent L. Lee

U.S. Navy (Retired)

Volume II

Copyright © 1990
U.S. Naval Institute
Annapolis, Maryland

Preface

In concluding the description of his naval career in this second volume, Admiral Lee devotes considerable attention to his two years in command of the USS Enterprise at a time when she was the only nuclear-powered aircraft carrier in the fleet. It was a job that offered virtually no respite, either mental or physical.

During the 1967-69 period described by Lee, the Enterprise made two combat deployments to Vietnam, ran a significant race with a Soviet nuclear-powered submarine, stirred protest while visiting Sasebo, Japan, lived through the seizure of the U.S. intelligence ship Pueblo, and suffered a devastating flight deck fire that took a considerable toll in both lives and property. Lee describes it all from the perspective of the man in charge. He tells of the fatiguing routine that included running the ship and her tactical formation off Vietnam, coping with the demands of Admiral Hyman Rickover and the news media, dealing with a succession of embarked carrier division commanders, and hosting a high-visibility visit from President Lyndon Johnson.

Before and after his afloat tour in the Enterprise, Lee served as an insider in the Navy secretariat in Washington, first as executive assistant to the Assistant Secretary of the Navy (Research and Development) and later as head of the Office of Program Appraisal for the Secretary of the Navy. As he talks about both jobs, Admiral Lee discusses their substance and also provides observations concerning the bureaucracy and personalities that influenced events of the time. His candid appraisals offer valuable insight into the period. For instance, he suggests that Admiral Thomas Moorer's approach to Secretary of the Navy John Chafee paved the way for Admiral Elmo Zumwalt to become Moorer's successor as Chief of Naval Operations, rather than someone more akin to Moorer's way of thinking.

In his first tour of duty as a three-star admiral, Lee returned to the Joint Strategic Target Planning Staff in Omaha, Nebraska. He had been there earlier as a relatively junior officer; now he was the top-ranking Navy man. When he arrived, the Navy representatives were still treated very much as second-class citizens by the Air Force officers of the Strategic Air Command. Part of Lee's legacy from that tour was to help build a more amicable working relationship between the services--cooperation rather than hostility.

The bulk of Lee's time as a flag officer was spent in the Naval Air Systems Command, first as assistant commander for maintenance and fleet support, finally as overall commander. In a way, these tours were the result of his youthful experiences as a farm boy and Navy airplane mechanic. Having in the meantime experienced naval aviation as a pilot and ship's captain, he now injected his concerns for maintenance and reliability at the highest level. He describes the vast NavAir bureaucracy and his need to go from one fire drill to another, including Grumman's continuing problems with the F-14 fighter. Finally, he tells of his considerable role in the genesis and development of the F/A-18 Hornet as a carrier-based tactical plane. Because of Lee's concerns, it is a reliable, maintainable airplane.

Throughout Admiral Lee's descriptions of his career are examples that define him as a man of character and integrity. His willingness to tell of that career in such a forthright and open manner makes this a particularly valuable oral history.

The transcription of the interviews contained in this volume was done by Ms. Joanne Patmore of the oral history staff. Admiral Lee and I both did a considerable amount of editing to the verbatim transcript in the interests of accuracy, conciseness, and clarity. This version has his full blessing. Mrs. Lee has also been of considerable help in the editorial process from raw transcript to finished volume. Ms. Susan Sweeney of the oral history department did the detailed index for the volume.

Paul Stillwell
Director of Oral History
U.S. Naval Institute
February 1990

VICE ADMIRAL KENT LISTON LEE
UNITED STATES NAVY (RETIRED)

Kent Liston Lee was born in Florence County, South Carolina, on 28 July 1923, son of R. Irby and Hettie Floyd Lee. He enlisted in the U.S. Navy on 15 August 1940 and became an aviation cadet (V-5) on 12 November 1942, entering the flight training program on that date. Completing flight training at the Naval Air Station, Corpus Christi, Texas, he was designated naval aviator and commissioned ensign, USNR, on 7 August 1943. He was promoted to lieutenant (junior grade) to date from 1 November 1944, and on 8 July 1946 was appointed in that rank in the U.S. Navy. He subsequently advanced in rank to that of vice admiral, to date from 29 January 1972.

After receiving his wings in 1943, he had duty at the Naval Air Station, Jacksonville, Florida, and the Naval Auxiliary Air Station, Cecil Field, Florida, until March 1944. He then joined Bombing Squadron 100 and in June 1944 transferred to Bombing Squadron 15, operating off the USS Essex (CV-9). On 19 August 1944 he was assigned temporary additional duty, to fly with Fighting Squadron 15, but remained on the roster of Bombing Squadron 15. He was awarded the Air Medal for participating in numerous strikes against enemy positions and shipping at Marcus and Wake in the Marianas, the Bonins, Palau, and Philippine Islands during the period 19 May to 24 September 1944, and a gold star in lieu of the second Air Medal for destroying an enemy plane in the vicinity of Formosa on 12 October 1944. He is also entitled to the ribbon for, and a facsimile of the Presidential Unit Citation awarded the USS Essex.

Detached from Bombing Squadron 15 in December 1944, he next joined Bombing Squadron 151, and in September 1945 transferred to Bombing Squadron 17. In August 1946 he was assigned to Attack Squadron 5B. Undergraduate instruction with the Naval Reserve Officer Training Corps unit, Columbia University, New York, New York, August 1947 until May 1949, was followed by a year's instruction at the General Line School, Newport, Rhode Island.

In May 1950, he reported for duty on the staff of Commander Carrier Division 15, and "for meritorious service as Flag Lieutenant and Aide . . . during operations against the enemy in the Korean Theater from August 3, 1950 to January 15, 1951 . . ." was awarded the Navy Commendation Medal. In February 1951, he transferred to the staff of Commander Carrier Division 17. Assigned in May 1951 to Attack Squadron 115, based on board the USS Philippine Sea (CV-47), he was awarded a gold star in lieu of the third Air Medal for completing 20 missions against enemy aggressor forces in the Korean area of hostilities during the period 8 February to 2 June 1952. He is also entitled to the ribbon with bronze star for the Navy Unit Commendations awarded the USS Badoeng Strait (CVE-116) and the USS Sicily (CVE-118).

Detached from Attack Squadron 115 in June 1952, he was a student for two months at the Naval Schools Command, Treasure Island, San Francisco, California, then continued his studies at the U.S. Naval Postgraduate School, Monterey, California, from which he received the degree of master of science in physics in June 1954. Duty with Air Development Squadron Three until April 1956 was followed by an assignment for duty in the Weapons Section, Fleet Training Center, Norfolk, Virginia. In May 1958, he assumed command of Attack Squadron 46, and in September 1959 became technical aide nuclear physics, Power Branch, Material Sciences Division, Office of Naval Research, Navy Department, Washington, D.C.

During the period November 1960 until March 1962, he served as operational planner, Single Integrated Operational Plan Division, Joint Strategic Target Planning Staff, Offutt Air Force Base, Nebraska. After a brief tour of duty on the staff of Commander Carrier Air Group Four, he assumed command of Carrier Air Group Six in June 1962, embarked in the USS Enterprise (CVAN-65). In 1962, he ejected from an A4D Skyhawk while participating in operations during the Cuban quarantine. From March 1963 until March 1964 he had instruction in Nuclear Propulsion at the Atomic Energy Commission, Washington, D.C. He next commanded the USS Alamo (LSD-33) and in May 1965 reported as executive assistant and naval aide to the Assistant Secretary of the Navy (Research and Development).

In July 1967, he assumed command of the USS Enterprise (CVAN-65) and from 3 January to 26 June 1968 also served as Commander Task Unit 77.1. He was awarded the Legion of Merit for the ". . . detailed planning and execution of extensive and sustained combat air strikes against extremely hostile and heavily defended areas in North Vietnam . . ." He is entitled to a facsimile of the Navy Unit Commendation awarded the USS Enterprise and is entitled to a second star on his Navy Unit Commendation Ribbon.

In August 1969, he was assigned to the Bureau of Naval personnel, Navy Department, and in November of that year reported as Assistant Commander for Logistics and Fleet Support, Naval Air Systems Command, Washington, D.C. He became Director of the Office of Program Appraisal, Navy Department in August 1970, and in January 1972 assumed duty as Deputy Director of the Joint Strategic Target Planning

Staff, Offutt Air Force Base, Nebraska. "For exceptionally meritorious conduct . . ." in that assignment, he was awarded a gold star in lieu of the Second Legion of Merit. The citation continues in part:

> ". . . Responsible for exercising direct supervision over the activities of the Joint Strategic Target Planning Staff, Vice Admiral Lee was highly influential in the formation of policy and in giving direction to the policies established by the Joint Chiefs of Staff (JCS) and the Director, Strategic Target Planning, leading to and governing the development and maintenance of the JCS Single Integrated Operational Plan and the Coordinated Reconnaissance Plan . . ."

On 31 August 1973, he became Commander Naval Air Systems Command, Washington, D.C., and held that billet until relieved on 31 October 1976. He was officially placed on the retired list of the U.S. Navy on 1 November 1976.

He was also awarded the Distinguished Service Medal for duty as Commander Naval Air Systems Command on 31 October 1976. His other awards include the Legion of Merit with gold star, the Air Medal with two gold stars, the Navy Commendation Medal, the Presidential Unit Citation Ribbon, and the Navy Unit Commendation Ribbon with two bronze stars, Vice Admiral Lee has the American Defense Service Medal; American Campaign Medal; Asiatic-Pacific Campaign Medal; World War II Victory Medal; National Defense Service Medal with bronze star; Korean Service Medal; United Nations Service Medal; Vietnam Service Medal; and the Philippine Liberation Ribbon. He also has the National Order of Vietnam Fifth Class, the Gallantry Cross with Palm from the Republic of Vietnam, the Philippine Republic Presidential Unit Citation Badge, and the Korean Presidential Unit Citation Badge.

He is married to the former Mary Edith Buckley, of Piedmont, California, and they have three daughters, Nancy Carolyn Lee, Barbara Ann Lee Eisenson, and Marion Denny Lee Leonard.

Authorization

The U.S. Naval Institute is hereby authorized to make available to libraries and other repositories of its choosing the transcripts of four oral history interviews concerning the life and career of Vice Admiral Kent L. Lee, U.S. Navy (Retired). The four interviews were recorded on 30 November 1987, 14 December 1987, 21 December 1987, and 21 November 1988 in collaboration with Paul Stillwell for the U.S. Naval Institute.

During the lifetime of the undersigned, permission must be obtained from the undersigned in order to cite or quote from the transcripts of the interviews in any published work. The tape recordings of the interviews are and will remain the sole property of the U.S. Naval Institute. The copyright in both the oral and transcribed versions of the interviews shall also be the sole property of the U.S. Naval Institute.

Signed and sealed this ___31st___ day of ___January___ 1990

_____
Vice Admiral Kent L. Lee,
U.S. Navy (Retired)

Interview Number 5 with Vice Admiral Kent L. Lee,
U.S. Navy (Retired)

Place: Logon Farm, Admiral Lee's home near Gordonsville, Virginia

Date: Monday, 30 November 1987

Interviewer: Paul Stillwell

Q: Admiral, the last time we met, you were about to describe the experience in the mid-1960s when the material bureaus were divested of their research laboratories.

Admiral Lee: At this particular time, I was aide to the Assistant Secretary of the Navy for Research and Development. The assistant secretary was a man by the name of Robert Morse, who was a Ph.D. in physics and was former professor of physics and dean at Brown University. One of the interesting items, during the course of my tour there, was the taking of the research facilities, namely the laboratories, away from the bureaus.

Through the years, the various bureaus--the Bureau of Ships, the Bureau of Aeronautics, the Bureau of Ordnance, even the Bureau of Supplies and Accounts--had built up laboratories. These laboratories were critical to the work of the bureaus. They helped with procurements; they helped with evaluating systems and weapons; they served on various boards. More important than any of that, they did basic and fundamental research in developing weapons of one type or another. Very often they would develop a weapon or a system, and it would then be put out for competition in procurement.

A typical example is the Sidewinder missile, which was invented by the technical director at China Lake, or, as it was called in those days, Naval Ordnance Test Station Inyokern. Sidewinder has been a great success. It was invented and developed in the early Fifties, went into production in the mid-Fifties, and for more than 30 years the Sidewinder missile has been one of the most reliable, one of the most effective, one of the most efficient and least costly missiles in our air-to-air arsenal. Later versions of it have even been used in surface-to-air work.

But the inventor of this Sidewinder missile was a very strong-minded individual who later became technical director of China Lake. In 1965 he had this job. He lined up the other technical directors of the Navy labs and, over a period of several months, lobbied and persuaded the Assistant Secretary of the Navy and the Secretary of the Navy, because the Secretary had to approve it, to take the laboratories away from the bureaus, and to set up a civilian director of Navy labs. Of course, the military, and for that matter the civilian bureaucracy in the various bureaus, were aghast at this, because the laboratories and the bureaus had worked as one for many years. The bureaus always supported the laboratories when it came time for funding. The laboratories got all their funding through the bureaus.

The technical director prevailed, and the laboratories were taken from the bureaus and set up under this civilian director of Navy laboratories. To this day that's the organization. The cooperation between the bureaus and the laboratories declined markedly after that. Very often the bureaus and project managers, program managers, rather than sending money to a laboratory to get work done, would find it easier to contract with one of the prime contractors than wrestling the bureaucracy which was set up to run the Navy laboratories. I think it was a great mistake, and I think it's hurt Navy research and development--and procurement, for that matter--to this day. But that's how it came about.

Q: Was that tied in at all with the initiative to do away with the bureaus themselves?

Admiral Lee: No. That was another issue. The chiefs of the various bureaus had limited statutory authority, and their appointments were statutory. During the McNamara era, the bureaus were abolished to get rid of that authority by law that the bureau chiefs had.* McNamara wanted to assume this authority. So the bureaus were

---
*Robert S. McNamara was Secretary of Defense from 1961 to 1968.

abolished, and in their place were substituted what were called the systems commands.* These are administrative organizations which have no statutory authority. Also, commanders of these organizations have no statutory authority. It was an administrative device to take away the authority of the chief of the bureau.

Q: Give him less autonomy.

Admiral Lee: Give him less autonomy. He had some authority in the contracting area, in the procurement area, which was statutory, in other words set up by the Congress, public law. Once these bureaus were abolished, of course, the law became meaningless, because these other administrative organizations were set up, and the laws didn't apply to them. That's why the bureaus were abolished.

Q: Interestingly, in the late Fifties, Aeronautics and Ordnance had been merged to form a Bureau of Naval Weapons, and now in the mid-Sixties, they were separated again into the Naval Ordnance Systems Command and the Naval Air Systems Command.**

---
*This change became effective 1 May 1966. For more detail, see Thomas W. Ray, "The Bureaus Go On Forever . . ." U.S. Naval Institute Proceedings, January 1968, pages 50-63.
**The merger of the Bureau of Ordnance and Bureau of Aeronautics became effective 1 December 1959.

Admiral Lee: Yes. That, also, was a mistake.

Q: Why do you say that?

Admiral Lee: Having had many tours in Washington and having endured many reorganizations, I can tell you that reorganizations are the most painful process ever to hit a bureaucracy. All work ceases for about six months to a year while the various Indians jockey for position.

That went on when the Bureau of Aeronautics was merged with the Bureau of Ordnance and became the Bureau of Naval Weapons. The idea was that, "Let's combine these two organizations, because a good part of the work done by the Bureau of Ordnance is for air so why not let's put it under one hat?" The powers that be were very unhappy at that time with the Bureau of Ordnance. But it was a great mistake. The Bureau of Aeronautics never really fully absorbed the Bureau of Ordnance.

To complete the story, at a later time a divorce took place. Three systems commands were established: Air, Ordnance, and Ship. Still later, in 1974, the Naval Ordnance Systems Command was once again abolished. A good part of it was merged with the Naval Ship Systems Command to form the Naval Sea Systems Command, and part of it was taken into the Electronics Systems Command, which had been set up in the meantime. So the Naval Ordnance Systems Command was an orphan for about 20 years, and that's one of the reasons it became so unproductive.

I was a party to some of those last shuffles. I tried to keep the Naval Air Systems Command out of it, because there's absolutely nothing worse for a big organization than a reorganization. Nothing. It's terrible on morale, no work gets done, and, of course, the things that the various engineers and division heads are battling for are their positions, their rice bowls, and that's number one. However you might look at it, I think Rickover was right in terms of how much of this is for me and how much is for the Navy. When it comes to the rice bowl, these fellows are going to look after their own interest about 99%, and that's what goes on in a reorganization. That's why they're so bad. I think organizations should be changed very slowly--a process of evolution rather than revolution. I've never seen a successful major reorganization.

Q: I think the rice bowl problem contributed to the creation of the Bureau of Naval Weapons when guided missiles came along. It was not clear whether they belonged in Aeronautics or Ordnance, so they were merged.

Admiral Lee: Yes, and the powers that be were unhappy with

Ordnance. That marriage never prospered. It was a sad period in the bureaus and in our technical communities in Washington, in my view.

Q: It's really ironic, too, because the Bureau of Ordnance was a kingpin in the Navy in the years before World War II.

Admiral Lee: I suppose you could look at it as the Gun Club, which was before my time. It ran the Navy for 30 or 40 years. This was the final defeat of the Gun Club, the abolishment of the Bureau of Ordnance. But even so, it was a mistake. It was all part and parcel of taking power away from the bureaus. This business of stripping the bureaus of their laboratories and setting up a technical director, so that the bureaus had no direct control over the laboratories, was all part of that.

Also, while I was in the assistant secretary's office, the F-111 brawl began to heat up. Of course, the assistant secretary was the Secretary's point man on this particular fight. As you might remember, McNamara had decreed that the Air Force and the Navy would have one airplane--the F-111. The Air Force would use it as a low-level attack plane--much like our A-6. The Navy would use it as a fighter.

The Navy fought tooth and nail--sometimes logically, sometimes illogically, sometimes emotionally--against the

F-111. While I was in this particular office, this fight was going on almost daily. Towards the end of my tour, McNamara himself took personal charge. The assistant secretary and the secretary, on many occasions, would go for a personal meeting with McNamara, to iron out the technical details of the two airplanes.

We even brought into the assistant secretary's office a very talented young officer that I had known on <u>Enterprise</u>. He was in the A-5 squadron. His name is George Jessen; he later became a rear admiral.* I thought he was one of the most talented young officers I had met. At this particular time, he had become an aeronautical engineering duty officer, an engineering specialist in aviation, and was over in the Bureau of Naval Weapons. We brought him over to the assistant secretary's office to be the assistant secretary's right-hand man for the F-111.

Q: Did you find yourself in a dilemma there, trying to support McNamara's idea on the one hand and serve the Navy's interests on the other?

Admiral Lee: Not really. I helped the assistant secretary in technical matters having to do with aviation. I really wasn't in the line of fire. OP-05, Admiral Connolly, and

---

*Commander George E. Jessen, USN.

the Naval Air Systems Command were involved.* They carried the fight. I, more or less, was running the office for the assistant secretary and making sure that he got and understood the various issues and papers. I never really was in the front lines on the F-111.

Q: Jerry Miller says that Admiral Connolly really sacrificed his fourth star in order to head up that fight.

Admiral Lee: I don't really believe that. I think Admiral Connolly was very well known as being pretty slippery. If Admiral Moorer had wanted to give Admiral Connolly a fourth star after McNamara left, he could have done so. I think once Admiral Moorer became the Chairman of the Joint Chiefs and Zumwalt became the CNO, then there wasn't a Chinaman's chance of Connolly getting a fourth star. I say that having had two tours in the secretariat and having listened to the secretaries and assistant secretaries discuss this sort of thing. I think Jerry is just being loyal to Connolly.

Q: Did you observe any of that slippery quality you mentioned?

Admiral Lee: A great deal, and when we get to the F-14,

---
*Vice Admiral Thomas F. Connolly, USN, Deputy Chief of Naval Operations (Air), November 1966-August 1971.

Lee #5 - 361

I'll talk about it.

Q: All right.

Admiral Lee: In January 1967, I was notified that I was to receive orders to be commanding officer of Enterprise. I was to spend February and March over in Rickover's organization and take part in a refresher course for commanding officers. All prospective commanding officers of submarines were brought into Rickover's office for two months, run through a refresher course in all phases of nuclear power, and given a final examination. I was to join one of these classes.

After having gone through the nuclear power program, and also having had command of Alamo, I realized that I was in the running to be commanding officer of Enterprise. But I hadn't discussed it with anybody, certainly not with the assistant secretary R&D, and certainly not with Rickover. I hadn't discussed it, period. But I was aware that there were only two candidates; I was one candidate and Max Harnish, who had been executive officer of Enterprise and had had an oiler at the time I had Alamo, also in the Pacific, was the other candidate. At that particular time, Max Harnish was an aide down in OP-90.*

---
*In 1965-66, Captain Harnish was Assistant to Director, Plans and Programs, Office of the Chief of Naval Operations.

Q: He was senior to you, wasn't he?

Admiral Lee: Max Harnish was class of '43. He was a classmate of Zumwalt's. I'm junior to the class of '44, so he was a year and a few months senior to me in terms of original date of rank. So I didn't know how it would go.

Q: Had you had any discussions with BuPers on a next assignment?

Admiral Lee: None. I very much wanted command of <u>Enterprise</u>. I thought the only thing to do was to do a good job over in the assistant secretary's office. I thought whatever I did, whatever moves I made would be wrong. I thought we'd just have to stand on our records. I don't know what Harnish did. I don't know if he spoke to his admiral about it or not. But my impression of that sort of thing is that sometimes influence hurts more than it helps.

Q: Especially with Admiral Rickover.

Admiral Lee: Especially with Admiral Rickover. So I never mentioned it to anybody, least of all Rickover. I was surprised but not shocked, because I knew that Harnish was a very strong candidate, and I wouldn't have been at all surprised to see Harnish get the job. But the orders came out, and Harnish was given Ranger, and I was given Enterprise.* I never discussed it with Harnish. But I would guess that it was a very great disappointment to him.

Q: Especially since he had had the advantage of being exec of the ship and you hadn't.

Admiral Lee: I don't know how this was ever sorted out. My guess is that Admiral Rickover decided, but I don't know that. My guess is that the bureau said that, "They're both qualified, they're both on the carrier list, and we think they'd both make good commanding officers." That's how the bureau does it. I wouldn't be at all surprised if Rickover made the choice, but I don't know.

Well, that was a great thrill, of course, getting those orders in hand. I can remember about the last thing that I did while I was in the Pentagon. The Under Secretary of the Navy, a fellow by the name of Baldwin who later became head of an investment banking firm of Morgan Stanley and Company, gave a luncheon for me before I left and invited all the aides. During the course of this luncheon, he said to me that he just wondered what my

---

*Harnish commanded the USS Ranger (CVA-61), 7 June 1966-20 October 1966.

thoughts were, what my plans were for Enterprise now that I was going out to take over this great command. I said to him that I'd been through that once or twice before and that I was just going to take one problem at a time-- remembering back to my speech to my young squadron on how things were going to be. But I decided that one problem at a time was the absolute best way to approach these things.

Well, in February, I went back to the N building and started the study routine with Rickover, classes and studies and examinations. Now it turned out that he gave me a break there. I understood that I had done very well in the year's academics with Rickover. I never saw the grades, but I understood that I got one of the highest grades at the prototype that they'd ever given out, and that might have had some bearing on my getting the job. But, anyway, when I went back over to Rickover's shop in February 1967, instead of being examined once a week as the ordinary candidates were, I was to be examined in only the radiological and chemical control areas. I had to take only the one examination over there, which was very different from my last time.

I also had another very interesting experience before I left. This was while I was in Rickover's shop. One Saturday morning, one of Rickover's Indians came down to see me, and it always happened in exactly this fashion--

"The admiral wants to see you." There was a saying among the prospective commanding officers in that, "When the admiral wants to see you, the first thing you do is put your mind in neutral, because whatever you think it is, that won't be it."

So, obeying our rules of conduct, I put my mind in neutral and went down to the admiral's office. He didn't hesitate for a second. He said "Lee [he always called everybody by their last names], how would you like to go out on sea trials with me tonight on the Ray?"* This brand-new nuclear submarine was at Newport News. This was a Saturday and we had to be aboard the submarine by midnight. She was going out for sea trials over the weekend, that is, leaving at midnight on Saturday night and coming back in by sunrise on Monday morning.

Immediately recognizing what a great honor this was, I said, "Why, yes, I'd like to go, but . . ."

He said, pointing at his secretary, "She'll get you a ticket. I'm going down on a plane at 5:00 o'clock." I was going to have a dinner party that night at my house, so after much effort I persuaded the admiral that I would meet him down there. I checked airplane schedules and found that I could get a plane about 10:00 from National Airport down to Newport News which would get me aboard the submarine on time. I arrived aboard the submarine, and got

---

*The USS Ray (SSN-653) was commissioned 12 April 1967.

very little sleep that night, because we got under way almost immediately after everybody was aboard--right after midnight. Rickover went to bed.

The next morning we were at sea, and the sea trials started. There was a representative from Newport News Ship Building and Drydock. There was a fleet commander's representative on board. Rickover used these two individuals as whipping boys the entire weekend. This was his standard procedure. He also, at some time during the course of it, put the submarine through its paces: full speed submerged, all back full. At a very crucial moment, he would kill the engineering officer of the watch, see what would happen, see how they handled that emergency. So I must say it was a very exciting weekend.

I was very glad bright and early Monday morning to have the ship come back into Newport News, and we departed in a drizzly rain. I took a taxi over to the airfield, got back to Washington to the N building, from National Airport about 8:00 o'clock, and right back to work. Standard weekend for Rickover.

Q: Did you learn some useful things during that sea trial?

Admiral Lee: Not really. I learned to stay out of Rickover's line of fire, if possible. I found it a very uncomfortable, a very embarrassing weekend.

Q: In what respect?

Admiral Lee: I found it embarrassing the way he treated the representative from the Newport News shipyard, and embarrassing the way he browbeat and treated the fleet commander's representative. I found he was just impossible: insulting, never a decent word, "those idiots from the shipyard, people like you," he'd say to the man. This went on all weekend. It was Rickover's recreation.

Q: How did he treat the skipper?

Admiral Lee: He treated the skipper fairly well this weekend.* The skipper didn't pay much attention to him. He went about his business and did his thing, didn't interfere with Rickover. But he ran the ship very well. Rickover really didn't take him into his line of fire. But I understand on other sea trials that he has taken the skipper of the ship into his line of fire and made a shambles of him. In this particular case, he did not.

Q: How important was the nuclear power training to you to be skipper of the Enterprise?

---

*The first commanding officer of the Ray was Commander Albert L. Kelln, USN.

Admiral Lee: I think the nuclear power training was invaluable for me for both _Alamo_ and for _Enterprise_. I had had a lot of technical training, but I had had a minimum of exposure to naval engineering. What I'd learned at Line School was the extent of my training. When I went to _Alamo_, I knew how a steam plant operated. I knew about turbines and steam pressures, and the nuts and bolts of it.

In terms of _Enterprise_, I never, obviously, operated the engines, but I think it's very important for a commanding officer to be able to talk the same language his engineers talk. I'd gone through the same training, had qualified as an engineering officer of the watch, so I knew what their problems were. I knew what they were talking about. I think that's important. In terms of my doing any of the work, no. Of course, I had more than I could handle up on the bridge and other parts of the ship.

But I would say one thing about the nuclear power training--I spent a total of 14 months in Rickover's office and then an additional two months on board _Enterprise_ before relieving Holloway. I don't think I needed that kind of training. I think five or six months total would have been adequate. But Rickover had a policy, one year to the minute, the original training. I will talk about that later on when I talk about the OPA job that I had, Rickover's fetish about to-the-minute tours of duty.

But in any event, I finished with Rickover in March, went to Naval Air Force Pacific for April, where I went through various courses, such as fire fighting, damage control, and other subjects useful for prospective commanding officers of carriers.

Q: You mentioned earlier that you had sat in on some of Admiral Rickover's interviews. Was it during this period in early 1967?

Admiral Lee: Well, I sat in on Admiral Rickover's interviews during the period '63-'64, when I was there for the year. Rickover's policy--and I guess this policy came about because of complaints about his interviews--was that he would always have a third person in the room. While we were there, going through the nuclear power course from '63 to '64, I took my turn as the straight man, as we called it. The straight man had to take notes from the interviews. We tried to write down the interview verbatim on a yellow legal pad. Same thing was true when I was back there for the two months. I took part in the interview system. Rickover usually conducted interviews on Fridays and Saturdays, and sometimes it was all day Saturday.

Q: That was more of his recreation.

Admiral Lee: Yes, that was part of his recreation. I think he thoroughly enjoyed it, harassing young naval officers and midshipmen.

Q: Why was it necessary to have a third person in on the interviews?

Admiral Lee: There was criticism by many people who had been interviewed that Rickover was brutal, that he was insulting, and that what he was doing was, in many cases, borderline illegal. Also there was criticism about this chair with two forward legs cut off by six inches or so. Rickover brought in the third person as a witness and to take notes. Then he would have a record of what went on during the course of the interview. That was the purpose of it. These notes were filed. We turned them in.

Q: So he could respond to the criticism if it came.

Admiral Lee: The interview system was an excellent system, a great system. I had no criticism of the interview system, but Rickover himself was something else. Once again, I think it was his recreation. He enjoyed pulling wings off flies, as we used to say. This was part of it.

After spending most of April in AirPac, I headed West, and sometime around the first week or two in May, I got to

Subic Bay and took one of those carrier-on-board transport planes out to Enterprise, which was in Tonkin Gulf. The plan was that I would spend two months aboard Enterprise as an observer, as a trainee, and then relieve Holloway back in Alameda in July. I reported aboard Enterprise feeling that the last thing any ship needs is two captains. It was a very awkward situation, being a prospective captain, wandering around the ship with, really, not enough to do. I tried during that period of time to visit all the departments on Enterprise and learn all about the air department, the operations department, the IOIC, the RA-5Cs, and the intelligence function to get as attuned as I could to the operations in Vietnam.*

Q: Did you live in the in-port captain's cabin during this time?

Admiral Lee: No, I lived in a room in the island structure--maybe on the 06 level. I didn't stay on the Enterprise for the entire time, which probably was a mistake, because Rickover later found out about it. For instance, Admiral Hyland came on board.** He was Commander Seventh Fleet during this period, and I had known him in Omaha. We played squash, and he invited me to go

---

*IOIC--integrated operational intelligence center.
**Vice Admiral John J. Hyland, USN, was Commander Seventh Fleet, December 1965-November 1967.

with him on his flagship. I went to various parts of Vietnam with him, including a couple of days in Saigon. I was away from Enterprise for, perhaps, a week with Admiral Hyland.

Then a little later on, Captain Jim Doyle, who was skipper of the Bainbridge, invited me to go to Singapore with him in his ship.* That would take about four days to Singapore and we'd have six days in Singapore, so I was gone from Enterprise during that period for about two weeks or maybe longer. We met Enterprise back in Subic Bay. I visited some other carriers just to see what their operations were like. So that I stayed on Enterprise only about half the time of this period, maybe less than half the time, which, when Rickover found out about it, he was not very happy about, because he wanted me down in the engine rooms, opening and closing throttle valves.

Q: There's more to running a carrier than just that.

Admiral Lee: Well, that's not what he thinks, but, anyway, I toured all the ships in Task Force 77 including the flagship, which Admiral Cousins began to run about this time.**

Q: Had Admiral Mehle departed already?
----
*Captain James H. Doyle, Jr., USN.
**Rear Admiral Ralph W. Cousins, USN.

Admiral Lee: Admiral Mehle departed while I was out there.* He was a very colorful character. It's my understanding that Mehle, in effect, got fired. I don't know the details of this but, supposedly, the Under Secretary of the Navy, Baird, was very upset with some of Mehle's antics, and he persuaded the Secretary of the Navy to fire Mehle. I spent a couple of days on Mehle's flagship, and it was the most tense flag mess I've ever been in. He was like a coiled snake, just--the whole flag mess was like that. It was very uncomfortable. I never worked for Mehle, nor with him. I just had that experience of about two days. Very shortly after that he was relieved, and Admiral Cousins became CTF 77.**

Q: Did you notice a change in atmosphere after he took over?

Admiral Lee: Yes. Admiral Cousins was a very low-key man, a very talented and very able man, who understood people and understood operations. He wanted his staff officers to express their ideas, thoughts, and recommendations to him. He wasn't one of those people who would shoot the

---
*Rear Admiral Roger W. Mehle, USN.
**The relief took place on 4 October 1967 on board the USS Constellation (CVA-64), which was the flagship for Carrier Division Five and Task Force 77.

messenger. I thought Admiral Cousins was just about the ideal man for the CTF 77 position, a very balanced man, very intelligent man. I had known Admiral Cousins at some time before this. I believe he was the operations officer for CinCPacFlt before going out. He was the ideal man, first-rate, and I think was a welcome relief to Mehle.

Q: Well, it was good for you to touch base with him to get his operational philosophy.

Admiral Lee: Yes. Cousins was just about the ideal in every way. I served with Cousins, in one way or another, two or three times after that. He was always the perfect gentleman, always did the right things at the right time, very loyal, very cordial to his subordinates, first-rate naval officer in every way. He was my candidate to be Chief of Naval Operations when Zumwalt got the job--not that I had a vote.

After two months on the line doing all these things that I've just described, we headed back for the West Coast and arrived on the West Coast around the first of July 1967.

Q: How was your relationship with Captain Holloway during that indoctrination period?

Admiral Lee: I would say cordial but formal. I tried to stay off the bridge. I saw Captain Holloway only when I had something I needed to talk to him about, such as permission to go to Singapore with Doyle, or if he wanted to see me about something. I decided the thing to do was not to presume on friendship. I saw very little of Holloway, and as I've said earlier, Holloway and I were never really close friends. We were colleagues; I'd put it that way.

Q: Did he have briefing sessions with you on various aspects of the ship?

Admiral Lee: None.

Q: So you really got that from the subordinates within the ship.

Admiral Lee: Yes. I thought Holloway could have done a better job there, because he made absolutely zero effort to give me any information on handling of the ship and navigation. When Petersen came aboard, I discussed all aspects of the ship with him. We had become good friends during the course of our nuclear power training and have remained good friends to this day.

Q: Well, and probably you had an appreciation for what you hadn't got and made an effort to give that to him.

Admiral Lee: But Holloway and I were never close friends. I don't think we were enemies, but we were not friends. As I said earlier, I don't think Holloway is the type to have close friends. He was a very political type, and political types don't have close friends.

Anyway, I relieved Holloway on July 7, 1967, and after a very few days, took Enterprise to Hunters Point Naval Shipyard for seven weeks, where we had a restricted availability, which is a Navy term for getting modifications and repair work done after a long voyage or a long cruise.*

Q: Did the crew members get a chance to go on leave following the deployment?

Admiral Lee: Oh, yes, we had a long leave period from the time the ship got back, which was around the first of July, until leaving Hunters Point, which was about two months altogether.

Q: The environment around there is not the most desirable. Did you have to take any precautions to protect your crew

---

*The Hunters Point shipyard was in San Francisco.

members?

Admiral Lee: Yes, Hunters Point was a miserable place to be. This was during the period in the late Sixties when black power was coming to the fore. We had to be very careful about going in and out of Hunters Point, because every once in a while people would stand outside Hunters Point and shoot inside. It was a difficult period, although we had no problems. We got our work done on time and got out on time. We had quite a few changes in the crew, as you would expect, officers and men. The crew had this two-month period for leave, and we probably took the ship down to about 50% of complement during the course of these leave periods and changeovers. We had a lot of new people and a lot of training to be done when we got out of the shipyard.

Q: Who was your executive officer?

Admiral Lee: Forrest Petersen had been Holloway's executive officer for one year. Sam Linder came in and was Holloway's executive officer for the second year.* Holloway was selected for admiral during the second year. Linder stayed on, of course, for a year with me. Sam Linder was a very bright guy, Naval Academy class of 1947,

---

*Commander Isham W. Linder, USN.

and had gotten a Ph.D. in physics from University of California at Berkeley. I had known Sam before, down in the special weapons school at Norfolk when I was an instructor down there. He and I, I believe, were in the same class. Anyway, Sam was a very talented man, very low key, and ran a good ship.

After Hunters Point, we had refresher training down in San Diego.

Q: Was that your first real chance to handle the ship?

Admiral Lee: First chance to handle the ship was when we brought Enterprise back to Alameda from Hunters Point.* We loaded up at Alameda, and then went to sea and headed south, and had refresher training down in the San Diego area. That was a very interesting period, about three weeks: damage control training, flight deck training. Every kind of training you can imagine goes on in the underway training group; it's very beneficial, very helpful. I don't think we give these underway training groups enough credit for the work they do.

Q: Well, they're normally viewed as the bad guys.

Admiral Lee: They're viewed as the bad guys, and at that

---
*The Alameda Naval Air Station, near Oakland, California, was the home port of the Enterprise.

time I sort of viewed them as the bad guys too. But they performed a great service for Enterprise and the Navy, and it gave me a fairly good idea of where our strengths and weaknesses were in the ship. I found that our strengths were in engineering and maybe operations and administration. Our weaknesses, as you would expect, were in damage control and maybe, to a lesser extent, in combat information. But we worked very hard at it. I got a report every day on all of these various exercises and sections, and we eventually got through the refresher training, getting a barely satisfactory mark in damage control. But many carriers fail the damage control, so our 62, or whatever we got, was kind of a high mark for aircraft carriers, because damage control is the most difficult thing there is on an aircraft carrier.

Q: The Forrestal fire took place during that period.* Did that help focus your attention?

Admiral Lee: Oh, yes. We worked very hard on damage control, and I instituted a training program after we left refresher training, so that we probably had more training in damage control and fire fighting, all aspects of it from the flight decks to the engine rooms, than any carrier in

---

*While operating off North Vietnam on 29 July 1967, the USS Forrestal (CVA-59) was devastated by a fire that left 132 crewmen dead and 62 injured.

the Pacific Fleet. We really worked at it. The performance of the ship in our fire the succeeding year attested to that fact.* Everything worked, and we fought it the way it should have been fought.

We developed, I thought, a fairly good damage control, fire fighting organization. But it's a constant struggle, constant struggle. You really have to stay with it. We had contests of one type or another. Damage control parties could win prizes which would involve extra liberty and leave. You have to be imaginative, because it's dull stuff--fire fighting and damage control, and various engineering drills, and flight deck drills. A carrier has more of that than any other three ships combined, I'm convinced, because they have all the things that other ships have plus all the flight operations--the hangar deck and the flight deck.

Q: And a lot of volatile things on board.

Admiral Lee: Yes, it's the most dangerous ship ever put together.

Anyway, in late October we had an unexpected visit. We were back in Alameda, and I got called one day by Vice President Humphrey's advance agent.** Humphrey was coming

---
*On 14 January 1969, the Enterprise suffered a damaging fire that Admiral Lee discusses in interview number six.
**Hubert H. Humphrey was Vice President of the United States, 1965-69.

to the West Coast at this particular time on a speaking tour, and his advance man thought that it would be a good idea if Vice President Humphrey came aboard Enterprise and talked. But he cautioned me three or four times that Humphrey wanted it low key--no ceremonies, no big deal, not having all the troops massed, no review of the colors--just a simple visit to Enterprise, and he would talk to the troops.

After discussing it with our people and discussing it with my bosses--with ComAirPac and a cardiv commander by the name of Bardshar, who was my administrative boss--we decided that the absolute minimum we could do was sideboys.* We'd put a stand up and let all the troops gather around Vice President Humphrey in the hangar deck. We would have it otherwise empty. Not in formation, not in rows, just let them gather around the way they would in Podunk County and listen to the Vice President.

So the day came and Vice President Humphrey came with his little entourage, came up the brow ladder, and I met him on the quarterdeck and we simply had sideboys, which in the Navy, you know, is the same as saying good morning. He was a little taken aback with these sideboys, but he didn't say anything. I welcomed him aboard and escorted him over to the stand, and we had all the troops gather around.

---
*Rear Admiral Frederic A. Bardshar, USN, Commander Carrier Division Seven, 1967-69.

Humphrey made a marvelous talk, all extemporaneous. He had a few notes on a card, but he was a marvelous speaker.

Q: What was the substance of it?

Admiral Lee: The substance was defense and Vietnam. He was one of the most articulate men I've ever listened to. As a matter of fact, we took this down on tape and later transcribed it, and it needed no editing. After Humphrey's speech, we took him up by elevator to the flag bridge, which was about on the sixth or seventh level in the island structure. We had a TV up there and we played back his speech to him, which he liked. He liked to see himself perform. You know, most politicians have big egos.

After that, we had some nice conversation and lots of pictures. He sat in the admiral's chair, and we took his picture. Then time to leave, he was the busy politician having to make his rounds. Down to the quarterdeck, and lo and behold, there were those sideboys again. Humphrey stopped and looked at those sideboys and looked at me and said, "This ship sure has a lot of protocol."

Q: Not knowing that this was the low-key version.

Admiral Lee: I had to chuckle a little bit. But without further protest, he went through the sideboys and left the ship. We have pictures of Humphrey, and I have a copy of the ship's magazine with a picture of Humphrey talking to the men on the hangar deck.

Our next big event during this workup period was the President's visit to Enterprise. Now this took place over Veterans' Day weekend in November.

Q: Eleventh of November.

Admiral Lee: It wasn't long after Humphrey's visit. Humphrey's visit was in October.

The President's naval aide came out to see us--very nice young lieutenant commander, and said the President wanted to come on board for Veterans' Day weekend or he had proposed to the President that he do this, but it had to be at sea. The President didn't want anybody else aboard. No admirals, no Commander First Fleet, no cardiv commanders or anyone. He didn't exclude the captain of the ship. So we, of course, agreed, because Admiral Moorer was in on it.*

It was decided by Admiral Moorer that Enterprise would be at sea off of San Diego, and we would have some highly experienced carrier pilots, a certain number on board, and airplanes, and that we would helicopter Johnson aboard in the afternoon, have a tour of the ship, flying at night,

---

*Admiral Thomas H. Moorer, USN, Chief of Naval Operations, 1967-70.

and then dinner after the night flying was over.*
Johnson brought McNamara, the Secretary of Defense; Admiral
Moorer, the Chief of Naval Operations; and a staff of
perhaps 15 or 20, including two women, one of whom was Liz
Carpenter, the writer, who was then Mrs. Johnson's staff
director. He also brought about 30 newsmen and
photographers. We had lots of room, because the air wing
in full wasn't aboard, and we were able to handle all of
these people.

I can remember saying to Admiral Moorer, "Well, we
have a choice. I can be the President's escort around the
ship and stay with him, or we can have the executive
officer, Linder, stay with him. If I stay with him, Linder
will run the ship from the bridge."

Moorer didn't even hesitate. He said to me, "You stay
with him." So I was Johnson's right-hand man during the
course of his visit, escorted him all around the ship, was
with him during the flight operations that night on the
bridge. There's a picture which was circulated throughout
the country of President Johnson, McNamara, Admiral Moorer
and me on the bridge.

I thought we had a very successful visit, a very
successful tour, and then that night dinner in the flag
mess. President Johnson had brought his own cooks, his own
food. They had their own menu, and we had cocktails and

─────────
*Lyndon B. Johnson was President of the United States from 1963 to 1969.

wine. I was a little taken aback to walk into the flag mess and see the stewards serving cocktails, but I must confess I joined right in and had one, too, and had a little wine with dinner.

But one of the interesting things that happened was that the executive officer, the naval aide, and I were talking, and we thought it would be a good idea to have some enlisted men have dinner with the President also. This was in the course of the afternoon, and the question was which enlisted men. So the exec and I talked to a couple of department heads, and we picked the enlisted men. One of them was a first class petty officer who was a machinery repairman that I'd gotten to know. He'd come up to the bridge and I would always talk to him, very intelligent young man from Texas. I thought he would be a good representative, and the executive officer thought so, so we picked him.

I've forgotten how many now, but we had four or five enlisted men that night for dinner and all of Johnson's staff so the flag mess was filled with people. There must have been 30 people for dinner, including Admiral Moorer. I was the only man from the Enterprise except for the enlisted men, I believe. Lo and behold, it came out during the course of the evening that this young man from Texas was from Johnson's hometown. Of course, that was great.

But a very interesting item appeared in Drew Pearson-Jack Anderson's column the next week.* The item was that Johnson insisted on having these enlisted men to his dinner, much to the chagrin of the Navy, and that he had insisted on having this boy come from Comfort, Texas. None of which was true.

Q: Johnson had a pipeline to Pearson so he could plant things.

Admiral Lee: Really?

Q: Yes, he did.

Admiral Lee: I'll be damned. He probably put this out then. Well, isn't that interesting. Well, I've just described to you how this boy from Comfort, Texas, happened to have dinner with the President.

Q: What were your impressions of Johnson from being his escort during that time?

Admiral Lee: The naval aide to the President said to me that, contrary to what you read in the newspapers, Johnson is a very reserved and wary man; he's a politician. He

---
*Drew Pearson and Jack Anderson were authors of "Washington Merry-go-Round," a syndicated newspaper column.

said, "He really won't have much to say to you until you've been with him a while." He said, "That's just his way; don't let it put you off." I found that to be true. I thought he was a very reserved, calculating man, very much a politician. But I'd say that after dinner with him, and breakfast with him, and touring him around the ship and the flight operations, I changed my mind. The next morning we had a formation on the flight deck, and President Johnson gave a sunrise speech. Remember that "We will meet on the seas" speech that he gave, which made headlines around the country?

Q: I don't remember it specifically.

Admiral Lee: It was in the newspapers. Big pictures, lots of photographers there, of course, and newsmen.

Anyway, I found toward the last third of the time with Johnson, that he realized that I had no political axes to grind, that I was doing what I thought was best for him. For instance, there's an open area behind the navigation bridge, and we went back there to watch the flight operations. Up above us were positioned all the newsmen and photographers. I thought Johnson ought to know that these newsmen were up there observing him. He didn't know it. So I told him. He didn't say anything, and he didn't do anything, but by and by he turned around and looked around and recognized one or two of them up there and spoke to them. He appreciated that. As I say, I'm not sure political types have close friends. It's the way they operate, because today's friend may be tomorrow's enemy.

But I think he trusted me. I found that once I broke down this reserve and he began to talk to me and began to trust me, I found him a very warm man. And I liked him.

Q: What sorts of things did you talk about?

Admiral Lee: We talked mostly about the Navy. I didn't try to get in his area of business, namely, politics and leadership of the country. We talked about airplanes, and the Navy, and anything that he wanted to talk about. I didn't presume on anything that I thought might be sensitive or that, as my daughter might say, was "getting me out of my tree." So we talked about the things that he wanted to talk about.

Q: Did he evince a good deal of curiosity about various parts of the ship?

Admiral Lee: You know, he did and he didn't. Like a good politician, he was interested. But I think in all of these tours, his mind was in neutral. My impression of politicians is that this is the way they make these tours. They go along for the tour and express interest and say all the right things, but their mind is in neutral. It's not something they really want to learn.

Now on the other hand, McNamara, who's a man with a very inquiring and, you might say, technical mind, was interested in everything.

But we had a very exciting couple of days with the President, and the ship and the Navy, of course, got tremendous publicity from it. I think Admiral Moorer was very pleased with the whole operation.

Q: Did you have to make any special arrangements with the Secret Service for his time on board?

Admiral Lee: They made the arrangements. They came aboard and told us what would be and what wouldn't be. For instance, when they answered the phone aboard the ship, it was the White House. We had a phone patch set up so that he could communicate instantly by telephone to shore. We had a ship-to-shore radio circuit locked in constantly. He slept in the admiral's in-port cabin. They came in and moved the shower nozzle about a foot up, took the old one out and put a new one about a foot higher. They did all kinds of things like that.

Q: Any other specific ones you remember?

Admiral Lee: Can't remember whether they brought his own mattress or not. (Laughter)

But they, of course, preceded him wherever he went and followed up. They had a Secret Service man at the doors to the flag cabin when he was there. I didn't have to get permission to go in, because I was the captain of the ship and they knew me, but you had to be invited in. Very tight security even on <u>Enterprise</u>. But it wasn't any big problem. I thought we handled it very well, sort of low key and didn't try to be things we were not. And I think the President really enjoyed it.

Q: What was his reaction to the flight demonstration?

Admiral Lee: You know, there's absolutely nothing more awe-inspiring than night flight operations from an aircraft carrier. I think during those night flight operations, even the politicians got their minds out of neutral and concentrated on what was going on. They were very good. We had one bolter. A bolter is when a plane comes in for a landing and misses the wire and has to go around again. We had one bolter during the night flight recovery, and that's always very spectacular. The plane hits the deck, the hook doesn't catch a wire, and in a fraction of a second he's airborne again down the angled deck. We had one of those. Of course, to the newcomer, your heart is in your throat, whether or not he's going to make it. Of course, they always make it. That's the plan. Because the minute they hit the deck, the procedure is to go to full power.

Q: Something you couldn't do in the straight-deck days.

Admiral Lee: No.

Q: Did President Johnson talk about the Vietnam War while he was on board?

Admiral Lee: Yes. We took him on a tour of what we called the integrated operational intelligence center. There we had all the pictures laid out of targets that we had attacked during the last cruise, and we showed him all of these. But this was the time when the heat was building up on the President, as you know, in late 1967. This was the time when McNamara had given up on the war, and I think this was the last supper for McNamara. You know, he left shortly after and became president of the World Bank. I think Johnson was easing him out.

McNamara had been the mastermind behind the war. He and his whiz kids started it, masterminded it, engineered it. Then came 1967. McNamara decided he had a loser, and he wanted to back out, and Johnson eased him out. I think for political reasons Johnson didn't think that he could pull out. He was in too deep. But we didn't discuss any of those aspects.

But Johnson has a good memory. As I will relate later, he called me some few months later, when we were in the Sea of Japan. I think that was about all the excitement for fall of 1967.

Q: I would like to get your reaction to what it was like to handle the Enterprise. She was obviously far bigger and more complicated than the Alamo.

Admiral Lee: Enterprise was a dream to handle. My first experience in handling ships was those twin-screw YPs at the Naval Academy. I went from that to Alamo. And Alamo was a twin-screw, single-rudder ship but with a flat bottom. You had to be very careful with Alamo in coming alongside another ship, or you'd be sucked in for an alongside collision.

But Alamo was a very nice handling ship under most circumstances. I found that Enterprise was even easier to handle than Alamo, was very responsive to power; very responsive to rudders; the engines were very responsive. I could go from full power to stop immediately and not have to worry about boilers. Or I could go from all-stop to full power immediately without having to worry about boilers. It was a marvelous ship to handle, a shiphandler's dream, Enterprise.

Q: But you also have to allow for a momentum when you get that thing going.

Admiral Lee: Oh, yes, it takes miles to stop it once you're doing 30 knots. Even with all power astern.

But it was a very fine engineering plant, and the ship was a little longer than the Forrestal class. The Forrestal class had four propellers and two rudders. But Enterprise had four propellers and four rudders, which made it a little more responsive to the rudder. Also, Enterprise was a little longer, had a little better fineness ratio, a little bigger and had lots more horsepower. Enterprise had lots of horsepower. We were rated at 280,000 shaft horsepower, that is, 70,000 shaft horsepower per two-reactor propeller, engine plant. However, we had more power than that. We were limited at top speed by torque on propeller shafts rather than power. In the first cruise, I guess we were limited in top speed to 32 or 33 knots because the bottom was a little dirty. In 1968, we went into Bremerton to get the bottom cleaned, and we probably had a top speed of 35 or 36 knots. Still limited by the torque on the propeller shafts.

We had Christmas in Alameda. Then on January 3, 1968, we loaded our air wing aboard. We had an air wing commander by the name of Paul Peck, who was a very able young commander, and a very aggressive wing commander.* The air wing assembled from all over the country. We had F-4s from Miramar, two squadrons; we had an A-6 squadron from Whidbey Island.**

I think we had A-4s in 1967 and 1968 from Lemoore.*** Then we had an RA-5C squadron of six planes from the East Coast. We also had some cats and dogs, such as helicopters, such as the radar planes, and we had our own COD planes.**** We had lots of airplanes on board and a full ship when we departed.

Q: How many people altogether?

Admiral Lee: Altogether about 5,500 people when we departed Alameda Naval Air Station on January 3, 1968. Our eventual destination was to be, of course, Vietnam.

As we went through the Golden Gate channel on the morning of January 3, we noticed the usual Russian trawler

---
*Commander Paul A. Peck, USN.
**The Grumman A-6 Intruder is a two-seat all-weather attack plane. The A-6A version then in the fleet had two Pratt & Whitney J52-P-6 turbo jets, a wing span of 53 feet, maximum takeoff weight of approximately 54,000 pounds, maximum sea level speed of Mach 0.95. Whidbey Island is a naval air station in the state of Washington.
***Lemoore is a naval air station in central California.
****COD--carrier on-board delivery.

sitting outside. These Russian trawlers were always outside the Golden Gate, monitoring the goings and comings of ships and picking up all the communications traffic they could find. As we all know today, we get great amounts of information from analyzing communications traffic. Most of our communications are in code, but we've been successful from time to time in breaking codes, and we have to believe that the Russians have been just as successful.

This trawler was waiting outside the gate. After about two days at sea, we got a message from the Chief of Naval Operations to the Commander in Chief Pacific Fleet, telling us that the Navy's intelligence organization reported that a Russian submarine was coming down from the Aleutian chain. It appeared that he was going to rendezvous with us. That was his mission from his track. If so, we were to wait until he got into position behind us and then increase our speed slowly to see just how fast the Russian submarine was, or to see at what speed he'd break off.

Q: But weren't you also supposed to avoid giving him the impression that you knew he was there?

Admiral Lee: Yes, we were also not to let on that we knew he was there. We did this, of course, by maintaining our normal course and speed until such time as he was locked on, which was maybe two days later.

A recent book written by Pat Tyler describes this entire exercise in great detail. Pat Tyler's book is called Running Critical, and it has to do with the 688 submarine.* Our race with the Soviet submarine was one of Rickover's tools in getting the 688 program approved. Now at the time I didn't know this. I didn't know how this intelligence had been used until Pat Tyler came down to see me about this particular run. I had never been told. In any event, the Soviet sub rendezvoused with us. We were probably doing 16 or 18 knots at the time. We slowly increased speed over a period of a day or so. I have subsequently checked the Enterprise deck logs and discovered that our top speed was 31 knots. At some point between 26 and 31 knots, the Russian sub broke off. Now Pat Tyler had all the information on this. Where he got it, I don't know. But he supposedly had a copy of the briefing that Admiral Rickover gave to Congress on this speed race with the Russian submarine.

Q: Was it put in the log that the submarine dropped off at a certain point?

---

*Submarines of the USS Los Angeles (SSN-688) class began entering the fleet in 1976. Patrick Tyler's book is Running Critical: The Silent War, Rickover and General Dynamics (New York: Harper & Row, 1986). It discusses many of the factors that went into the design and construction of the Los Angeles class.

Admiral Lee: No. That was not put in the log. The only things in the log were the courses and speeds, and the other information was reported to the CNO by message.

Q: Would you say that Tyler's book is correct, insofar as you know, concerning that incident?

Admiral Lee: I'd say Tyler's book is 100% correct. What we did was run the race and report the results. Rickover then put this together with his colleagues and, I'm sure, with Admiral Moorer's approval. They probably briefed Admiral Moorer and then took this briefing to Congress as proof that the Russian submarines were much faster than we had believed up to this time.

Q: I would imagine you weren't allowed to share this with too many other people on board the ship.

Admiral Lee: No, I've forgotten the circumstances, but also, as I explained to Pat Tyler, which he decided not to use in his book, we had a flag officer on board by the name of Spin Epes.* He was getting the messages from Washington telling us what to do and when. He was the task group commander and also our carrier division commander.

---

*Rear Admiral Horace H. Epes, USN, Commander Carrier Division One.

He was also aboard, of course, when we later had our visit in Sasebo, and the Pueblo.

But, anyway, we got into Pearl Harbor, and we were expecting to have our operational readiness inspection, but after only a very few days in Pearl Harbor, we were told that our operational readiness inspection would be postponed or cancelled and that we were to set sail for Sasebo, Japan. Visits to Japan by nuclear-powered ships were not routine. They were very sensitive. The Japanese had agreed to allow Enterprise to go into Sasebo. The dates had been picked, so we needed to take right off from Pearl Harbor and head for Sasebo. It was decided that this was politically very important.

Q: In this operational chain of command, you mentioned Admiral Epes's orders on things like the race and going to Sasebo. Did they go step by step in the chain of command, or was it jumped in those cases?

Admiral Lee: Usually items would come from the Chief of Naval Operations to CinCPacFlt, asking CinCPacFlt to do this or that. Now, technically the chain of command was from Secretary of Defense to the unified and specified commanders. The Chairman of the Joint Chiefs and the CNO are not in the operational chain of command. That's the way it is legally. So that technically it would have gone from the Secretary of Defense to the CinCPac, who was a different admiral, to CinCPacFlt, then to the numbered fleet commanders, either First Fleet or Seventh Fleet, then to the cardiv commander, then to Enterprise. Now, as a practical matter, if Moorer wanted something done, he would probably tell us to do it and info CinCPacFlt. Moorer didn't pay much attention to the technical, legal chain of command. There wasn't any question that if Moorer sent to CinCPacFlt a message to do this or do that, it was done.

Q: So if you got an info copy, you'd better prepare to do that.

Admiral Lee: That's the normal way it was done.

Q: Did you get any State Department input preparing you for the Sasebo visit?

Admiral Lee: Yes, as a matter of fact, we had the ambassador to Japan.

Alexis Johnson was flown out to Enterprise the day before we entered Sasebo.* We had a whole group of Japanese members of the Diet, maybe members of the Japanese State Department, flew to Enterprise the day before we entered Sasebo. We found Alexis Johnson a very intelligent

---
*U. Alexis Johnson was U.S. ambassador to Japan, 1966-69.

man who was aware of all the nuances of our visit.

Q: He was a career Foreign Service officer.

Admiral Lee: Yes, very impressive man. I thought of all the career Foreign Service officers I've met, and I've never met all that many--you know, we meet them along the line--he was the most impressive. I thought he was the most operationally minded. Most State Department people that I've met were status quo people. Alexis Johnson was a very aggressive man, very energetic, very outgoing. But we had his people come aboard, and he brought a whole group of Japanese aboard.

We also had a terrible storm en route to Sasebo. So we were one day late getting in. It was the worst storm I was ever in in the Enterprise. It was one of those typhoons, and we just slowed down to near steerageway for about 24 hours as we sat there and let the storm beat us to death. Salt water up to the bridge. We suffered some damage from it.

Q: Did you try different headings to see which worked the best?

Admiral Lee: I tried everything. And I found that headings and speeds make a great deal of difference. I finally found a speed of maybe five or six knots, mere steerageway, and a heading where Enterprise rode more smoothly than otherwise. You don't want to turn one of those big ships in seas like that, because you can get your sides bashed in. I tried to put the seas on one quarter or the other; that's the best. In this particular case, I think I put the seas on the port quarter.

Q: How big were the waves?

Admiral Lee: They were huge--50 or 60 feet. Huge. They were the equal of some of those typhoons that I ran into in World War II. During the two years I had Enterprise, that was *the* biggest storm I ran into. They're no fun. You can wreck a ship, a big ship. If you keep the power on and plow into those mountains of water, you can push your whole front end in. The ships and the waves are that powerful. The bows of those ships above the waterline, and especially up towards the flight deck level, are not all that strong. And a wall of water will push them in and fold your flight deck back.

Q: Had you gotten any briefings or technical information before this on things of that sort, vulnerability in a storm?

Admiral Lee: Yes. The education to be a commanding officer of an aircraft carrier is a kind of do-it-yourself thing. I got all the literature. There are various things like that that you're supposed to read when you go through AirPac. There are various instructions on how to handle storms, and you get all the books on ship handling. But I think all ships' captains do a great deal of reading in this area, especially carrier captains. So yes, I had read and reread all the instructions and books in this area. You have to play with it a little bit, but all captains have impressed on them, especially of aircraft carriers, that you don't plow one of those big ships into these walls of water at high speed. You can wreck your ship. We've had carriers wrecked like that, flight decks peeled back. You just want to sit there where the ship rides as comfortably as possible and maintain steerageway and wait it out.

We went into Sasebo one day late, and we really had a very enjoyable five days in Sasebo.* This particular visit also made great headlines, and there were all kinds of news people, both American newsmen and Japanese in the Sasebo area, because it was a big event. Made all the newspapers. The various protesters, nuclear protesters, Communist protesters, and all the left-wing protesters

---

*The Enterprise arrived at Sasebo on 19 January 1968 in company with the nuclear-powered frigate Truxtun (DLGN-35) and the conventionally powered frigate Halsey (DLG-23).

would take the train into Sasebo every morning. The trains would be loaded with these young people.

Q: It was like that was their job.

Admiral Lee: Their job, and they probably were paid for it. But the trains every morning would be absolutely filled to overflowing. They probably ran extra trains, bringing all these youngsters into Sasebo every morning.

Q: Did you brief your crew on special ways of behaving ashore in view of this?

Admiral Lee: Oh, yes, we spent a lot of time briefing the crew. We put it in the plan of the day and put out information brochures, so that the crew was well prepared for Sasebo--what to expect, what our conduct should be, how important it was not to have an incident. Oh, yes, that sort of thing goes without saying. We spent a lot of time educating the crew. We had a very fine crew on Enterprise. Very proud of the ship, very responsive. As I was saying, these protesters came in by the thousands every morning and were no doubt joined by a certain number of protesters from the Sasebo area.

Meantime, the Japanese had beefed up their Sasebo police detachment, and it was like a staged play. The choreography was predictable. Every day the protesters would converge on a given area and a given point. The police would be on the other side of this given area or given point down towards the naval base. They would push each other back and forth all day. Sometimes the police would use water cannon on them, but the idea was to make a scene, do something for the TV cameras and the newsmen. The policemen went out of their way not to injure any of the protesters. I think the protesters knew the limits which they were permitted to go in terms of flogging policemen and in terms of location. So it was sort of a game that was played for five days.

Q: Ritual is very important.

Admiral Lee: Good point. Ritual is very important in the Orient. It was important that the police not lose face, and it was important that the protesters made their point. This went on every day. Then, at a given signal towards the end of the day, these youngsters would all break off their protesting and head back for the trains, move out of town, so that at night Sasebo was relatively peaceful. We went about our shopping. The shops were all open at night, and we tried to avoid the town during the day. But at night we went into the clubs and into the stores, and I thought we had a very good visit.

Q: It must have been fascinating for you to watch these sides go back and forth at each other.

Admiral Lee: You have to have a sense of humor to appreciate that, but everybody seemed to understand it. Both sides of the Japanese seemed to understand it fully well, and nobody got too emotional about it. The police were doing their job; the protesters were doing their job. So a great time was had by all.

Q: Did your crew have any interactions with the protesters?

Admiral Lee: None that I knew about. They didn't want to get hit over the head with a club. But I guess the best measure of how well indoctrinated our crew was was that we had no incidents. We had none of our crewmen leaving Enterprise. You know, some Americans, military, were enticed to desert in Japan. There were organizations in Japan who were working on American servicemen to get them to desert because of Vietnam and lots of other reasons. We had no deserters from Enterprise, and we had no incidents that ever came to my attention that required shore patrol action, or police action, or reports to higher authority. So I think under the circumstances, our youngsters did fairly well. We also had two frigates with us, Truxtun and Halsey.

After our five-day visit to Sasebo, we were ready to depart, and our orders were to leave Sasebo. We were to get under way about 8:30 or 9:00 o'clock on this particular morning and head south and join Task Force 77 off Vietnam with a stop in Subic Bay on the way. Our departure was relatively routine. All liberty parties were to be back aboard by midnight, and we were to depart first thing in the morning, so that we had no people left ashore and had had what we thought was a very successful visit and some good shopping. Shopping in Japan in those days was still reasonably good.

Q: Certainly compared with today.

Admiral Lee: Today, yes.

Q: The exchange rate, I think, was 360 to one back then.

Admiral Lee: Three-sixty to one; that's what it was.* The prices in Japan were relatively cheap in terms of yen. A beer was just a few cents.

After hoisting anchor and heading outbound from

---

*At the time of this interview, the exchange rate was averaging around 135 yen to the dollar, only a little more than a third of what it had been in 1968.

Sasebo, we picked up a very strange message. By "we," I'm talking about the ship's communication system. This message was from a ship by the name of Pueblo, and the message was saying something about, "I'm being attacked. Help, help!" And let me say at the outset that we had a rear admiral on board by the name of Spin Epes, Horace H. Epes, and he was in charge of the formation and operations and in command of the task group. By then it was a Seventh Fleet task group.

Spin Epes was not one of my heroes. I didn't think he was operationally one of the best admirals that I worked for. But he had a chief of staff by the name of Frank Ault, who had had command of Coral Sea in a Vietnam tour, and I thought was one of the most able captains in the Navy. Frank Ault had also had command of a ship in the amphibious squadron that I was in. He went from command of that ship to command of Coral Sea and had had a WestPac tour. It was just a great shame that he never made rear admiral. I don't think it was because of his ability. I think it's one of the few cases in the Navy where bad publicity and some personal black marks prevented him from achieving that rank. But he was Epes's chief of staff, and I daresay ran about 90% of it. So when I say that Epes wasn't the best operator, I am in no way criticizing the decisions that were made, because Frank Ault was really running things as chief of staff. We couldn't have had a more able man out there.

When we got the Pueblo message, number one, we didn't know that there was such a ship as Pueblo; number two, we didn't know that Pueblo was up in the Sea of Japan. We had no idea where Pueblo was. Another factor was that Enterprise's deck was not spotted for launch. We'd been in port, planes were being worked on. Primarily the flight deck was filled with airplanes, and the hangar deck was relatively empty. We had just maintenance going on in the hangar deck. All we had were perhaps two planes, as we always had in the Pacific--two F-4s on the catapults which could be launched as CAP, combat air patrol, in a very short time. We might have had two backups, but as for A-6s or any other types ready to go, or F-4s, except for those two cats, we had none. Also, we had no information on Pueblo.

Hindsight is good stuff. It's been suggested that Epes should have launched on receipt of the message. He could always recall those airplanes. That's true. But, anyway, by the time we waited for clarification on the messages and by the time we found out that Pueblo was a U.S. Navy ship, was in the Sea of Japan, that it was a trawler-type, communications intelligence ship, it was too late to launch.

Q: How long did it take you to find out all those things?

Admiral Lee: I would say two or three hours. In the meantime, we were getting our flight deck all set to launch. Now the other odd part of this is that Pueblo didn't report to Commander Seventh Fleet. Pueblo reported to Commander Naval Forces Japan, which was a shore-based command.

Q: Rear Admiral Frank Johnson.

Admiral Lee: Pueblo reported to Johnson. He had operational control over it. Johnson, I believe, reported to CinCPac rather than to CinCPacFlt or Seventh Fleet, so that Pueblo was not one of Seventh Fleet's ships, unfortunately.* How much knowledge Seventh Fleet had of Pueblo, I don't know. But we had zero, which was unfortunate. Our intelligence people didn't even know, hadn't even been informed. That was unfortunate, because we should have been informed of everything out there, but we were not.

Q: Well from what you're saying, no direction came from higher authority to do something. It would have had to have been Admiral Epes's own initiative to launch.

---
*CinCPac--Commander in Chief Pacific.

Admiral Lee: Nothing came from higher authority. We just intercepted this message. Epes could have launched on reception of the message, and in hindsight, I suppose that's what he should have done. Decided to launch the two F-4s we had on CAP and vector them up. Our F-4s probably could have reached the Pueblo, and Enterprise could have made best speed towards that site. That would have looked good.

But by the time it was sorted out, we were in touch with Commander Seventh Fleet and Commander Naval Forces Japan--then it was too late. I think it's problematical whether or not we could have done anything anyway. But that, essentially, is what went on in Enterprise.

Q: Admiral Hyland said it would have been better, if only for the sake of appearance, to have launched.

Admiral Lee: Yes.

But, anyway, by the time this was sorted out by the powers that be in the chain of command, it was too late. We were then ordered to head up through Tsushima Strait into the Sea of Japan. There we started low-level flight operations, exercising our pilots and our planes primarily CAP and the various other planes that needed a little practice.

Q: The Navy put on a large show of force in the wake of that seizure on the 23rd of January.

Admiral Lee: We steamed around in the Sea of Japan, and additional ships were sent up to join us, from the 23rd of January until maybe the 13th or 14th of February. Meantime, Russian ships came down from Vladivostok and other Russian ports in the northern areas of the Sea of Japan. We saw the Russian ships almost every day, because we had gone fairly high up into the Sea of Japan.

We steamed up north to perhaps opposite Wonsan, Wonsan being a big North Korean port where Pueblo had been taken.

We were moved out of the Sea of Japan in a most unusual manner. One evening I was on the bridge at perhaps 7:30--I would assume this would have been about 7:30 in the morning in Washington. I was told that I had a telephone call in the little tactical plot area behind the navigation bridge. I went back to take the call, and much to my surprise, the call was from Washington and from President Johnson.

Q: Your friend.

Admiral Lee: My friend of the previous November. He wanted to know about those fellows from the north; were they giving us a problem? I told him no, that there didn't seem to be any problem, that we were doing very well. I didn't think there was any great danger. He told me then that what he wanted us to do was to turn south and head out of the Sea of Japan. The duty officer from CinCPac was on the line, and he asked me after the President had hung up if I fully understood what we were to do. I said, "Yes," and that I would immediately turn the formation south and head towards Tsushima Strait.

Q: Was this communication authenticated so you were absolutely sure it was the President?

Admiral Lee: No. It was not authenticated. That's why CinCPac said they would send an operational immediate message, which came in in a few minutes to authenticate it. I felt it would do no harm to turn south.

But, anyway, we had an admiral on board and, of course, you don't make such dramatic changes without his approval and usually his direction, although I was the officer in tactical command, as was done out in the Seventh Fleet in those days. Admirals and their staffs worked on the strike operations, and the flag captains ran the ships and the formations. That was the sort of division of labor.

Anyway, our admiral, Spin Epes, liked to have his

movie every night. The instructions were very firm that the admiral was not to be disturbed while he was having his movie. But I thought this message important enough that I go disturb the admiral. I went down to the flag cabin, and called the flag lieutenant aside and said that I had to see the admiral. This was very important. The flag lieutenant turned a little pale, knowing that this might be a problem, but he agreed that the movie would be stopped and I would see Admiral Epes.

I then went in to see Admiral Epes when the lights were turned on, and I told him that he wouldn't believe this, but that I had just talked to President Johnson on the telephone. The President had ordered us to head south out of the Sea of Japan. That CinCPac said that a confirming message would be sent immediately. Admiral Epes was a little bit taken aback, as you can understand, and a little bit miffed that orders having to do with his task group came in this fashion, but we still headed south out through Tsushima Strait.

On February 15, _Ranger_ came up to join us, and Admiral Epes was moved to _Ranger_, and _Ranger_ was left in the Sea of Japan area, and _Enterprise_ headed south, first to Subic Bay and then out to the Tonkin Gulf and to Task Force 77, so-called line.

We also got a new admiral on board, Rear Admiral John P. Weinel, better known as Blackie Weinel. Admiral Weinel was perhaps the best operator that I worked with during the Vietnam War, and I worked with a number of them. He was very knowledgeable about airplanes and weapons. He was also very well informed about the politics of what we were doing: what was going on in Washington; and what was going on in the world; and the importance of the various things we were trying in Vietnam.

First and foremost, he was a very fine operator. Any important event that happened in Vietnam with our pilots, Admiral Weinel would talk to them about it, interview them, and he was very sensitive to losses. Also he would come up to the flag bridge, at least once a day, and send his aide up to tell me that the admiral was on the flag bridge. That was the time for the two of us to talk. So, all in all, we had a very good introduction to the Vietnam War through Admiral Weinel and his staff.

Q: Were these talks to bring you up to speed on tactical arrangements and so forth?

Admiral Lee: These talks were about any and everything. We talked about the Navy--usually for an hour each day-- about the Vietnam War, about the squadrons, about the pilots, about what we should do in various areas. He wanted to hear my thoughts and ideas on all these things. Sometimes he was influenced by my thoughts, and sometimes he wasn't. But he was certainly a good listener, and I thought the decisions he made having to do with operations were the best of my time out there.

Q: Do you have any examples to give?

Admiral Lee: During our time out there, it became popular to hit Hanoi, and the idea was that we had these A-6s, which were built for night attacks. We knew that if we sent lone A-6s up into Hanoi, they would be picked off. We were forced to send some A-6s. And, you know, A-6s at night operate by themselves. There were no other planes operating in North Vietnam at night in this fashion. It wouldn't be all that difficult for the North Vietnamese with their Russian help to pick off the A-6s.

After we had lost several A-6s--and, as a matter of fact, a very interesting item, one of these young pilots from an A-6 was shot down and became a prisoner of war in 1968. In 1986, I visited America for a weekend, the carrier operations, and this young man, who spent four years in Vietnam as a POW, had come back when the POWs were released, was now number two officer, executive officer, of America.* He remembered me very well, and I was sorry

---

*In June 1968, Lieutenant (junior grade) Joseph S. Mobley, USN, a naval flight officer, ejected during a mission in an A-6 and was captured. In 1986, as a commander, he was executive officer of the USS America (CV-66).

to say I didn't remember him. But he accused us of leaving him in Vietnam in 1968.

But, anyway, Admiral Weinel was, I think, very instrumental in bringing some sense into our A-6 attacks in North Vietnam at night. Yes, we could send our A-6s up there, but by and by we wouldn't have any left. It was a very dangerous operation. A better way to attack North Vietnam would be with a big group of planes in the daytime, rather than sending those lone A-6s at night, because we would lose them all. I daresay we lost four or five. I've forgotten the numbers, but we lost quite a few.

Q: That's not very good for morale in your A-6 squadron.

Admiral Lee: Terrible.

But in all justice to them, they kept coming back. We had a very professional group of naval aviators for that Vietnam War--I think far better than we deserved. I was tremendously impressed with them in all three tours I was out there. I was out there two months with Holloway, and then I had two tours with Enterprise myself, so I saw three different air wings. I was very impressed.

Q: Did the ECM planes offer any kind of a solution on those strikes?*

---

*ECM--electronic countermeasures.

Admiral Lee: Yes and no. The trouble with Vietnam was that the North Vietnamese didn't have any air power to speak of. Their planes were really not a menace, their fighter airplanes. But what they did have was their surface-to-air missiles. They could move them around all over North Vietnam and could set one off when you were least expecting it. The surface-to-air missiles, and, of course, small arms fire, AA, knocked down the great bulk of the planes we lost. We really had no good defense against surface-to-air missiles.

We had various black boxes in our airplanes, which would deceive the surface-to-air missile. We had ECM airplanes, which would jam the radars needed by these surface-to-air missiles. But you must remember that we had 24-hour operations over Vietnam, day and night, and it was just impossible to have the radar planes every time they were needed.

I think it might be worthwhile to describe the operations in Vietnam. They really were almost unbelievable. Each aircraft carrier flew a 12-hour day. This meant that we normally launched our first flight of the day at noontime or midnight, depending on which 12 hours of the day we were assigned. Every hour and a half we might launch 12 or 15 planes at noon, and then at 1:30 launch 12 or 15 more. This would go on all afternoon and evening until midnight. We would launch our last flight at 10:30 and recover this particular flight at midnight. We always commenced the recoveries at midnight. Sometimes it would take us 20 or 30 minutes to get them on board.

After that we would refuel and replenish. Enterprise wouldn't need fuel oil but we'd need aviation gasoline or jet fuel, and we needed ammunition and bombs. We were unloading bombs in Vietnam at a rate unheard of before the Vietnam War, because these jets would carry big loads. We were sending hundreds of them over there every day. After the last recovery each day, we would do the replenishing and any other work we needed. So that the average work day on a ship like Enterprise was 16 or 18 hours a day for those people who didn't have an alternate. By an alternate, I mean there was no alternate for the captain, and for most of the crew, they were either on a watch basis, or they were on a shift basis. For instance, our aircraft maintenance group were on a 12-on and 12-off shift basis. We had about half our maintenance crew come on at noontime and work through until midnight. The other half would come on at midnight and work through the next day.

The people on the watch, such as officer of the deck, and engine room, and CIC were usually on a one-in-three watch basis, and then they did their regular work besides. This went on week in and week out, seven days a week. The weather was always marginal, never any good weather.

Sometimes we'd have to delay a launch or cancel a launch because of the weather, but not very often. Night and day in terrible weather we'd launch these strikes, weeks on end, months on end. It took a terrible toll on everybody. We would stay on the line for three weeks, a month, and then go into Subic Bay--that was our diet--for maybe five days, and then back to the line again.

Now one of the great treats we had on <u>Enterprise</u> for this particular cruise was a trip into Hong Kong. Maybe half to two-thirds of the way through our tour in 1968, the British Governor General in Hong Kong decided that <u>Enterprise</u> could come in. <u>Enterprise</u> in its previous tours had not been allowed in Hong Kong. So that <u>Enterprise</u> had been restricted to Subic Bay as sort of a home port. But, in this particular case, it was decided to let us in. We went into Hong Kong and had about five or six days there. That was a great treat for all hands. As a matter of fact, my wife and some other wives came to Hong Kong during our visit there. But other than that, it was Subic Bay and Olongapo, and Olongapo and Subic Bay, and back to the line.

This went on until perhaps the first week in July, when we left for home. I know we arrived home on 18 July, home being Alameda. After having left on 3 January, we arrived back on 18 July, which meant we were gone about six and a half months.

Q: Did it make a difference in your operations when the bombing halt came in at the first of April 1968? The northern part of North Vietnam was put off-limits.

Admiral Lee: No, we then concentrated our efforts on selected targets in South Vietnam. I don't think that made a great deal of difference to our efforts. I've forgotten the circumstances of it, but, as you say, in April we had a bombing halt which halted operations in North Vietnam.

Q: Well, not all North Vietnam; the southern panhandle was still available.

Admiral Lee: Yes.

Q: I guess there was a big alfa strike on the 31st of March, the last day before the halt.

Admiral Lee: I've forgotten the circumstances, but in any event we didn't stand out. We kept moving along. If we weren't attacking North Vietnam, we were hitting the strong points along the border, the DMZ I guess you'd call it, and the various points where Vietnamese were known to be assembling their forces.* So that, for us, it didn't make a lot of difference. But I've forgotten how long it

---
*DMZ--demilitarized zone.

lasted. Maybe, perhaps you know.

Q: I don't remember specifically.

Admiral Lee: Perhaps a month, three weeks, six weeks.

Q: Well, longer than that. At the end of October--all of North Vietnam was put off limits. This was, I think, one of President Johnson's moves just before the election, to try to help Humphrey.

Well, you talked about the effect of those long hours on the crew. You were someone who didn't have an alternate. What was the effect on you from a physical standpoint?

Admiral Lee: Well, you got what sleep you could.

Q: Which amounted to how much?

Admiral Lee: Well, very often as soon as flight operations were over and replenishment was over, I would, of course, approve the night orders and go to sleep.

Q: Would that be, say, 2:00 or 3:00 in the morning?

Admiral Lee: Perhaps 2:00 or 3:00 in the morning if we had

that particular shift. We would begin flight operations the next day at noontime. Chances are I would go to bed at 2:00 or 3:00 in the morning and be awakened once or twice during the night, and wake up the next morning at 8:00 or 9:00 o'clock and start in again. Now very often we would have to land aboard CODs and other aircraft. The captain of the carrier always is on the bridge or right there when flight operations are going on, so that I suppose I got five or six hours a night of sleep. Then, when we went into Olongapo I'd rest up. But it's a 24-hour-a-day job.

I can remember one night we had launched a strike into Vietnam, and this was one of the more spectacular nights. A plane radioed over Vietnam that he was on fire, and that he was heading for the ship, and he had an escort. So we told him to come ahead, and we could see him coming over the horizon, flaming. When he got to within a few miles of the task force, we told him to eject--this was at night-- and leave his airplane and let it crash into the sea, and we would pick him up. He ejected and ejected safely and landed in the water, and our destroyers picked him up and had him back to the ship within a very short time. That was sort of routine for operations in Tonkin Gulf. Meantime we went ahead with our launch and recovery.

Q: Could you describe a night unrep, please.*

---

*Unrep--underway replenishment.

Admiral Lee: Well, night unreps weren't very different from day unreps. The ammunition ships and refrigerator ships, stores ships, oilers were all right there. We went alongside one or more of them almost every night. The idea was that you don't have time to do them all at one time. So tonight we had an oiler, and tomorrow night we had an ammunition ship, the next day we would have a stores or grocery ship, although we didn't have to go alongside the stores or refrigerator ships more than once a week or ten days if we could get enough. We also loaded up when we were in Subic Bay. But the ammo ships and the oilers every third day usually, because we never liked to get lower than half full of the ammo and jet fuel, so, as a minimum, every third day.

We would be told the location of the oiler or replenishment ship, and we would then try to spot him about 10:00 or 11:00 at night. We would move toward him before our last recovery. From our last launch to our last recovery, which was from 10:30 to midnight, we would move towards this replenishment ship so that he would be within a few miles of us. We also knew what our recovery course would be, and we would take charge of this replenishment ship and move him out in front, in the direction we would be going to recover aircraft.

So that as soon as we recovered the final aircraft, if

we had done our planning properly, the replenishment ship would be within a few miles of us, and we would then give him course and speed to take up for replenishment. I would normally go to 27 knots and make an approach on the replenishment ship. There's a system of lights for making an approach on a replenishment ship. After doing it every night for months on end, you get pretty good at it. I would come in normally at 27 knots, because that was an easy speed for Enterprise and easily controlled, and we normally would replenish at about 12 to 15 knots, depending on circumstances and the ship. Perhaps half a mile back I would go down to 20 knots, and then maybe 15 knots as we were approaching the other ship. The plan was to get alongside as quickly as possible. After a while, we got very good at it.

Within a few minutes after recovery of aircraft, while the mechanics are refueling the aircraft from the last flight and getting organized there, our people down on the hangar deck would be ready. As soon as you go alongside, the line is shot over, and they have two or three or four replenishment stations. The replenishment ship would be all ready for us; everything that we had coming would be there. By the time the two ships were alongside each other, the produce and merchandise and the oil would be flowing across. It got to be routine. We used floodlights.

I found out that at the night, distances can be very deceiving. I always used radar to approach a replenishment ship until the final approach. Then for the final approach I would come out to the wing on the aircraft carrier and observe the wake of the ship ahead. A wake is absolutely indispensable, because night vision is not all that good. You'd use binoculars, but your depth perception at night is not very good. Once you get the wake nailed down and after you've made a few approaches, you can come to within a few feet of where you should be. I also had one of those alidades made so that all I had to do, if I wanted to be 120 feet out, was put that 120 feet on the edge of the wake, come right alongside, and there you were.

Q: I presume that you always came along the port side of the replenishment ship, your starboard side.

Admiral Lee: Always port side, because we couldn't come along the starboard side, and we were looking down on him from our bridge. But we got very proficient at replenishing, night or day, both in rendezvousing and going alongside, and in moving the ammunition and oil and produce, whatever else we had across, and people.

Q: Did you habitually take the conn during the approach?

Admiral Lee: As you can understand, the first few times, until I was confident that I could do it and would recognize errors, I made all the approaches. After I had confidence in my judgment and in my own eyes, both night and day, then I always let the executive officer, department heads, including the air wing commander and squadron commanders, come up and take their turn. I let them conn the ship alongside. They liked that. It was a chance to talk to them.

So I really didn't make many approaches personally after the first eight or ten, because I thought it was important to let the others do it; the department heads, the commanders always looked forward to this. It was a challenge, something to talk about in wardroom. I thought it was very important to them too. It was long hours for them and their only chance to conn the ship really. Most of them got very proficient at it, the engineers.

Q: Plenty of opportunities.

Admiral Lee: Yes. Oh, Lord, plenty of opportunities.

Q: There's a special relationship between a skipper and his officers of the deck. Could you describe that, please?

Admiral Lee: You know, I put together a system on Alamo

for qualifying officer of the deck. First off, we had a study outline, and it was sort of patterned on Rickover's qual card system training. We had a written exam. They had a certain amount of studying they had to do; then we had a written exam for them, and then we had an oral examination, where we would give them various problems. The oral exam board was made up of the department heads and one OOD, the engineer, executive officer, and me. I started that on Alamo. I wanted everybody to qualify as an officer of the deck. When I moved to Enterprise, I did the same thing. Yes, it was a way to get to know the junior officers. We started this qual card system, and it was great. As a matter of fact, we had a Marine captain who was the son of the Commandant at that time.

Q: General Chapman?

Admiral Lee: Chapman.* Leonard Chapman III was on Enterprise. He wanted to become an officer of the deck. Now I don't know if it's generally known, but Marines are not required to stand officer of the deck watches under way. They're required to stand officer of the deck watches in port, but under way they're not. There's some question as to whether or not it's legal. Only line officers who are eligible for command are supposed to stand officer of

---
*General Leonard F. Chapman, Jr., USMC, Commandant of the Marine Corps, 1968-71.

the deck watches under way. But, anyway, he wanted to be an officer of the deck.

So I said, "Fine. Why not?" He ran through our training program. These people had to go down to the engine room and become acquainted with it, stand some watches down there, damage control. They had to learn a lot about the ship. Then they had the written exam and the oral examination. We either passed them or failed them, primarily on the oral examination, how they responded. Meantime, they were standing watches on the bridge as assistant officer of the deck. And, yes, we ran dozens and dozens through our training program. And many of them, you know, didn't then stand watches on the bridge after they completed the training program. Although Chapman, the Marine captain who was the commanding officer of the Marine detachment, did. He stood watches for months and was one of the best.

But, yes, the captain always has a very special relationship with his officers of the deck. You have to have confidence in them, and you have to take them into your confidence. It's most important that they not be afraid of the captain, that if they're in doubt, call him. I let them deal with the ship just as I did the department heads, make approaches, maneuver the ship. Many of them became very proficient. I had a very fine group of OODs.

Had a good training program.

Q: How large a group did you have as a regular rotation?

Admiral Lee: Five.

Q: And what was the pattern of operations for the ship during the air strikes? Would you operate in a small box back and forth?

Admiral Lee: Yes. We had a point. Each carrier was assigned a point--point alfa, point bravo, point charlie, in Tonkin Gulf. There were some points up in the north and some points down south. We were expected to operate within about 50 miles of that point, something like that depending on any wind or weather. We did. We operated within a circle of 100 miles of those points, I'd say, all the time. Replenishment ships and CODs coming out and so forth, knew generally where to find us. We would be at point charlie, and we could pick up ships and aircraft always out there on our radars.

Q: Did you have any concern about submarines in those points?

Admiral Lee: Yes and no. I learned a long time ago that,

"Don't worry about things that you can do nothing about." And there was absolutely nothing we could do about a submarine. Our destroyers were out there looking, listening. One time or another we had ASW carrier groups up there, and we had P-3s, and we had all the intelligence community looking and listening, but there was absolutely nothing I could do on Enterprise.* So it wasn't one of the things I worried about. I had enough to worry about on things that I could influence.

Q: Since you were in this relatively confined area, it was predictable where your strikes would be coming from. Did Admiral Weinel try to vary patterns to deceive the enemy?

Admiral Lee: Yes. We tried never to repeat our strikes. This sort of thing went on every day. Our pilots tried all types of deception: high, low, various routes; every day was different. Weinel was very good at that. We were bombing Vietnam, both North and South Vietnam, 24 hours a day. So every day somebody was over there. So it would be hard for them to miss our planes day in and day out. I don't know how many sorties we sent over North and South Vietnam during that long period but a tremendous number. It would stagger the imagination--the cost--because Enterprise had four full tours out there alone. I don't

---
*The Lockheed P-3 Orion is a land-based patrol plane used primarily for antisubmarine warfare.

know when the first strikes started in Vietnam, and I don't know when the last ones ended. But it seemed to me as though it went on forever. I almost made a career of it, starting with <u>Alamo</u>.

Q: You know that some losses are going to be inevitable. How do you keep that from interfering with what you have to do as part of your job?

Admiral Lee: That's a good question, and I think if you're going to be a naval aviator and a naval officer, you have to come to terms with that sort of thing fairly early in life. We had losses in World War II, really very large losses. In one squadron I was in of about 50 pilots, we lost 22, 23 pilots. Not all out of that group of 50, because as we lost pilots, replacements came in. The other squadron I was in in World War II, we lost about the same number, VF-15. But the point I'm making is, you come to terms with this, or you become ineffective. You have a nervous breakdown. And people do that. So you have to come to terms with this if you're going to be a naval aviator, because you have not only combat losses but accidental losses through the years.

I think most naval aviators come to terms with it in the sense that it's not that they don't mourn the loss of their friends and their colleagues. It's not that they become hardened, but it's the fact that in order to carry on--which is most important in the military, you can't quit; otherwise, you get clobbered. I think you sort of compartmentalize your mind. You're grieving greatly, but you put it aside and go on with the job at hand. Those people who can effectively do that, survive and become very capable combat leaders and the like. Those people who cannot, who become emotional about losses, become very ineffective. Now, that may seem a very hard way to look at it, but I think it's about the way it happens.

Q: You have to force yourself to accept the inevitable risks.

Admiral Lee: Yes. You're going to have losses and you can't dwell on them. You have to move on. That's just about the way it is.

Q: Your executive officer has to play a very large role, while you're concentrating so heavily on the operational things, on all the other things that need to be done on an aircraft carrier.

Admiral Lee: The executive officer is a very key man. All the department heads are key, but the executive officer is the manager of the hotel. The captain is running operations, and meeting the dignitaries, and doing all the things that only the captain can do; but the executive officer is the man who has to run the whole machine. He has to keep close track of his department heads, and division officers and men; he has to handle discipline and the chief master-at-arms; he has to handle all the visitors and the wardroom. I think being executive officer of an aircraft carrier is the toughest job in the Navy. It's tougher than being captain, I think. That was why I wasn't all that eager to be executive officer of Enterprise, because I had seen many executive officers. It's a very difficult job. I was lucky to have two very fine executive officers.

I mentioned before that my first executive officer was Isham Linder, better known as Sam Linder, who later became a rear admiral. He was an ASW-type aviator, so he was never really seriously considered as commanding officer of Enterprise. The next executive officer I had was a fellow by the name of John Alvis, who was just as talented in his way as Linder was.* Both were highly educated people, both Naval Academy graduates, both in the top of their class. Linder got a Ph.D. from Berkeley, California. And Alvis got a bachelor's degree in aeronautical engineering and then went down to Oak Ridge, studied nuclear

---
*Commander John H. Alvis, USN.

engineering down there, and got a master's degree. Rickover always made light of these people in the Navy who were over-educated. But, almost without exception, he always picked them for these jobs. Alvis and Linder are two very good examples.

Q: I think that must have been a big factor with Linder, because coming from an ASW background, he normally wouldn't get into an attack carrier.

Admiral Lee: I think he was the only man who got into the nuclear navy, aviation navy, who wasn't an attack carrier aviator, only because he had such marvelous academic tickets.

Q: I think he was later superintendent of the PG school.

Admiral Lee: He's the man. Very able man and a good friend. Alvis and his wife came down and spent the weekend with us the weekend before last, and we went down to the Virginia and North Carolina game--good man. But Alvis later joined me in NavAir, and I'll talk about that more later.

Q: You mentioned discipline briefly. I take it nearly everything was handled before it got to you.

Admiral Lee: Well, not entirely. This might be a good time to talk about discipline.

Discipline is a big factor on an aircraft carrier, but I sometimes think that we had a minimum of problems on our aircraft carriers in that period. It's hard to understand. But the executive officer, of course, controls the ship. In accordance with the Uniform Code of Military Justice, only the commanding officer, or the acting commanding officer, can hold captain's mast and award nonjudicial punishment. Now that's another major chore that a commanding officer has to do. When squadrons and an air wing move aboard, only the captain of a ship can hold mast. So at sea I normally held mast once a week. I'd hold mast on the flag bridge and I might have 20 or 30 people there.

But with the exception of some completely amoral individuals, we didn't really have any problems, no court-martials to speak of. We might have had one or two court-martials in the two years I was aboard. It was mostly young men telling a petty officer where he could jam it, that sort of thing. Maybe after a trip into Olongapo, or Hong Kong, or Singapore, we would have more cases than usual, because people would be absent over leave or get in fights ashore.

But there were a certain number of men who were, as I have often said, amoral. They don't recognize right from wrong, and you see them back at mast, time after time after time. You begin to recognize them. You also recognize a youngster who's never been at mast before and who did something that he knows is wrong, whatever it might be, and who wants to take his punishment like a man and not do it again.

I think captains holding mast by and by get a pretty good grasp of when they have one of these amoral types and when they have a good sailor who made a mistake. I think captains should be given great leeway in this, because there are some youngsters that are absolutely first-rate sailors, but they have too many beers. Something happens, they get into trouble. If you get them back aboard ship and then take them to mast, and really hit them a hard lick, you can ruin them. They can become very discouraged.

So I think a captain has to be very perceptive in how he handles this. Men who had a good record, who were good performers, usually got a warning. It was always good to have the chief petty officer come to mast and describe the man. If the chief petty officer gives the man a good recommendation and it's a first offense, I would be very reluctant to do much, unless it's something really gross, borderline felony. But these amoral types, we showed no mercy on them. We tried to make a record, so to speak, and get them out of the Navy and off Enterprise as quickly as possible. You recognize them fairly quickly. They take so much division officer time and chief petty officer time, and they take so much of our time, so that as soon as we could pretty well recognize one of these characters, we tried to move them off the ship. I thought that was very good for Enterprise, good for the Navy, and good for discipline.

Q: Their presence is really counterproductive.

Admiral Lee: Yes. In the two years I was aboard, we probably transferred 50 or 100 of these types.

But other than that, the bad apples, discipline was never a problem. It was less of a problem on Enterprise than I ever would have guessed, whether we were in port or otherwise. Never a problem. There's absolutely nothing wrong with the American youngster of that generation, and I'm sure they haven't changed much to this generation. If they know they're getting a fair shake, they're willing to work hard. If you keep them fully informed, and let them know and let them see that whatever comes about, they're going to get their fair share, and they're going to get a fair shake if they make a mistake. Discipline certainly wasn't a problem in those years. I still am amazed at how many disciplinary problems the Navy apparently had during the Zumwalt era. Because we had no problems with blacks or anyone else before the Zumwalt era. No problems.

Q: Well, you say you got rid of maybe 100 men, and you're probably speaking out of a population of 10,000 if you consider turnover and different air wings.

Admiral Lee: Probably.

Q: That's 1%, which is pretty small.

Admiral Lee: Yes. As a matter of fact, nowadays, on my visit to America, I learned the entire Navy has gone to this view that when we find a sour apple, let's get him out of the Navy. Commanding officers are now allowed to discharge them directly from their ships during a certain period of the year. In that way the Navy gets rid of these difficult youngsters who can't adjust to discipline, are amoral, or won't work. The Navy gets rid of them very quickly. I think it's a very good thing. It certainly lightens the load of the commanding officer, and the executive officer, and the chiefs who have to deal with these people. But during the Vietnam War, I thought discipline and morale were amazingly good.

Q: What role do your chaplains play in that overall picture?

Admiral Lee: Chaplains handle the emergency leave business. On a big ship, such as Enterprise, that's pretty big business. They have to sort out those people who should be allowed to go on emergency leave and those people who shouldn't. For instance, if you have a youngster 19 years old whose grandfather dies, we normally would highly discourage his going on emergency leave. We let the chaplains know what the ground rules are. If we had a young man whose son died, we let him go home. Our rules were that if he could be of benefit, he could go. But if a mother died or a father died, not ordinarily. Because by the time he got home, the funeral would be over. Nothing he could do, provided he wasn't an only son, and he had to help his mother get settled.

So our chaplains were the first line in that area, emergency leaves and problems with wives and dependents. They also did lots of other things, such as handle the recreational items. They held religious services, of course. There are a certain number of youngsters who grew up in highly religious families, whether Catholic or Southern Baptist, or Mormon who would need to go talk to the chaplain. They would get emotionally upset.

So the chaplains, I think, played a very important role, and we had some first-rate chaplains. I was very pleased with all the chaplains we had. They did their jobs and didn't try to be the commanding officer. I never had cause to criticize one of our chaplains for anything that he wanted to do or recommend. After we'd got confidence in them, we really rarely questioned their recommendations. Because we found they were good. So, yes, we had very active chaplains. They were very much a part of the administrative structure of the ship, and played a key role. We always had two chaplains.

Q: They can be useful in discovering problems and communicating those to you.

Admiral Lee: Chaplains are very useful in discovering problems and letting the division officer or the executive officer or the captain know. They oftentimes can detect problems before other people. On a big ship like Enterprise, the chaplains worked very closely with the executive officer in this area. So I have nothing but the best of words for our chaplains. They were very important to us.

Q: The drug situation wasn't as big then as it later became. Was that a problem at all during your time?

Admiral Lee: Not really. Of course, we were in the San Francisco area and Haight-Ashbury, and I think some of our people tried LSD and marijuana. But drugs were not a big problem and not a big issue. We kept our eyes open for it, and supposedly they were available in the Subic Bay area. We had a few people caught with drugs. Once again, it was never a problem on Enterprise. We never had any big drug busts, or any big drug agents, or any big gambling rings. That's the sort of thing that your chiefs and your chaplains and your division officers have got to keep their ear to the ground about. They've got to let you know if they see a problem building up in any one of these areas.

Q: You had the protesters in Japan. Did you have to deal with any anti-Vietnam War protesters?

Admiral Lee: Yes, we had all kinds of anti-Vietnam War protesters in the Bay area. Remember the broken cross sign and all of that. They'd meet us with boats, with signs on boats. We had our share of protesters in the Bay area. But it was never a problem for us. I was asked two or three times about the protesters by newsmen, and I never had much to say about it. My comment always was that, "The Navy doesn't like war either. We hope we can have a peace in Vietnam and not have to go back out there." But the protesters, at least during my two years there, were always present. They were building up steam during these two years, because I didn't leave until July '69. But it wasn't a problem for us. It never caused us any heartache.

It never caused us any disciplinary problems that I know about.

Q: You touched on yet another facet of your job, dealing with the news media. Could you discuss that more fully, including the role of the public affairs officer?

Admiral Lee: Enterprise, as opposed to most carriers, had a full-time professional public affairs officer, commander in both cases, because it was in the public eye so much. We had newsmen aboard frequently. Most of the time when we went to sea, we had one or more newsmen aboard. Everybody from Gene Roddenberry who puts on "Star Trek" to TV newsmen, to columnists.* We had lots of newsmen aboard all the time.

When we went into a city we hadn't been into before, such as San Diego, or Seattle, or Sasebo, we had dozens of newsmen and TV reporters. Our public affairs officer had our standard brochure we'd hand out. I usually had a news conference--TV, or radio, or columnist. We would have a talk. I would answer their questions about the ship, about the Vietnam War, and had news conferences, of course, after the flight deck fire, which we haven't gotten to yet. News conference in Sasebo. We had lots of newsmen aboard. As I

_____
*Eugene W. Roddenberry was the creator and producer of the popular television series of the period, "Star Trek," that included a spaceship named the Enterprise.

say, Enterprise was the center of attention just about everywhere we went.

So dealing with newsmen became second nature with us. We didn't look on it as any big chore. We talked to them anytime they wanted to talk. Took them around the ship if they wanted a tour, talked to me, the executive officer. We talked to them very frankly, very honestly. No, it wasn't a big problem.

Q: Did you generally find them to be fair and open-minded?

Admiral Lee: Yes, I thought so. I never had any problems with newsmen. I thought they were very fair. I don't ever remember getting a bad press personally. I didn't see a third of it, but I don't remember getting a bad press. My impression of newsmen is that if you treat them courteously and in gentlemanly fashion, they don't take potshots at you. Most of the newsmen that we knew were not aiming at captains of ships and Enterprise and the crews. They're bigger people than that. If they had any disagreements, it was with Johnson and people making the big decisions. I got an interesting quote fairly recently. I knew a newsman by the name of George Wilson who writes for The Washington Post.* He told Pat Tyler about me, and Pat Tyler says,

---

*George C. Wilson later wrote a book titled Supercarrier: An Inside Account of Life Aboard the World's Most Powerful Ship, the USS John F. Kennedy (New York: Macmillan, 1986).

"Well, what should I know about Admiral Lee?"

He said, "Well, he was the last of the gentleman captains." That's what Pat Tyler told me.

But, I don't know, my impression was that people who get in trouble with news media are people who don't play fair with them. We never had any problems that I knew about.

Q: Your friend Ed Snyder was descended upon by the media when he had command of the New Jersey, and he took essentially the same approach that you did and had a good press.* I think some senior officers tend to view the news media as the enemy, and that leads reporters to become suspicious and to dig in to see, "Well, is there something I should be trying to find here?"

Admiral Lee: You know, the first flag officer that I ever knew was like that, Ruble. He wouldn't have a thing to do with the press, wouldn't talk to them. He and I went on a trip together on a plane, and newsmen were at one end and he was at the other, never talked to them. Whereas, the fellow who made four stars--Jimmy Thach--as the saying goes, "He'd walk a mile to meet a newsman."

---

*Captain J. Edward Snyder, Jr., USN, with whom Lee had previously served in Washington, was commanding officer of the battleship USS New Jersey (BB-62) from April 1968 to August 1969. The New Jersey received a great deal of news media coverage during that period.

I found that if you treat them courteously, do all you can for them, because they've got a job to do, you'll never have a problem with them. They're not shooting at you. Now, the President--that's different--people, I think, in responsible positions, the newsmen are trying to trip them up. They put a little English on their questions. But that doesn't happen on my level, that is, commanding officer of a ship. Most of the newsmen coming aboard aren't very knowledgeable, and they want to write a good story, and they want to learn about the ship and the ship's personalities. I thought we did our very best to make them feel at home, make them feel welcome.

Q: Well, and it's an opportunity for you to educate them.

Admiral Lee: Yes, and we did that. We worked on that. I think we did some pretty good things. Keyes Beech wrote a column about _Enterprise_ and it was an excellent column. He interviewed me on _Enterprise_ in Tonkin Gulf. As a matter of fact, it was so good that Rickover had it put in the _Congressional Record_ by Senator Jackson.* It gets to be a chore to see these newsmen, but I felt we did a good job

---
*Senator Henry M. Jackson, Democrat from the state of Washington, was a great supporter of Admiral Rickover and the nuclear power program. The article was titled "Six Months in Tonkin Gulf--Big E Wins Case for Rickover, Supporters of a Nuclear Navy." It appeared in the _Philadelphia Inquirer_, 18 June 1968, and was reprinted in the _Congressional Record_, 9 July 1968, Volume 114, Part 15, pages 20276-20277.

in that area thanks to the two executive officers I had and these two commanders, these professional people. I think people who have trouble with newsmen are people who don't play the game.

Q: Well, frankly, I was a little surprised at your candor when I read Tyler's book, because it was obvious that you'd been cooperative with him, or he wouldn't have gotten that story.

Admiral Lee: Told him whatever he wanted to know. That is, to my knowledge. I didn't play coy with him.

Q: Well, and you didn't get into anything that was still classified either.

You mentioned Captain Chapman, just in passing, among the OODs. What was your relationship with the Marine detachment on board?

Admiral Lee: The captain of the Marine detachment on board is a division officer. They are just like another division, and I had a Marine orderly. The exec had a Marine orderly from the division. The Marines handled the brig, the prisoners, and manned weapons; they were our landing force. We had Captain Chapman for the first year, and another captain the second year. Captain Chapman was a very fine young man. As a matter of fact, I saw General Chapman after I got back to Washington, and I told him that I enjoyed having his son aboard, that I just wished I had one just like him. He was a fine young man. Unfortunately, he died in a swimming accident in the Far East a few years ago.

Q: I saw his dad a few weeks ago and he looked sort of frail and had his arm in a sling.

Admiral Lee: He was a good Commandant. But the Marines were just another division, and we had first-rate young officers. I think the Marine Corps very carefully selects their officers for shipboard duty.

Q: I know that's true.

Admiral Lee: You just wouldn't find better than we got. I was tremendously pleased with them and impressed with them.

Q: Did the detachment provide security for nuclear weapons?

Admiral Lee: Yes, they provided security for nuclear weapons, security for prisoners, ran the brig, and were our landing force. When we had guns, they'd man one of the gun mounts. Marines were part of the damage control organization. Marines were just a part of the ship, just another division. They were a division within the weapons department.

Q: The presence of Marines on board can set a good example for the sailors too.

Admiral Lee: Yes. Although they were always getting in little scuffles ashore.

Q: Friendly rivalry.

Admiral Lee: Friendly rivalry, but it wasn't something that we took too seriously.

Q: With all the ammunition and bombs that you were running through, why would you take up some of your magazine space with nuclear weapons?

Admiral Lee: That's a good question, but we did. We had a magazine full of nuclear weapons on all of our cruises to WestPac. We had a magazine set aside for them. I've forgotten what number we carried but--it wasn't just one or two; it was probably 60 or 70 in those years.

Q: Because you don't know for sure that you'll be operating only against Vietnam.

Admiral Lee: Yes, we prepared for any eventuality.

Interview Number 6 with Vice Admiral Kent L. Lee,
U.S. Navy (Retired)

Place: Logon Farm, Admiral Lee's home near Gordonsville, Virginia

Date: Monday, 14 December 1987

Interviewer: Paul Stillwell

Q: Admiral, today we resume your time as captain of the Enterprise, and you are ready to discuss the procedures involved in moving from the home port up to the naval shipyard at Bremerton.

Admiral Lee: Enterprise was home-ported in Alameda, in the San Francisco Bay area, and on prior tours the Enterprise was able to go into the Hunters Point Naval Shipyard for restricted availability between tours to WestPac. This meant that our men were at home with their families during the six months between tours.

This particular year, 1968, Enterprise was scheduled to get home on 18 July and on 27 July to depart Alameda and go to Bremerton, Washington, for about two months dry docking and restricted availability. I thought that would be very tough on families. We had been gone since the first of January, so after six and a half months away, we then would have only two weeks with families. Sailing off to Bremerton was difficult.

We started thinking about this on the way back from

the Western Pacific. Since the air wing would not be on the ship, we came up with the idea that we take dependents with us--automobiles, household effects, wives, and children--all to Bremerton. Those who wanted to stay in the Bremerton area could do so. Those who just wanted to ride the ship up and come home again in their own automobiles could do that. In any event, it would be a nice trip for them and a good vacation. This hadn't been done before. We requested permission, through Commander Naval Air Force Pacific Fleet, to the Chief of Naval Operations, outlining our reasons and the fact that we had plenty of room, and we thought we could run a safe cruise. It was immediately approved, much to our pleasure and somewhat to our astonishment.

We went into high gear in planning for this trip. We did indeed take everybody's automobile, all the household effects they wanted to take, a rock and roll band, all their wives and children--a total of 700 dependents. We planned entertainment all the way from Alameda to Bremerton. The trip was for two days, getting under way on 27 July in the morning, and arriving in Bremerton on the morning of 29 July, which would be two nights at sea and three days. It was a remarkably successful cruise. We had a cookout on the fantail. We had shows, and a dance, and tours of the ship.

All enlisted men who had wives and children along were

put up in officers' country. We had enough rooms available so that I think everybody was happy with the trip. It was one of the best things we ever did. On the way home we were able to come directly from Bremerton to Alameda and off-load them. That was the highlight of our summer.

Also, while at Seattle, Rickover came with Dave Leighton, and he was all sweetness and light, very pleased with our first cruise.* He had nothing but good words for us, as opposed to later on.

After getting back to Alameda from Seattle, we went to San Diego for underway training, and then had operations off the coast until ready to depart for the Western Pacific once again.

Q: Are there any highlights to mention from the period in Bremerton? Were there any updates or changes in the ship?

Admiral Lee: We had lots of updates and changes in the ship. For instance, we had to convert to the test facilities and equipment for a new airplane. We were going from the A-4 to the A-7. None of it was of major proportions, but we had dozens and dozens and dozens of changes that had to be made before the next cruise, for one

---

*David T. Leighton stood 23rd of the 1,046 graduates in the Naval Academy class of 1946 and subsequently entered the nuclear power program as an active duty naval officer. He resigned his regular commission as a commander in 1962 and remained with Rickover as a civilian.

reason or another, in electronics and in some of the machinery. We were put in dry dock and our bottom was scraped, because <u>Enterprise</u> had been out of dry dock since coming out of overhaul in Norfolk three years previously, so her bottom was getting pretty dirty, three cruises to WestPac. But other than that, it was a routine availability. We had no problems to speak of.

Q: How much work gets done on the nuclear plant during a routine availability like that?

Admiral Lee: Very little, although we did have some work going on in the nuclear plant. We tested 16 generators, we put in some new pipes. <u>Enterprise</u> has 32 steam generators, four per reactor. So always there's work going on in a big ship like that. We worked on overhaul of a good section of the ship in every area. We had work going around the clock for eight weeks. But we went in in good shape and came out in good shape.

We went through underway training again, operations off the West Coast--not very different from the previous year's, so I won't go into any of that. I think what I'd like to do is go directly to departing for Western Pacific on 6 January 1969.

Now the night before that, I made a great mistake--in retrospect. On the night of 5 January, the reactor officer, whose name was Commander Ned Kellogg, called me at home and said that they had an unusually high chlorine count in a steam generator.* Or it might have been the four steam generators involved with one reactor; it just involved one reactor.

What I should have done was call Rickover and tell him. But I didn't do that. What we did was start cleaning it up. Chlorine comes from the salt water, so somewhere or other we had a leak of salt water into our steam generators in that one reactor, which was we later found out to be a sort of overboard exhaust line. The water came backwards into the steam generator, but we didn't know that at the time. But I didn't call Rickover and report to him or Leighton by telephone. That was the beginning of a very difficult relationship with Rickover, because when we subsequently reported to him via an incident report about this chlorine in the steam generator, he really hit the roof. And I had a very difficult time with Rickover from then on.

We left Alameda on the morning of 6 January, had about five days to Pearl Harbor, and then several days in Hawaii while we prepared for our operational readiness inspection. On the morning of 13 January, we got _Enterprise_ under way from Pearl Harbor to head out to the operating area and begin our operational readiness inspection.

---
*Commander Edward S. Kellogg, USN.

On the morning of 14 January, we had a launch at 0700--fully armed airplanes. This was our final examination before another trip to Vietnam--new air wing and lots of new people. The first launch, about 20 airplanes, went off at 0700 to attack some targets in the area southwest of Pearl Harbor. There was a wind of 12 or 15 knots, and we were headed downwind at about ten knots so that the wind was blowing over the flight deck, getting ready for our second launch, which was to go at 0830, and we were to recover the first launch.

At 0819 I was in my sea cabin, probably doing paperwork, when I heard a very sharp explosion. It was sort of like the explosion that's set off by underway training group people when they start an exercise. But the captain was never supposed to be surprised by any of those because the underway training groups and ORI people would tell him beforehand. Nothing like that was scheduled. So the moment I heard this, I immediately went to the bridge, and in the very few seconds in walking from the sea cabin, which is not more than five steps away, I got out to the wing of the navigation bridge, and the whole aft end of the flight deck was enveloped in smoke and flame.

I immediately realized what had happened. We had had a very bad accident. Something had set off an explosion on the flight deck, and it had punctured fuel tanks and ignited a great big holocaust on our after flight deck.

The first thing I did was take the conn and turn the ship into the wind and order general quarters immediately. Now there was a problem with ordering general quarters, because when a ship like Enterprise goes to general quarters, it's sealed up from stem to stern. We had a lot of people from the air wing on the 03 level, just below the flight deck. Since we were on a 12-hour basis, many of them would be locked in their compartments.

We had about 15 or 20 aircraft on the after part of the flight deck, all loaded with full fuel, full ammunition, Zuni rockets, and bombs.* We had this horrendous blaze going. There wasn't any doubt in my mind that the safety of the ship was paramount, and that what we should do is go to general quarters, flood the hangar deck with the overhead sprinkler system, and try to prevent the fire from spreading from the after part of the flight deck to the rest of the ship. Because once those fires get going with the minimum fire fighting equipment that we had on the flight deck, there isn't anything you can do about it. Also, metals like aluminum and magnesium begin to burn at very high temperatures, so piles of molten metal were growing back there.

Further, we had a number of Zuni rockets and 500-pound

---

*The Zuni is a 5-inch, folding-fin, air-to-ground rocket carried in pods for launching from aircraft. It is characterized by high speed and high accuracy, which made it useful against small hard targets in Vietnam.

bombs loaded on various aircraft back in the pack at the after end of the flight deck. After a certain period of time in this intense heat, they cook off. When they cook off, they blow the airplane to which they're attached into 1,000 pieces, and sometimes off the ship and in the air, and blow a hole in the flight deck. The flight deck is a steel plate, perhaps two inches thick, inch and a half, solid steel. But these 500-pound bombs going off two feet above the flight deck blow holes in that metal.

So we got turned into the wind, and I regulated the speed of the ship so that we would not have any smoke coming forward. We didn't need a lot of speed, so I just kept speed on of about ten knots, and did the things that I've described earlier. There really wasn't any way we could fight the fire on the after flight deck. We just had to let it burn out, especially with those Zuni rockets, bombs, and ammunition. In the meantime, we were taking pictures of all this with the various TV cameras available to us in the bridge area so that we would have a complete record of what was going on.

We were making every effort to prevent the spread of the fire, which was crucial. If it got on the hangar deck, we could very easily lose the ship. So we didn't want it to go below the 03 level, which is the first deck below the flight deck. But there wasn't any way we could keep it out of there, and we had to man our damage control forces to those compartments that got blown through on the 03 level. We had to spray water on the bulkheads around them to make sure that they didn't flash into flame and that would spread on down below.

Also, burning fuel was pouring off all sides of the flight deck. So we had to keep water sprayed on those sides and on the fantail. The equipment that we did have all worked. Our people had just finished underway training, and we'd had hundreds of drills. That training paid off so that we were able to confine the fire to the after part of the flight deck. After about three hours, the fire had burned itself out. We then headed in towards Pearl Harbor and in the meantime, destroyers came alongside and tried to spray water on us and help us fight the fire. Their efforts were greatly appreciated, and took great courage on their part and great seamanship, but they just didn't have the water power to do us much good.

In an article that I wrote for Wings of Gold several years ago--for those of you who are interested, I described the fire fighting equipment that ships prior to the time of the Forrestal had and how it was used--especially to fight flight deck fires.* I described what Enterprise had and how it was used. Then I described what Nimitz has and how

---

*"An End to Catastrophic Flight Deck Fires," Wings of Gold, Spring 1983, pages 22-36.

she managed her flight deck fire.* I further went on to describe what we really need to manage a flight deck fire. That article was in an issue of Wings of Gold, and I believe a copy of it should be attached as the appendix of this particular oral history.

Q: It will be.

What advantages did you have fighting your fire as a result of what the Forrestal had gone through a couple years earlier?

Admiral Lee: Very little. We had those trucks on the flight deck with fire fighting foam, a mixture of water and fire retardant chemical. But it wouldn't have made any difference if we hadn't had it. We weren't any better off than Forrestal, Enterprise was not, and Nimitz was no better off than Enterprise. The changes that were made were largely cosmetic and ineffectual.

What we really need is a dramatic change, such as is described in that article--a new piece of equipment. What you really need is a water cannon that can throw at the fire thousands of gallons per minute or water mixed with a flame-retardant chemical. That's what you need, which we don't have. Our sources of water for fire fighting are

---
*On the night of 26 May 1981, while the USS Nimitz (CVN-68) was operating 60 miles off the Coast of Florida, a Marine Corps EA-6B electronic warfare plane crashed on the flight deck while attempting to land and started a fire.

rather puny compared to what you really need--people manning fire hoses on the flight deck. That's ridiculous.

Anyway, after about three hours, the fire had burned out, and we began to count crewmen, count noses, to see how many people were missing, how many were killed, and how many injured.

Q: What can you say about the skill and courage of the crew in fighting that fire?

Admiral Lee: I think the skill and courage of the crew were absolutely superb. The senior investigator, appointed by Commander Naval Air Force Pacific Fleet, was Rear Admiral Bardshar. His report is a matter of record. For somebody interested in this particular phase of it, it makes very good reading. He goes into how we fought the fire, and he gives great praise to the crew. All equipment worked, the crew was well trained, they showed great bravery. He especially had praise for the flight deck crews and the air officer who directed their efforts. I personally had no criticism for any aspect, or any person, or any phase of it. And neither did the investigator.

I was about to say that after we had counted noses, we had 28 killed and 343 injured, with 15 aircraft destroyed and 17 damaged. I've looked up those numbers from that paper I wrote for Wings of Gold, and I had previously done the research to put those numbers together.

We then headed for the Pearl Harbor Naval Shipyard. After any naval disaster, there's a board of inquiry. This is called in the vernacular, "around the green table." Such came to pass after the Enterprise fire. The president of the board of inquiry was Rear Admiral Fred Bardshar. He had two or three lawyers to assist him. Other members of the board were specialists from around the Pearl Harbor area. The investigation went on for about five or six weeks while we were in the naval shipyard. I was around the green table a fair amount of time.

I was made an interested party to this board of inquiry, as were the air officer, the executive officer, and other senior officers responsible for the ship. As interested parties we were informed that we could have counsel, and we didn't have to testify unless we wanted to. We were afforded all our legal rights, in other words.

But I decided that I thought we had done a good job in training our crew; I thought we had fought the fire very well; and my whole desire was to get to the bottom of the fire, find out just how it started, and what went wrong, what caused this. I decided to testify freely to the board of inquiry and not have a counsel, and that if I later needed a counsel for a court-martial, I would get one. But at this stage the board of inquiry merely fixes blame, and court-martials would come later. I told my senior officers who were also interested parties what I was going to do, but I invited them to make up their own minds about having a counsel. As it turned out, none of the senior officers, the officers on <u>Enterprise</u>, elected to have counsel.

The inquiry went off about as scheduled, and, I think, got to the bottom of what caused the explosion and fire. It's very simple. We had a 19 year old driving a tractor with a small jet engine mounted on the rear. These jet engines put out a great volume of fairly high-pressure air which is channeled through a big hose to start a modern huge jet engine such as in an F-4 aircraft. These tractors are normally also used to tow jet aircraft around. The tractors have a sizable diesel engine as motive power.

This youngster backed this tractor with the little jet engine on the top of it up under the wing of an F-4 aircraft. On the wing of the F-4 aircraft were mounted Zuni rockets. As luck would have it, the exhaust of that small jet engine was coming out in such a way that it impinged directly on the warhead of a Zuni rocket. In a little more than a minute this hot exhaust cooked off the Zuni rocket.

The board of inquiry ran tests to see how long it would take one of these jet exhausts to cook off a Zuni rocket warhead. Each one took something a little more than a minute. They cooked off regularly, never a misfire. It was decided that without a doubt that this is what started the whole thing. The Zuni rocket warhead split into a thousand pieces when it exploded, and those little pieces of hot metal traveling at high speed were scattered all around the flight deck, wounding crewmen, puncturing fuel tanks, spilling JP-5 all over the flight deck, and igniting it. So in a matter of two or three seconds, the whole after flight deck was blazing with JP-5.*

Q: How was it determined that that was the cause? Were there witnesses who saw the Zuni go off?

Admiral Lee: There were witnesses who saw the young man back the tractor up to the F-4. The pilots had manned aircraft, and we lost no pilots. The pilots were protected from the blast since they were in the cockpits. But the explosion took place at a particular F-4, and the pilot was there. So, yes, we had witnesses for all of this. We knew where it started, and we knew that it was that Zuni warhead that went off. The pilot escaped, fortunately.

Q: But the 19-year-old man was killed.

Admiral Lee: The 19 year old who was sitting in an open tractor was killed by the shrapnel from the Zuni warhead. He was killed instantly.

---
*JP-5 is a type of fuel used for jet aircraft, among other things.

As luck would have it, the board of inquiry had great praise for the ship and the way the fire was handled. None of us were, to use legal terms, indicted. None were court-martialed or got letters of caution or reprimand, or any other disciplinary action. The general feeling was that we had done about as well as we could do in a very difficult situation, that our crew was well trained, that we had fought the fire the way our equipment was designed to be used to fight fires, and that we had done all that was possible to do in such circumstances.

Of course, that came as a great relief to all of us, because it had been a very traumatic experience, and as we all know in the Navy, the captain is responsible for whatever goes wrong on his ship. I was fully prepared to take whatever medicine was coming my way, whatever disciplinary action was coming my way as a result of it. Much to my surprise, none of us were disciplined, and as a matter of fact, we got great praise for the way we handled the whole thing--we, the crew, the officers of the ship.

Q: How had you spent those three hours while the fire was burning? What all had you done?

Admiral Lee: I was on the bridge the entire time, of course. I was monitoring everything that was going on. I was monitoring what was happening on the flight deck, and our air officer was running the fire fighting going on on the flight deck. I was monitoring what was going on in the hangar deck to make sure that we didn't have a fire down there. I was monitoring what was going on in the other parts of the ship, fire main pressures. I directed that the water wash-down system be turned on up forward. We couldn't get to the valve to turn on the water wash-down system back aft, but it wouldn't have made any difference. That water wash-down system was like pissing into the wind, if you'll pardon the expression.

But during these three hours, and especially during the first hour, I was monitoring, through various listening posts, what was going on throughout the ship and what needed to be done and what we could do. We had settled the ship on a steady course and speed, so there wasn't anything that needed my attention there. Also, I was in touch with the various destroyers around, to have them pick up people who had jumped over the side or to come alongside and spray us with water.

Q: And undoubtedly with higher authority as well.

Admiral Lee: Yes. We, of course, reported this immediately to Pearl Harbor, and they sent helicopters out to take off our injured and dead. You're helpless up there on the bridge. There's just not much you can do to help anybody. I really didn't have enough to do on the bridge, because everything that could be done was being done by the commanders in charge of a given section.

The engineer officer was running damage control, and our air officer was running the flight deck, and our assistant air officers were running what was going on in the hangar deck. And our medical team, of course, was taking care of the wounded and injured. We had a very competent team handling all phases of it. I was primarily ensuring myself that all the things that needed to be done were being done.

Q: You mentioned that some air wing personnel were sealed in their spaces. What became of them?

Admiral Lee: Some of them were among the fatalities and the injured because bombs cooked off above them. Others got out. When we went to general quarters and they heard what was happening, they probably opened watertight doors and escaped, because if you look at the number of killed for such an inferno, it was surprisingly low. We had nine or ten 500-pound bombs go off high order. We had a lot of other bombs, but some of them didn't cook off high order. But we had only 28 people killed. Now when I say "we only," I'm not being insensitive about it, but we had a potential for killing hundreds, maybe even thousands, and we lost only 28.

Q: Do you think that would have been a likely consequence had that space not been sealed off?

Admiral Lee: Very possible. We had to bend every effort to keep that fire isolated to the after part of the flight deck. Keep it from getting into the living compartments; keep it from getting into the hangar deck.

Q: Did some men go overboard because they had no place else to go?

Admiral Lee: Yes. Not many, but a few went over the side because the fire just covered the after part of the flight deck, and they were in a position that they had to go over the side. They were picked up by helicopters and destroyers.

Q: How long did it take to get back in to Pearl after the fire was out?

Admiral Lee: We were about 90 miles south. We were in to Pearl by the end of the day. We came in late on the afternoon of the 14th.

Q: Then how soon did the repair work start?

Admiral Lee: We went into the shipyard immediately, and the repair work started almost immediately, and it went on around the clock for six weeks.

Q: That's fantastic to get a ship fixed up that quickly after she was damaged so badly.

Admiral Lee: Yes. The shipyard did a great job. They didn't completely repair it. We had one elevator that was not repaired, and we had one catapult that was not repaired, and I believe one arresting gear engine that was not repaired. But for all practical purposes, we had a fully operational ship, since we had a total of four elevators, and we didn't have any problems operationally afterward in the Western Pacific.

The most embarrassing thing in my naval career happened on March 5. The ship was fully repaired. We were very pleased with everything that had gone on. Early on the morning of March 5 the ship was to get under way from the Pearl Harbor Naval Shipyard and go out into the operating area, and operate with our air wing for about two days and then come back and head west for the Western Pacific.

The channel goes all the way around Ford Island. That morning we were going around the north and the west side of Ford Island. All of our condensers pulled mud up--Pearl Harbor is not very deep--and plugged us up, and all of our reactors came off the line. <u>Enterprise</u> had to be pulled by tugs back in to the pier while we cleaned our condensers.

Q: Did you lose the electrical load also?

Admiral Lee: We lost electrical load, but we had eight diesel generators and they picked up the electrical load. But we lost power and had to be pulled back in to the piers with tugs. It took us about eight hours to clean out the condensers, and then we got under way again. The second time out, we turned the ship in the channel and headed out back by the Navy yard rather than going around Ford Island, and we never went around Ford Island again. But after being in the shipyard for more than six weeks, really from 14 January to 5 March, then to have that embarrassment of clogged condensers on the way out and having to be pulled back by tugs to the pier, in effect running aground right in the channel, was more than our share.

Q: How had that happened? Was it silted or what?

Admiral Lee: This happened with some frequency in the

Pearl Harbor channel with the aircraft carriers. You have to be very careful. Aircraft carriers have flat bottoms, and the intakes are right in the bottom, and they just pull thousands of gallons of mud and water right off the bottom. If you run across a mud bank, all four intakes clog up with mud and fish and debris. Now we've had this happen before going into Pearl but usually only one or at most, two. But on this particular morning, all four.

The water might have been a little low. Might have been low tide going out. But the tidal range at Pearl is not large, but it's a couple feet; that would make a difference. It probably was low tide, and we didn't give it a thought. We never should have gone around the north side of Ford Island, anyway. We never did again. We always came in from the south, turn right, right into the shipyard. When you turn around and go back up that same way, you don't have to go around Ford Island, where all the muck is. It's supposed to be dredged to 45 feet, but Enterprise would draw 38 to 40 feet, and if there's any mud coming in, floods, you're going to pick it up. There isn't much margin for error.

But, anyway, that was a great embarrassment for me personally and for the Navy.

Q: Was there any inquiry after that?

Lee #6 - 471

Admiral Lee: Yes, there was a little inquiry, but it didn't amount to anything. But the big embarrassment was the newspapers. There were all kinds of newsmen watching us leave. It was on national TV. It was the greatest embarrassment of my naval career.

Q: There was one item that had happened by then that you haven't mentioned. You'd been selected for rear admiral. What do you remember about learning of that?

Admiral Lee: I believe we were out on the line in Tonkin Gulf. The selection board had met in maybe April of 1968. The list of selectees was sent out by message around the first of June, 1968. My name was on the list. I had been selected for rear admiral. Of course, it's the thrill of a career. I had hoped I might be selected, but you never know about these things.

I later sat on two admiral selection boards and two admiral plucking boards, and I would like to postpone my thoughts on the selection process until a later time, after I had sat on the four different admiral boards.

Q: Did you have any celebration when you got that news on board ship?

Admiral Lee: No, no celebration. LBJ wasn't aboard with

all his booze.* Of course, there were great happenings on the bridge when we saw this list. There's great happiness for those selected, and then there's sadness for those good friends of yours who don't make it, such as the chief of staff for one of the cardivs, who was a very able man, Frank Ault. He didn't make it.

Q: You mentioned him before.

Admiral Lee: But, yes, that was a great, that was a great thrill.

Q: You must have known it was a good possibility, because your predecessors had all been selected.

Admiral Lee: Yes. I thought it was a good possibility, but you never know about these things. You never know.

Now it just so happens that I got a letter from an unlikely source. His name was Charlie Martell, vice admiral, retired. After my selection for admiral, I got a letter from him. I had known him in Washington. He was in charge of the Navy's ASW efforts. He was the ASW king and OP-95. Charlie Martell, better known as "The Hammer." He had sat on the previous year's admiral selection board, and

---
*LBJ--President Lyndon Baines Johnson.

I think in the meantime he retired.* I got a most unusual letter from him. I really didn't know that he would remember me, because I was an aide for two years to assistant secretaries of the Navy, and he never acknowledged my presence in all the two years I was there. He was one of the big wheels in OpNav. But I, of course, talked to him once in a while. He was always very formal.

But then I got this very warm letter from him in 1968, after my selection. He told me that he wasn't surprised that I was selected. He expected it, he said. He had sat on last year's selection board, and he told me that without a doubt I would have been selected on this board he was sitting on, except that I was going to Enterprise. They didn't want to select anybody who was en route to a major ship.

Q: After all that training, there would have been no payoff.

Admiral Lee: Yes.

Q: And I think, if you'd had a choice, you wouldn't have wanted to pass up the ship command either.

---
*Vice Admiral Charles B. Martell, USN, retired from active duty in 1967. His last active duty billet was as Director Anti-Submarine Warfare Programs, Office of the Chief of Naval Operations.

Admiral Lee: No, I wouldn't have.

Anyway, we got the condensers cleared out and got to sea late on the afternoon of March 5. Now this next tour to WestPac, second tour for me, only had one unusual occurrence. It wasn't very different from the previous three cruises that Enterprise had had out there. We were going to Tonkin Gulf. Operations would be about the same. The only difference in this particular cruise was that an EC-121, an intelligence plane, was shot down by the North Koreans off the coast of North Korea in the Sea of Japan.* Once again, Enterprise was sent to the Sea of Japan to have a show of force opposite North Korea. It was winter and cold and miserable. And we stayed up there for a reasonable period of time, three or four weeks.

Q: So it was a replay of the Pueblo after that.

Admiral Lee: A replay of the Pueblo. It really wasn't very different from the Pueblo incident, in the sense that the Russians came down to greet us. We steamed back and forth and had flight operations in the Sea of Japan, once again, for two or three weeks, and then finally were relieved by another carrier and, once again, returned to Tonkin Gulf.

---

*On 15 April 1969, a four-engine propeller-driven EC-121 electronic reconnaissance plane disappeared from radar screens about 90 miles southeast of Chongjin, North Korea. On board were 30 Navy men and one enlisted Marine.

We had only one liberty port on this particular tour of the Western Pacific, other than Olongapo and Subic Bay. Since we weren't allowed into Hong Kong for this particular cruise, we were allowed to go down to Singapore for about a week. That was a very nice diversion, very nice change of pace.

Q: You talked a previous time about Admiral Weinel and trying to solve a problem with losing A-6s. Had things improved about plane losses by 1969?

Admiral Lee: In 1969 we weren't sending the A-6s on night missions singly up to North Vietnam to bomb their capital. That's where we were losing all of our A-6s. I've forgotten the details of our bombing missions and our effort in 1969. I've also forgotten the details of the moratorium on bombing north of the dividing line between North Vietnam and South Vietnam, but we were fully employed when we were in Tonkin Gulf on various types of missions, bombing the trails of the North Vietnamese coming south, bombing trucks night and day.* It really wasn't very different except that we weren't losing A-6s into the North the way we did on the first cruise.

---

*On 1 April 1968, a bombing and shelling halt was put into effect by President Johnson for all of North Vietnam except the southern panhandle. On 1 November 1968, shortly before that year's presidential election, Johnson put the rest of North Vietnam off-limits for U.S. bombing and shelling.

Q: Did it make any difference having A-7s instead of A-4s for light attack?

Admiral Lee: Not a lot of difference. The A-7 could carry a bigger load, had greater accuracy, and better range. It was a good airplane. But, insofar as carrier operations, not a lot of difference. I think they're more effective, but there weren't many good targets out there. A very difficult war on all counts. Once again, not very different in '69 than in '68.

There is one item that I became greatly concerned about during these two years with <u>Enterprise</u>. That was the maintenance problem of our aircraft aboard aircraft carriers. I made many hangar deck tours down to see how maintenance was coming along, and it was just backbreaking. We just could not maintain the RA-5C, which was a dog of an airplane in the first place. But the F-4s, and the A-6s, and the A-7s, always we had a hangar deck full, the A-7s being a little better than the F-4s and the A-6s. But almost without exception, an A-6 would make one flight and have to go to the hangar deck for repairs, maintenance--F-4 almost as bad. Maintenance manhours per flight hour were running for those airplanes around 40-45, which is just unbelievable. The RA-5C was a hopeless cause.

I decided that something had to be done in this area. We were failing. We had to carry just altogether too many maintenance people on our aircraft carriers to keep these planes going. So I decided that I would like to seek a job in naval aviation which had to do with procurement, maintenance, reliability, and see if I could, over a period of my few remaining years in the Navy in flag rank, do something about this. I applied for work in that particular area on leaving Enterprise.

Enterprise got back in to Alameda early in July, and I was relieved by my good friend, Captain Forrest Petersen, in July. As I mentioned earlier, Petersen and I went through the nuclear power training program together, and he had also been an executive officer of Enterprise, going to Enterprise directly from the nuclear power program. A very able man, well qualified in every way, and, having perhaps as much formal and informal education in the aviation field as any man in the Navy, and also having a year, of course, in Rickover's nuclear power program.

Q: I have some more questions about the Enterprise before we get completely away. You've mentioned some of the division commanders you had embarked. I wondered if you wanted to go into any more detail. I think you talked about Admiral Weinel pretty well. Any more to say on Admiral Bardshar?

Admiral Lee: Admiral Bardshar never rode <u>Enterprise</u> as a task force commander, although he was in the Pacific at the same time we were and directed our efforts. But Admiral Bardshar was a very imaginative man and was about like Admiral Weinel in his great interest and great knowledge of naval aviation, tactics, and weapons. He was a very talented operational commander.

Q: What can you say about his handling of the inquiry?

Admiral Lee: I was very pleased with Admiral Bardshar's handling of the inquiry, because I thought he showed great concern and compassion for all of us who were interested parties. He also is a very generous man and a very gracious man, and he made it easy for us. There isn't any doubt in my mind that if he had found us culpable in any way, we would have been, to use a legal term, indicted. But I had great confidence in him, and my confidence grew as I saw the type man he was in his handling of this inquiry. He had some able people helping him. So I saw a lot of Admiral Bardshar in a lot of different ways, and he was certainly one of the more able young aviation rear admirals of that time.

Lee #6 - 479

Q: You talked previously about Admiral Epes and his reaction to the message about turning that you got from President Johnson. You talked, also, when the recorder wasn't running, about his desire for creature comforts.

Admiral Lee: Some admirals are known as creature comfort admirals. They're people who want new drapes, and new curtains, new tablecloths, and new silverware. They like nicely appointed flag quarters. Admiral Epes was one of those people. When he found out he was going on <u>Enterprise</u> to the Western Pacific, he would send his aide up to check on the flag mess and flag quarters about once a week until sailing time. He also made inspection to make sure everything was up to the Epes standards. But, yes, Admiral Epes was what I call, and what is generally known in the Navy as a creature-comfort type. What you have to do in a case like that is grin and bear it.

Q: How would you describe the general nature of your relationship with these cardiv staffs? How much communication did you have with them?

Admiral Lee: We never had any problems with any of the carrier division staffs. I didn't think Admiral Epes was a very talented operational commander, but he had a chief of staff who more than made up for it. By and large, the staffs were very talented and they were very helpful.

We had Admiral Cagle with his staff on board; we had Admiral Weinel with his staff on board, and there might have been another at various times. But, without exception, the chiefs of staff were people who had had command of a carrier. The operations officer was usually a captain who'd been a wing commander or something like that, so that the carrier division staffs were very helpful to the ship. I'd give them high marks. They made life easy for us.

Q: In what ways?

Admiral Lee: They handled all the messages. If we had not had a carrier division staff aboard, my officers, operations officers, air operations officers, would have had to communicate with Task Force 77 and Seventh Fleet, and make all the arrangements for all the strikes and all the planning. We were stretched thin. We really couldn't do it justice. With a carrier division staff aboard, they could handle all the communications with the Vietnamese-American types that we had to coordinate with; they could handle all the communications with Seventh Fleet and Task Force 77; they could do all the debriefing and fill out the necessary action reports every day, and our people could help. It would then become a joint exercise. They would be there to debrief the pilots and make decisions or recommend actions to Commander Task Force 77.

When you're flying combat missions 12 hours every day, there's a tremendous amount of paperwork that goes on, a tremendous amount of planning. You have to make decisions on weapons and tactics. Although every day we would get a message from Commander Task Force 77--our target assignments--we had to translate those into a flight plan and into our actions. Having a carrier division staff on board lessened the load on our ship. At first I had some misgivings about having a staff aboard. But after operating out there without a staff a few times and operating, for the most part, with a staff, I don't think that the captain in the individual aircraft carrier is equipped to handle it all. You don't have the people. What really happened during the Vietnam War is that the captain ran the formation and the operations of the ship in the task group. The admiral and his staff ran the war.

Q: Some admirals have the temptation to usurp the captain's prerogatives. Did you have any problem with that at all?

Admiral Lee: None. I never had any problems like that.

Q: Did you typically sit in on their briefings and planning sessions?

Admiral Lee: I could sit in on anything I wished to sit in on. If I wasn't there, my executive officer was there and the wing commander. There were no secrets between staff and ship. We worked together. Never once did I feel that my authority was usurped. Not once. I have to give the staffs, and the admirals, and the chiefs of staffs great credit.

Q: Is there anything else you want to mention about Admiral Cagle?

Admiral Lee: No. I thought Admiral Cagle was not a very good operational commander. He didn't have a great knowledge of the weapons and aircraft. But he had a very good staff once again, so that we didn't have any problems with them. But I thought Weinel and Bardshar were sort of in a class of their own, from my observation, as operational commanders. The staffs were uniformly good.

Q: That's the relationship up. Now the one down to the air wing commanders. Could you describe their relationship to you?

Admiral Lee: The average captain of an aircraft carrier tries to have a very close relationship with the air wing commander and the squadron commanders. The ideal, I thought, happened on USS Intrepid when I was a squadron commander, when Admiral Masterton was the captain. I thought he had the closest and perhaps the ideal relationship with the wing commander and the squadron commanders. I tried to emulate that on Enterprise. I tried to get to know the wing commander and the squadron commanders and have them for dinners in the captain's mess, and discuss with them their problems--space problems, pilots, so that I thought that we had a very good relationship. I was just tremendously impressed with the quality of the wing commanders, and the squadron commanders, and executive officers of the various squadrons.

Q: Any that you especially want to identify by name?

Admiral Lee: Paul Peck was the first wing commander, and he later went on to make rear admiral, and well deserved, very able man, Paul Peck. Another squadron commander of great talent was a fellow by the name of Dick Seymour.* Dick Seymour was executive officer of an A-4 squadron. On a mission over Vietnam the skipper was shot down. That's a

---
*Commander Ernest R. Seymour, USN.

very traumatic time for a squadron. Dick Seymour rallied that squadron around, and they didn't miss a beat. Seymour later was promoted to rear admiral and vice admiral, and became Commander Naval Air Systems Command. Seymour worked for me two or three times after that. We had a very fine group, and I think Paul Peck and Dick Seymour sort of epitomized the quality of the leadership we had in naval aviation for that period. It was of a very high order, because it was a difficult war for the Navy, and especially naval aviation.

Q: Seymour was the man you were later trying to sell your firefighting system to.

Admiral Lee: Seymour was trying to sell it to the Navy. He was Commander Naval Air Systems Command at the time, and he liked it. He knew what happened to <u>Enterprise</u>. It made sense to him. He tried to take over and sell this thing to the Navy. I offered to help him by writing this article and the letter to OP-05 in doing the research for it. I wrote the article; he provided all the research materials. I then wrote the article and gave it to him to edit and criticize, and let his experts look at it. They changed it hardly at all and sent it back, and we had it published.

To sum up my thoughts on air wing commanders, and squadron commanders, and executive officers, and pilots, too, for that matter, I thought we had a very high order of courage, of professionalism, of skill, of all the qualities that we wanted in our naval officers, in the leadership of those air wings and squadrons out during the Vietnam War. It did take great courage to fly over there and face those missiles day in and day out, hundreds of missions and to take a chance of being a POW in Vietnam.

During the time I was over there, I never saw any flinching on the part of our pilots. I came back with nothing but the greatest admiration for the young group of pilots that were doing all of this in the Sixties and Seventies.

Q: The Enterprise was at that point the only nuclear-powered carrier. Do you think she had a tendency to get the cream of the crop in terms of personnel and air wing?

Admiral Lee: No, I think in terms of personnel in the engineering department, we got better quality. But the rest of the ship, especially the air wings, I think was the same quality as all the carriers, because we didn't know from one cruise to the next which squadrons we would have or which air wing. I think the quality was uniformly high. I just can't say enough for those young men who were flying those airplanes off aircraft carriers day and night during the Vietnamese War. They were the finest set of young men

I've ever run across--ever.

Q: How does a captain go about exerting leadership over an outfit that's as large and diverse as an aircraft carrier? Was closed-circuit TV effective by that time?

Admiral Lee: No, I didn't use closed-circuit TV, but I'd say leadership, number one, is effected through your department heads. The captain has to maintain close relations with his department heads. He has to encourage them to come see him at any time, and through the executive officer. I'd say that's number one: close relations, daily meetings, making sure that they understand your wishes, and that your wishes get carried out.

Number two I'd say is relations with the junior officers. You must work very hard to do that, and you do that through meetings with the junior officers, through talking to your officers on the bridge, and any other way you can communicate to these junior officers.

Lastly, and perhaps most important, is your relationship to the crew. I had a number of ways to do this, and I used the 1MC more than most captains. Before we began any operation, or the morning we began it, I would go on the 1MC, which is the loud-speaking system for the ship, and start my pitch. I would usually do this after dinner at night and before the movies began. I'd say,

"This is the captain speaking." I would tell the crew exactly what we were going to do for the next week or two weeks in some detail, everything that I knew about the events for the next two weeks, our at-sea period, our next port, flight operations. I tried to tell the crew exactly what I knew, in simple language and in detail. I found that to be very effective. There were very few questions, because if there was a change to our schedule, I immediately went on the 1MC and made a correction, gave them the proper information. So that that was a very effective tool.

Another tool, of course, is through your daily newspaper or some type of ship's magazine, and the TV. But I didn't use the TV. The executive officer and other officers used it, but it was the inconvenience of leaving the bridge and going down to the studio. I liked the 1MC, sort of the way I grew up. I liked that and I used it frequently.

The other thing I tried to do was have eight or ten enlisted men--some chiefs, some first class--that I would talk to from time to time, have a cup of coffee with, some engineers, maybe the chief quartermaster, maybe the chief master-at-arms. As I've described earlier in my relationships with enlisted men, I tried to establish, not covertly, but just as a matter of course as you'd meet people and try to establish a relationship with them, namely a conversation, and that sort of thing. But it's a lot more difficult on a big ship like Enterprise with 5,500 people than it was on USS Alamo with 250 and 25 officers. It's a lot more difficult. You have to be imaginative. You have to work at it, because there's absolutely no daily contact with all those people as there was on a small ship such as Alamo. But I think if you work at it, you can be very effective.

Q: What were examples of an imaginative approach for leadership?

Admiral Lee: The dependents' cruise from Alameda to Bremerton.

There were other events, such as smokers on the hangar deck, and I always went down for those, and sometimes I made a talk.

We published an Enterprise newsletter. I wrote a letter once a month for all the families. I still have copies of them. There are two other ways that we communicated on Enterprise which I thought were useful. We put out a monthly magazine--and I have copies of those--which described some of the departments on the ship as you'd expect a monthly magazine to do. Sort of a mixture of current events and profile of the department or of an individual, and maybe a short piece by the captain. I found one or more officers who could write fairly well, and I would have them give me a rough draft; we would talk about it. Then I would do the editing and put it in final form. We would send this letter to every dependent once a month. I thought that was very important, because they would hear from me, and that would give them confidence in the ship. They, in turn, would write their men. Those were the tools that I used. We worked at it.

Q: You were fighting this war against the North Vietnamese. What sources of intelligence did you have and how would you evaluate their usefulness on targets, possible threats, antiaircraft, etcetera?

Admiral Lee: Our sources of intelligence were not all that good in North Vietnam. It was a guerrilla-type war, and our intelligence was very poor. The one area where our intelligence was better than most places was missile sites and the like. But the one thing we did have was good photography, and we could take our own pictures. The locations of missile sites was pretty well pinpointed and kept up to date. But in terms of movements of troops, and movements of convoys, and movements of trucks and the like, intelligence was poor, very poor. It wasn't a war where intelligence was really used, not like World War II, where we used various types of intelligence to defeat the

Japanese, first at Midway. In the German war we used intelligence to a great extent.

Q: How would you assess the ship's communications?

Admiral Lee: I'd say ship's communications were very good. We really had no communications problems, either internally or externally, excellent.

Q: Any engineering problems other than the clogged-up condensers?

Admiral Lee: None. My two years aboard we never had any engineering problems of any magnitude.

Q: Regarding the two years, this is another thing you told me when the machine wasn't running, that you really regarded that as too long for a skipper to be in command during wartime.

Admiral Lee: Yes, I think one Vietnam tour, one cycle, is about enough during wartime. It's a 24-hour-a-day job, and after one complete cycle, I was pretty well worn out. I was tired. It just takes a while. I was emotionally, physically, and mentally tired after the first tour. There's very little time to rest up. You get in the saddle and start all over again. After the second tour, I was doubly tired, mentally, physically, emotionally. It's very draining emotionally to see these people disappear, and to have to write the letters to their dependents. Very draining emotionally. Two years of that is a really tough grind. The end of those two years and with the fire I know I was completely exhausted. All I wanted to do was go find a corner and rest up for a month or so. Get my perspective back.

Q: Do you think your effectiveness was impaired during the latter part of the command tour?

Admiral Lee: I think so. I think I was a better commanding officer the first tour than the second tour. Primarily because I was fresh and had lots of energy. The second tour, I think I was tired to start with. The best job in all the world is to be commanding officer of a ship. It's the best job there is. It's a great job. So under normal circumstances, I would say a two-year tour would be great, but with the war going on where you have 12 hours of flight operations every day, seven days a week, you get worn out. That's the point. So that I think two years of that is too much. There are no breaks for the captain; even back in the States there were no breaks.

Q: What happened back in the States to keep you from having breaks? What sorts of things?

Admiral Lee: You're in and out of Alameda, so about the only time the captain could take any time off is when you're in the shipyard. In 1967 and 1968 I took a break each year during the Christmas holidays while *Enterprise* was in Alameda. But you don't want to be too far away in any event, especially with eight nuclear reactors there. You're responsible for them. You know, a captain can take time off in those circumstances, but even though he gets away physically, the load is still there.

Q: You can't relax mentally.

Admiral Lee: You can't relax mentally, because the executive officer feels obliged to let you know of any untoward events. So, no, I think under those circumstances for a carrier captain two years is too long.

Q: You mentioned a problem you had with Admiral Rickover after the high-chlorine count. How was that manifested, the difficulty in the relationship?

Admiral Lee: Rickover immediately came to Pearl Harbor when he got the incident report. He personally inspected the ship and had Leighton go down and chase through the leak. He gave us all a very bad time. Then in the spring of 1968 he sent a nuclear propulsion examining team aboard. They hadn't had one aboard for two or three years, and they gave us a clean bill of health. He was very unhappy about that. He didn't feel that after he inspected our spaces that the spaces were as clean as they should be. I thought they were very acceptable.

He then sent another team out in the spring of 1969 and gave us another shakedown while we were on the line or coming back from the Pacific. He made life unpleasant for us in every way after that chlorine incident. I made a great mistake--I'm the first to admit it. I should have called him immediately that night on the telephone and told him what the problem was and asked for his advice, tell him what I'd like to do is continue to investigate it and get under way. But if he had said not get under way, I wouldn't have gotten under way. I didn't do any of those things. I didn't call him, and he didn't know about this until three or four weeks later when he got the incident report. Then he just flew apart. I made a tactical error there, an error in judgment which he didn't let me forget.

Q: So in retrospect you could have forestalled it probably with one telephone call.

Admiral Lee: If I had handled it properly, I wouldn't have had a problem, but that's the lament of everybody who makes a judgmental mistake.

Q: Now are you saying properly on his terms or your terms?

Admiral Lee: He would have been happy if I had handled it properly. I would have been much better off if I had handled it properly. I didn't handle it properly. I made a mistake.

Q: We talked about the admiral's fine quarters. What about those for you as the captain?

Admiral Lee: I thought the captain's quarters for Enterprise were very nice. I didn't do any refurbishing while I was captain. I thought they were perfectly adequate. I'm not a creature-comfort type, either clothes or quarters. My in-port cabin was absolutely superb-- dining room, bedroom, galley, office and sitting room-- beautifully done. I had many dinner parties there at various times.

Q: Could you describe the setup for one of those parties? It sounds like a fantastic atmosphere for entertaining.

Admiral Lee: Oh, it is. When we were in Alameda, we would have one dinner party a week on Enterprise. I had Filipino steward, cook, and servants. We would normally have about six couples, maybe a total of 14 people, which is about the maximum for the captain's quarters dining room. We would invite various people from the Bay area. We would rendezvous at the officers' club, have a few drinks, and then drive down to the pier and go aboard ship for dinner.

The various people that we invited from the Alameda area were very pleased. This was a very fine invitation. We invited leaders of the community, people who had done things for Enterprise, retired officers, personal friends, and we did this the two tours of duty we had in Alameda. They weren't short. We probably had a total of ten or 20 dinner parties there. At sea I had some dinner parties for the wing commanders and squadron commanders and executive officers. But it's a wonderful place to entertain, except you don't do much entertaining in Tonkin Gulf.

Q: No. Just to wrap up this section on the Enterprise, what was your relationship to your family during this operational tour? How much time could you spend with your wife and daughters?

Admiral Lee: I had very little time with them. I assumed command in July. Enterprise immediately went to the

Hunters Point Naval Shipyard and was there for about six or seven weeks. We spent a good part of our time from then until we deployed at sea. We would come in for weekends or for a few days at a time. The same thing was true for the next in-port period, you might say. The two years I had command, of course, I was in the Western Pacific for one year total, and the other year I was in and out of Alameda, except that part of that time we were in San Diego underway training, total of maybe two months up at Bremerton. So I had very little time in the two years with my family. I'd say at the most three months out of two years.

Q: That can't help either, piled up on top of all this exhaustion you've described.

Admiral Lee: Yes.

Q: Well, when you got away from the ship, did you have a chance to recharge your batteries?

Admiral Lee: Yes. Each December we went skiing at Lake Tahoe and stayed in a cottage owned by one of Mimi's cousins. That was good fun. We went up there for a week at Christmastime each year. That's probably the best battery recharging that I did.

Lee #6 - 497

Q: What sort of assignment did you get upon being relieved? Were you promoted to rear admiral right away?

Admiral Lee: Yes, I had been on the selectee list for a year. So I made my number almost as soon as I was relieved on Enterprise.

I first got orders to be Commander Fleet Air Alameda before Enterprise ever got back to the States. I let it be known that I wanted to come back to Washington and work in the material business for the rest of my career. So those orders were changed, and I was ordered back to Washington without a job, just ordered back to BuPers to wait until something turned up. That's how assignments are made.

So after being relieved by Captain Petersen, I came back to Washington, having about 30 days' leave, and we went down to South Carolina and had a cottage on the beach there for two weeks or so, and we got rested up. I reported in to Washington, perhaps in August of 1969 to the Bureau of Naval Personnel. My first assignment was to be on a selection board, a lieutenant commander to commander selection board. That took about six weeks. I won't comment on the selection boards at this particular time. I'll save that until we get to the admiral selection.

I went to OP-05 for temporary duty. Vice Admiral Thomas Connolly was OP-05 at the time. After I'd been there a couple, three weeks, I got orders to go to Air-04, which was a division of Naval Air Systems Command, which was what I wanted to do. Air-04 is in charge of logistics and fleet support. That job was a disappointment in the following sense. I wasn't able to do much along the lines that I had planned, because the Commander of Naval Air Systems Command at the time was Rear Admiral Thomas Walker, and he wasn't interested in my ideas about improving maintenance and maintainability and reliability, and really working hard in this area, and especially on new procurements, or doing what we could do for the old systems.* Wasn't interested. He had another agenda. I did do some interesting things, so I did what I could at Air-04, but I didn't have the power in Air-04 to do the things that ought to be done.

I sat on a selection board, a joint selection board, where we picked an engine in a competition between Pratt & Whitney and General Electric. It was my first competitive selection board in the procurement business, which was in 1969, and we picked Pratt & Whitney to build the F-15 and F-14 engine.

I did have a couple of interesting items. First thing I did when I got to Air-04 was look at the various programs we had. Air-04 runs all the naval air rework facilities, and they probably employ 30,000 people, and spend several

---

*Rear Admiral Thomas J. Walker III, USN, was Commander Naval Air Systems Command from 20 February 1969 to 1 April 1971.

hundred million dollars every year. In addition, we run contracts for various types of work. In looking at all of our civilian contracts in our various programs, to the tune of several hundred million dollars, I ran across three or four that interested me a great deal. For instance, I ran across the H-2, which is a helicopter built by Kaman, and Kaman had been overhauling these helicopters for years.* The prices for overhaul were fantastic. When I compared these numbers to the numbers that we were getting out of our overhaul facilities, I couldn't believe it.

Another was the H-46 and Boeing, very high prices for overhauling one of those helicopters.** There were two or three others like that. Then I started looking into what it was costing us to have them done by these particular people and what it was costing us in an overhaul facility, and what it was costing us in commercial work in the so-called aircraft shops down in the Southeast, where a lot of it's done, rather than having it done by these aircraft manufacturers. I decided that what we needed to do was re-compete these contracts and move the H-2 to Quonset Point. We would move one and see what it would cost us to

---
*The H-2 Seasprite is a small helicopter built by the Kaman Aircraft Corporation, first delivered to the Navy in late 1962. The UH-2 version has been used for utility work and the SH-2 for antisubmarine warfare from destroyers and frigates.
**The CH-46 Sea Knight helicopter, built by the Vertol Division of the Boeing Company, was first delivered to the Navy in 1964 and the Marine Corps in 1965. The Navy has used it for replenishment at sea and the Marine Corps for transporting troops and cargo.

do it there, and then move them all if we could get a better competitive contract.

I ran into my first bit of political pressure at this particular time. I announced what we were going to do to both Kaman and Boeing. There were great howls of anguish from Kaman. They'd had this helicopter overhaul contract for several years at this time, and the more I looked at it the more I felt that it was a sweetheart contract. I announced that we were going to re-compete it, and I was going to put it up at Quonset Point until such time as we could get a good baseline on it. Then they went to see their congressman, which is standard procedure. The congressman called the Assistant Secretary of the Navy for Logistics, and his name happened to be Sanders.* So then I had to go explain it to him. This was my first experience with the political machinery in Washington.

In the Kaman case, Charlie Kaman, who owns the company or owns a big chunk of it (it's a publicly traded company), even came to see me and told me that he was letting the president of this company go.** I tried to explain to him the president didn't have anything to do with it, that I was dissatisfied with the prices. Their quality was good, but we were doing essentially the same thing for half the

---

*Frank P. Sanders, Assistant Secretary of the Navy (Installations and Logistics).
**Charles H. Kaman, chairman of the board, Kaman Corporation.

price elsewhere.

Q: At the air rework facilities.

Admiral Lee: Yes, and in some of the air workshops in the Southeast; there are a lot of shops in the Southeast that do this kind of work, overhaul engines and aircraft for the Air Force and the Navy.

But, anyway, we went ahead with moving this stuff around. But there was great anguish, great pressure, because these are rice bowls. These people had had a very good thing at Kaman with the H-2. There were some others, too, but I just merely tell you about the H-2 to cite the problem. But I think the services have a tendency to get locked into contracts like this. They're doing a good job; the money's not coming out of the individual's pocket; Kaman is making a great profit on this, so they liked it. I decided I would break this up. But it's not that simple. I got a few brickbats in the process. The secretary, the assistant secretary who had to handle this had some very uncomfortable moments with Congress.

Q: Was he supportive of your effort?

Admiral Lee: He didn't direct me to do otherwise, because I pointed out to him the cost. If he had directed me to do otherwise, then he would have put himself in an untenable position. I pointed out to him that we could do this work for about $60,000 per copy, and we were paying Kaman anywhere from $120,000 to $160,000.

Q: That's more than double.

Admiral Lee: Well, some of that work was what is called over and above, extra work we were having done for one reason or another, which wouldn't be included in my $60,000 either. But for comparable work, roughly twice as much.

Now 15 or 20% more, even 25% more, is kind of standard, because they pay taxes, and the Navy's overhaul facilities don't pay taxes. We had had studies done, and we figured that 25% more for commercial rework was about par for course--$100,000 for us. We should pay them $125,000. But I learned. It was a very interesting procedure, and I competed both helicopters. Kaman and Boeing lost.

I had one other interesting experience in Air-04. We had just had a competition for the overhaul of some equipment. We were ready to announce the winners; I've forgotten how many competitors there were, but there were several. I got a call from Rear Admiral Baldwin who worked for Connolly in the office of the Deputy Chief of Naval

Operations for Air.* He told me that this was an order, that I was to make sure that Company X got some of this business. I am positive the order came from Connolly. I told him that we had had a fair competition, and, unfortunately, Company X didn't win. Company Y won. Company Y was going to get all the business. I said that if he wanted somebody to do that sort of thing, why, they'd better give me another job and send somebody else in. After that phone call, I called over to the Deputy Chief of Naval Operations for Air and told Rear Admiral G. E. Miller, OP-05B, what had happened. I believe he discussed it with Connolly.

In my several years at the Naval Air Systems Command, a lot having to do with procurement and competitions, that was the only case that I had of pressure being applied to me in a competition. I never had any pressure from congressmen, never from the Chief of Naval Operations or the Vice Chief, never from anybody in OSD.** There were billions and billions of dollars worth of procurements that we ran in NavAir and a great percentage of them were competitively done. That was the only case in my entire time in this area in the Navy that I received what I thought was improper pressure in a contract or in a competition.

---

*Rear Admiral Robert B. Baldwin, USN, Director Aviation Programs Division, Office of the Chief of Naval Operations.
**OSD--Office of the Secretary of Defense.

Q: It could be that your resistance of it the first time prevented there being a second or third.

Admiral Lee: It's very possible, because I was never approached again by anybody.

In June of 1970, right out of the blue, I was invited over to be interviewed by Secretary of the Navy Chafee, who had been in office since January 1969. Chafee was the Secretary of the Navy, and Warner was the Under Secretary, Bowsher was Assistant Secretary (Financial Management). I went over for this interview, and it turned out he was interviewing me and two or three others, including Rear Admiral Donald Engen, to relieve Ray Peet, who was then head of the Office of Program Appraisal, which is sort of a systems analysis office for the Secretary of the Navy.* I was interviewed by Secretary Chafee.

At this particular time, Moorer was moving up to be Chairman of the Joint Chiefs, and Zumwalt was coming in from Vietnam to be Chief of Naval Operations, and Ray Peet was being promoted to vice admiral and going out to be Commander First Fleet. Hence, Chafee was looking for a new rear admiral in his immediate office there. The job, as I said earlier, was called Director of Office of Program

---

*Rear Admiral Donald D. Engen, USN, Director Strategic Plans Division, Office of the Chief of Naval Operations. Raymond E. Peet, USN; the oral history of Peet, who retired as a vice admiral, is in the Naval Institute collection.

Appraisal. But you're sort of Chafee's right-hand man in budgeting and systems analysis matters.

During the course of the interview, Chafee asked me if I'd like to have the job. I said, "Yes, I had one two-year tour, roughly two-year tour in the secretariat once before, and I'd be very happy to have the job."

Next day I was called up and said that I had the job, and they'd like me over there tomorrow. I left Air-04 almost overnight and moved over to the Office of Program Appraisal.

I don't have a lot to say about the Office of Program Appraisal. I found Secretary Chafee to be a highly intelligent man. I would say a little bit on the liberal side for a Republican, but a graduate of Yale, Harvard Law School, was a Marine during World War II, and no doubt a good one, and I thought a highly effective Secretary of the Navy and a very thoughtful man.

Warner, who was the Under Secretary, and later Secretary, I found not so effective. Warner, in the entire time that I knew him, never did his homework in any particular project that I knew. He had a memory span of about two microseconds. It was just impossible for him to sit down and do any hard studying or hard work, except on speeches. He loved to make speeches and was very good at it. He was a great public relations-type man and liked to take trips.

Frosch was still there as research and development; Sanders was the I&L type, and Bowsher was the financial management type. I had lunch once a week with the Secretary and all the assistants and the Under Secretary. We discussed whatever the problems were. Once again, I had a sort of a ringside seat in the Pentagon on the decision-makers. I'd had two years there as an executive assistant and aide to the Assistant Secretary for R&D. And, believe me, there's very little that goes on in the Department of the Navy that those senior aides to the CNO and the Secretary don't know about.

Obviously, I worked on a daily basis with Mr. Chafee, and very little went on there during those times that I didn't know about. I didn't always have a vote or get a recommendation in, but when you're in the secretariat, you usually know what's going on in the Navy--who is in disfavor, who's in favor, who's being promoted, who's not being promoted, and all that sort of thing.

Q: You told me previously your theory on how Admiral Zumwalt got to be CNO when Chafee was the Secretary. I think that's an interesting thing to put on the record.

Admiral Lee: Stan Turner was Mr. Chafee's executive

assistant and aide.* Stan Turner is a Naval Academy graduate, Rhodes scholar-type, very personable, very persuasive individual, and an 1100.** I believe that he persuaded Mr. Chafee to give the CNO job to Zumwalt.

There's another factor there. I don't believe that Admiral Moorer had too much of a vote, because I think Zumwalt would have been his last choice. When I got there, I gathered that the relations between Admiral Moorer and Chafee were not the best. Moorer sort of looked on Chafee as a boy scout. Chafee had sort of a liberal agenda he wanted to bring forth in the Navy, and Admiral Moorer didn't want any part of a liberal agenda, and hence, they had come, in my view, to a sort of parting of the ways.

I found Chafee to be a very reasonable man. And, in my view, Admiral Moorer--and I have great admiration for him--made a mistake with Chafee. I think that if he had gone along with Chafee and some of his boy scout ideas, some of his liberal ideas--and they weren't all that difficult or far-reaching or revolutionary--and had supported Mr. Chafee in a number of these areas, and had maintained cordial relations with him, that Admiral Moorer could have picked the next CNO. But I think as it was, Secretary Chafee was determined to get his own man,

---

*Captain Stansfield Turner, USN. Turner eventually became a four-star admiral and served as Director of the Central Intelligence Agency during the Carter Administration.
**Turner stood 25th of the 821 graduates in the Naval Academy class of 1947.

somebody who would be amenable to his agenda, and his outlook--and especially in the personnel policies area, and in the racial area. This is what Chafee was working on. Zumwalt came in, and he had the same sort of ideas, and we were off to the races.

But there were a couple other little incidents that I would like to relate. One day I got a call from Admiral Rickover while I was director of OPA. He brought up the case of a lieutenant who was a reserve officer. We'll call the lieutenant, Baker, and this lieutenant wanted to get out of the Navy 60 days early, out of his nuclear power program and out of the Navy to go to graduate school. Rickover said, "Absolutely not. You signed on for three years in my program, and your three years are not up until 60 days after the graduate school starts, and that's tough."

This young man appealed Rickover's decision to the Chief of Naval Personnel and then to the Secretary of the Navy. Rickover called me up to ask me to help him, make sure that Chafee didn't overturn this, because the Bureau of Naval Personnel was going to go along with Rickover and set a precedent.

Q: Well, since you were on the outs with Admiral Rickover, why would he call on you for help?

Admiral Lee: I think he thought I was his only hope.

But, anyway, he called me up, wanted some help, and I was noncommittal. I didn't promise any help. I just said I'd see what I could do, that I didn't normally get into that circuit.

But, anyway, as luck would have it, the Secretary called me over to talk about this. He asked me what he should do. I said to the Secretary, "Any reasonable man would let young Lieutenant Baker go. If he doesn't get out now and start graduate school on time, he's going to be delayed by at least six months, maybe longer. But," I said, "Rickover is not a reasonable man."

Mr. Chafee smiled and directed that the boy be let go 60 days early. The very next day, Rickover was over to see Chafee, furious. He thought this was a bad precedent. Mr. Chafee chuckled about it a little bit, and that was the end of that. No precedents were set.

Q: Did you get any flareback from Admiral Rickover on that?

Admiral Lee: Never discussed it. I never told him that I'd had a role in it. I never brought it up.

Q: How much relationship did you have in that job to the Program Planning Office, OP-090, and Systems Analysis,

OP-096?

Admiral Lee: Worked every day with them. We handled the POM at OPA and any anything else that Chafee wanted us to work on, had about 20 people over in OPA, all analysts, and most of them civilians.* We worked any projects he wanted worked.

Q: The Navy did not gracefully accept the systems analysis discipline. How was it by that stage of the game, 1970?

Admiral Lee: Well, we didn't accept it gracefully, because we thought they were arriving at wrong answers. But we had to fight back. The CNO set up a systems analysis office--OP-96. The Secretary set up his own office, which was OPA. We had about 20 people there to handle the Secretary's part of it, the POM, systems analysis. That's the office that I headed.

I had another interesting experience there, but we had some very able people in OPA. We had maybe two or three line officers, two or three aviators, two or three submariners, and all the rest were civilian analysts--good team, and very talented people, and I think we did excellent work for the Secretary.

---

*POM--program objectives memorandum, a basic planning document for upcoming budgets.

Q: Did you work with Charlie DiBona in the Center for Naval Analyses?

Admiral Lee: Charlie DiBona was Zumwalt's think tank man. Charlie DiBona was at the Center for Naval Analyses during my tour at OPA.* He was somewhere else before that, but we worked very little with him. OP-96 worked mostly with him, and he did studies for Zumwalt.

Q: You were talking about the systems analysis people coming to wrong conclusions. Do any examples especially stand out in your mind?

Admiral Lee: Yes. There was one study where they showed beyond a doubt in their systems analysis logic that what we should do is buy nothing but 250-pound bombs. We didn't need to buy 500-pounders and 1,000-pounders, because it was more cost-effective to buy 250-pounders. Well, any aviator who's ever dropped bombs knows intuitively that the bigger the bomb you can deliver on a target, the more chances you have of knocking it out. Also, they didn't take into account the losses to aircraft. They merely took into account CEP, which sometimes is a good number and sometimes

---

*Charles J. DiBona stood second among the 681 graduates in the Naval Academy class of 1956. He subsequently resigned his regular commission and continued to work with the Navy as a civilian. He served as president of the Center for Naval Analyses from January 1968 through February 1973.

it isn't, and the cost of the bombs, and how many we could carry, and came to the conclusion that we should buy nothing but 250-pound bombs.* If you go through the numbers on it, you save money buying 250-pound bombs.

Q: Well, this is the great argument that the experienced line officers raised, that it doesn't take into account operational knowledge.

Admiral Lee: This didn't. That is a typical one, where following their numbers and their assumptions, they arrive at what is for them a good answer, but for us operators, a very wrong answer. That's a typical one; there were many others.

Q: Were you working the F-14 problem while you were in that job?**

Admiral Lee: Mr. Chafee was very concerned about the F-14 and about Grumman. He was afraid Grumman was going bankrupt, which they very nearly did. Grumman had won the F-14 competition. They had a fixed-price R&D contract, and a fixed-price production contract for the first five or

---
*CEP--circular error probable, a measure of accuracy in dropping bombs in relation to the target.
**The Grumman F-14 Tomcat fighter entered the fleet in the mid-1970s and has been he Navy's principal carrier-based air defense plane since then.

seven lots of aircraft. Some people believe that Grumman was given inside information on the competition. They lowered their prices by about $370 million dollars in their best-and-final bid on production lots. The irony of it is they would have won anyway without that. But they lowered their prices, and if they hadn't done that, they would have been all right.

Grumman was losing millions of dollars in the F-14 program while I was at OPA. I used to talk to Mr. Chafee about it, and he used to go down and see David Packard, who was Deputy Secretary of Defense. David Packard gave him some very good advice: "Settle with Grumman; don't draw it out. Grumman cannot give you an F-14 under this contract. You'd better settle with them now, because it'll be more painful later."

But for one reason or another, Chafee couldn't do it. There was a political problem. There were a whole bunch of congressmen and senators who wanted to hold Grumman's feet to the fire. But the problem with that is they're not going to give you a good airplane if you hold their feet to the fire and they're losing millions of dollars.

Subsequently, Mr. Chafee sent Bowsher and me up to Grumman with the program manager. He wanted us to look it all over and come back and give him a presentation on the F-14. I really hadn't seen the F-14 before that, so we went up. We spent a day or so with the program manager and went to Grumman to go over all their problems. Then Bowsher and I came back and put together a presentation for Mr. Chafee, only for Mr. Chafee. We listed all the problems and what we thought of the program. I said that I thought the F-14 too sophisticated, too complex, and would be a monster to maintain. Besides that, Grumman had rushed the research and development, and I felt the F-14 was going to be a terrible problem for the Navy. That was the gist of my presentation. And that I had grave doubts about the wisdom of the F-14 program.

Q: Did you have a recommendation?

Admiral Lee: My recommendation was to settle the contract with Grumman, and then see what we could do about the F-14, if we really wanted to buy all those numbers. Because I could see nothing but dollars going down the drain with the F-14 the way it was going.

Once again, not very much happened, except about two or three weeks after this Admiral Connolly, who was OP-05, had his secretary call up one day and say that he was coming down to see me. Admiral Connolly walked into my office, on the D-ring, sort of inboard from the Secretary of the Navy's office one ring, and said he heard I'd been making some comments on the F-14, and that he wanted to read me what his charter was. So he pulled out of his pocket his charter as OP-05. The charter says that he's the chief adviser to the Chief of Naval Operations and the Secretary of the Navy for matters involving naval aviation. That he wanted me to stay out of his bailiwick. Then he turned around and walked out.

But that was my last experience with Admiral Connolly while he was on active duty. I had a round with him after he retired.

Now those are about the only items that I would like to comment on in my OPA tour. If you have some other questions, why, I'd be happy to answer them.

Q: Now my understanding of the original rationale for OPA was to give the Secretary an independent source of judgment and information so that he wouldn't have to be dependent on the CNO and the OpNav organization. Did you function in that fashion?

Admiral Lee: Yes.

Q: Would that F-14 report be a good example of that, running counter to what Admiral Connolly was saying?

Admiral Lee: Yes.

Q: Any other examples that come to mind?

Admiral Lee: Secretary Chafee used the office of OPA a great deal. The director of the office has to be very careful, because sometimes the CNO--and especially Zumwalt--puts a little twist on the things he wants to do, a little spin, if you will. You have to be careful that you don't get the CNO upset by shifting his programs around, and yet you're working for the Secretary. You have to give him your thoughts. So you have to be very careful.

Now the way I worked that problem was to work directly with 090 and my counterpart down the street who did the work for 090. He had a rear admiral--John Tierney was the first one and then Worth Bagley was the second.* We worked out a system so that whatever projects or programs they were working on, they'd let us see them. If we had any things that the Secretary was interested in or something that we knew the Secretary wouldn't accept, we would let them know. So we tried to prevent our OPA making recommendations contrary to what the CNO had recommended. We tried to do this by working the problems out early, before it got to that stage. I think we were very successful, except in the Connolly and the F-14 bit, but in

---

*Rear Admiral John M. Tierney, USN, Director, General Planning and Programming Division, Office of the Chief of Naval Operations. Rear Admiral Worth H. Bagley, USN; Bagley eventually became a four-star admiral. His oral history is in the Naval Institute collection.

that particular case I told Mr. Chafee exactly what I thought, which was very different from what Connolly was pushing.

Q: What was he pushing?

Admiral Lee: The F-14 had 10,000 problems, number one, the engine. The Navy had planned to use an engine which was being developed for the F-15 and the F-14. It was called the F-401 engine, and the Air Force was calling it the F-100. The engine was a failure. Now, meantime, the Navy was to buy the first 70 airplanes with an engine called the TF-30, which is the same engine that was in the F-111.*
The TF-30 wasn't a very good engine, and the F-14 with the TF-30 was very under-powered. We put $300 million dollars into the F-401 engine, and it was still a failure.

The F-14, in spite of what people might think, was really just a warmed-over F-111; it had the same weapons system. The Phoenix weapon system and the radar of the F-14 were designed for the F-111. The F-111's engine and the swing wing were used in the F-14.

Q: But the F-14 was designed to be a carrier plane.

Admiral Lee: Designed to be a carrier plane and it had

---
*The engine was the Pratt & Whitney TF30-P-412A turbofan.

tandem cockpits, rather than side by side. But the F-14 was really a sort of a redesigned F-111 by Grumman. Because Grumman was General Dynamics's partner in building of the F-111. But the F-14 had lots of problems. I thought it important that we point out all these problems to the Secretary, and I did.

Plus the contract was a terrible burden. There was no way that Grumman was going to fix all these problems losing all those millions. But Admiral Connolly wanted business as usual. The F-14 was a great airplane; it had no problems. The TF-30 was a perfect engine for the F-14. We really didn't need the F-401, although we'd put $300 million in it and it was a failure. These little problems that the F-14 had, why, we'd work those out as we went along. That was Admiral Connolly's pitch.

Mr. Chafee wanted a better look at it, and he didn't want to go down and give Mr. Packard this Connolly line on the F-14; he didn't believe it. So he had Bowsher and me go look at it. That's really how it came about.

Q: What would you say about Secretary Chafee's working style. What kind of a man was he? Was he decisive, forceful?

Admiral Lee: I thought Mr. Chafee was a very kindly man, he was a very friendly man. He was a very moral person, great integrity--that sort of an individual.

Q: I'm sure you and he got along well then.

Admiral Lee: I became a great admirer of Chafee's, but he really had no experience in the technical end of things. He was a lawyer, and he had never worked in a technical area, never did anything like that. He was a lawyer and governor of Rhode Island before coming down. He was a little liberal for the taste of some. Admiral Moorer called him a boy scout, because he wanted lots of programs that sort of liberalized, you might say, the Navy, and especially race relations in the Navy. Admiral Moorer didn't approve of that, so they didn't get along very well.

But I'd say, first of all, that Mr. Chafee wanted to learn all about problems. He didn't want a superficial look at them. He especially wanted to learn all about problems involving people, such as the Rickover lieutenant who wanted to get out. He had great courage. He didn't hesitate in letting the young boy go 60 days early, even if it did raise the ire of Rickover, and against the recommendations of the Chief of Naval Personnel, who went along with Rickover.

I'd say his great weakness was in the program management and weapon systems and the technical side. He had no experience, no training, no technical background.

But I don't think the Secretary of the Navy needs that. I thought he worked very hard with the senators and representatives and other parts of government for the Navy, which is what the Secretary of the Navy is supposed to do. I think when the Secretary of the Navy gets into managing projects, we're all in trouble, and he didn't do that. Mr. Chafee worked hard at his job. I would give him high marks.

Q: And by that you mean he did his homework and investigated things thoroughly?

Admiral Lee: Yes. He always did his homework. He learned his programs. If he had to go testify on a given program--F-14, some ship program--we spent hours going over these things, things he ought to know so that he'd make a good impression. In every other area that he had to personally make a decision on, such as the Pueblo case, he spent a lot of time at it. He did his homework. He didn't have any trouble making decisions. I thought all of the decisions he made were very good.

My only criticism of Chafee would be that I think he let Zumwalt run wild. He didn't rein Zumwalt in when he saw that Zumwalt was getting too liberal, even for Chafee in the Navy. Moorer was absolutely turning purple down as Chairman of the JCS watching what Zumwalt was doing to the

Navy.* I think the one criticism I would have of Chafee is that he had a chance to rein Zumwalt in early on, and he didn't take the chance.

Q: Did you talk to him about that aspect?

Admiral Lee: No, I didn't.

Q: Did your purview limit itself more to the technical and systems analysis and program planning types of things?

Admiral Lee: In the position I had, the only time I gave Mr. Chafee advice was when he asked for it. I think anybody in the aide business, in the assistant business which I was in--and especially since I was a military type--if you start giving advice on every subject and in every area and in every matter, the first thing you know, they don't want to see you. They think you're trying to run them.

I found it a good policy when I was two years in the secretariat as an executive assistant and aide, never give unsolicited advice. Only advise them on the matters that they ask you about, or they have assigned to you. I followed that with Mr. Chafee. And when you do that, and

---

*After Admiral Zumwalt relieved Admiral Moorer as Chief of Naval Operations, Moorer served as Chairman of the Joint Chiefs of Staff from 1970 to 1974.

if you establish a good personal relationship--such as I used to play squash with him a couple times a week, and that was good fun; he was a great squash player--why, they come more and more to you. They ask you questions that they ordinarily wouldn't ask. It depends on the personal relationship. But never unsolicited advice, no.

Q: Well, this might have been an opportunity for you to sell some of your ideas about reliability and maintenance. Did you try any of that?

Admiral Lee: Yes, I did.

Q: Did you have any successes?

Admiral Lee: Well, yes, as a matter of fact, I did, because one of Mr. Chafee's assistants was a man by the name of Charlie Ill, who later became Assistant Secretary of I&L.* He's the one who brought me back to be Commander Naval Air Systems Command.

While I was there, Tom Walker was transferred to California to be Commander Naval Air Force Pacific Fleet, promoted to three stars. He was Commander Naval Air Systems Command. The Navy was looking around for a successor to Tom Walker. Tom McClellan was at that time

---
*Charles L. Ill, Assistant Secretary of the Navy (Installations and Logistics).

Air-01, which is a kind of a program manager-type; he runs all the program managers.* I persuaded the Chief of Naval Personnel and the powers that be that Tom McClellan would be the right man to have the Commander Naval Air Systems Command job. I didn't know at the time that they were considering giving it to me, from OPA back to Naval Air as the commander. I learned that later. But it's just as well; it was better that I not go there at that time.

Q: Was Admiral McClellan somebody in sympathy with your ideas?

Admiral Lee: No, he wasn't, but he was a good man. There weren't many people in sympathy with my ideas at that time. But I was in Naval Air Systems Command with Admiral McClellan. He was a Naval Academy graduate, very quiet man. Had a patrol plane career; was an aeronautical engineer, very bright guy, very able, I thought he would do a good job. I believe I persuaded the hierarchy to give him a job, because he relieved Tom Walker.

Q: You said Admiral Walker had his own agenda. What was that?

---

*Rear Admiral Thomas R. McClellan, USN, Deputy Commander, Plans and Programs and Comptroller, Naval Air Systems Command.

Admiral Lee: He was a very hard man to pin down. I could never get him to sit still for any of my thoughts and ideas. He had to play golf every day. He let Naval Air Systems Command run by itself. So, yes, he had his own agenda.

Q: Well, rather than get the NavAir job at that point, you went back out to SAC and JSTPS. How did that come about?

Admiral Lee: I really don't know except what the aide told me. The Secretary's aide and I became very good friends, a fellow by the name of Thor Hanson.* I later sat on an admiral selection board which picked him for rear admiral. I like to think I was instrumental in getting him picked.

But he told me that Zumwalt came in to fill the spot in Omaha and had another man on the list, and that the Secretary persuaded Zumwalt that I was the man for the job. True story, I'm sure, because the aides don't miss much around there. I was called up one day and told that I was being promoted to three stars--and at that time I was still a lower half rear admiral--and going out to Omaha in January 1972. I was very pleased with that.

Q: Did you have any kind of a personal relationship with Admiral Zumwalt? Did he know you?

---

*Captain Carl T. Hanson, USN.

Admiral Lee: Oh, yes. I knew Zumwalt. You see, I had been aide in the office of ASN(R&D) when Zumwalt was aide to Nitze, so I got to know him then. I believe Zumwalt was OP-96. He went out to the West Coast.

Q: He was. He had a cruiser-destroyer flotilla and came back.

Admiral Lee: Anyway, I had been around Zumwalt since 1965 in one way or another; 1965 to '67 I was aide. We had been colleagues, I'd say--not friends, but never had a problem. But as I understand it, he came in with his plans to fill the job in Omaha, going to move Michaelis down to Norfolk.* Chafee persuaded him that maybe I ought to go out to Omaha, that I'd done a good job. As I understand it, that didn't give Zumwalt a problem. Yes, I talked to Zumwalt frequently.

As a matter of fact, he called me in to talk to me about it. Typical of Zumwalt. He wanted to know about what sort of a guy I thought Warner was. He wanted to know about OP-05, Mickey Weisner; what I thought--Mickey Weisner had replaced Tom Connolly--how I felt about Mickey Weisner and OP-05, and Warner.** That sort of thing. He would

---
*Vice Admiral Frederick H. Michaelis, USN, was Deputy Director Joint Strategic Target Planning Staff, 1969-72, and Commander Naval Air Force Atlantic Fleet, 1972-75.
**Vice Admiral Maurice F. Weisner, USN, Deputy Chief of Naval Operations (Air), 1 September 1971-4 August 1972.

call me in and ask me my opinion on these things. So, yes, I had a good relationship with Zumwalt. I wasn't one of those in his inner circle; I don't think any aviators were. But I didn't have a running battle with him as did Jerry Miller, which probably started in the days when we were aides together, and maybe earlier.

Q: Well, evidently, he had confidence in you, though, even though there was not a close personal relationship.

Admiral Lee: I don't think there was a problem in promoting me and sending me out there with Zumwalt. I just think that--I was still a lower-half rear admiral and they had other plans. They had in mind sending an upper half rear admiral.

Q: Well, before you get out to Omaha, I'd appreciate it if you could talk about the VCNO, Admiral Cousins, please.

Admiral Lee: The first VCNO with Zumwalt was Admiral Clarey.* Admiral Clarey was relieved by Ralph Cousins, who was OP-03 and then moved up to be VCNO.** I worked with Admiral Cousins when he was VCNO, and I was in OPA. Later, when I went to Omaha, I worked with Admiral Cousins

---

*Admiral Bernard A. Clarey, USN, was Vice Chief of Naval Operations, 17 January 1968 to 30 October 1970.
**As a vice admiral, Ralph W. Cousins was Deputy Chief of Naval Operations (Fleet Operations and Readiness). As a four-star admiral he served as Vice Chief of Naval Operations from 30 October 1970 to 1 September 1972.

frequently, because OpNav wanted to know what was going on out there. I worked with him on getting people out there.

I thought Admiral Cousins was just about the ideal Vice Chief of Naval Operations for any CNO. I think he had a very difficult time with Zumwalt. But he was 100% loyal. Whatever Admiral Zumwalt decided on, Admiral Cousins supported, which is the way the VCNO should be. He was always in a good humor. He was a very courteous man, very efficient, always did his homework, and never seemed to be in a big rush. But he got the job done. And a very talented man. I always regretted that Admiral Cousins wasn't made CNO to relieve Admiral Moorer. Because I think he would have been just the ideal CNO, very smooth man, very sophisticated, very intelligent. I thought he had it all. I think anybody who could be about the perfect VCNO for Zumwalt has real talent, because that was a tough job. But he handled it well, both from my observation when I was in OPA and also when I was out in Omaha. I give him very high marks. He was one of the finest naval officers I ever knew, I think. He's not a close friend, but I had great respect for him, admiration.

I was relieved in OPA by Rear Admiral Thomas Hayward who succeeded Holloway as Chief of Naval Operations.*

---

*Rear Admiral Thomas B. Hayward, USN. Later, as a four-star admiral, Hayward was Chief of Naval Operations, 1978-82.

Lee #6 - 528

Q: You described, when you were in Omaha before, the frustrations of trying to deal with General Power from the Navy side. Had that climate improved with the passage of time?

Admiral Lee: No. I won't spend too much time on the JSTPS in this particular tape, because I've already described the organization out there. When I left the Joint Strategic Target Planning Staff in 1962, I was a commander, and Vice Admiral Roy Johnson was the deputy director.* When I went back in January of 1972, I relieved Vice Admiral Michaelis, who went down to ComNavAirLant, and I became the deputy director. There was absolutely no change. It was just as bad in 1972 as it was when I left in 1962--namely, that the Navy participants were being treated like second-class citizens. The place was being dominated and run by the SAC types. I made it my mission to change it.

The commander out there was a tactical Air Force general, Bruce Holloway.** When I approached him on it, we got absolutely nowhere, complete stone wall. My proposal was that the Navy be treated as more than second-class citizens, that we be given a meaningful role in the organization, and be given some reasonable jobs. I said

---

*Vice Admiral Roy L. Johnson, USN. Johnson eventually became a four-star admiral; his oral history is in the Naval Institute collection.
**General Bruce K. Holloway, USAF, Commander in Chief Strategic Air Command, 29 July 1968 to 30 April 1972.

that we ought to have a study to reorganize the place and see what we could come up with. Zero. Stone wall. Relations cooled off between us.

After I was there about six months, Holloway retired, and a fellow by the name of J. C. Meyer, World War II fighter ace, Dartmouth graduate, came in as the boss.* J. C. Meyer was also in Omaha when I was there in '60, '61, '62. I went over with J. C. Meyer exactly how unpleasant it was in those years and how very little had changed since then. I said that what we should do is put together a team to look at the organization and see if we could come up with some reasonable accommodation to give the Navy a meaningful position out there. I suggested that the same kind of plan would be turned out, and I thought, as I said to him, the SAC fanatics were pushing things too far. I went to see Zumwalt and Cousins about this. I went to see Admiral Moorer about it. I was trying to line up support. I didn't get much help from Admiral Moorer. He had other problems.

But, anyway, much to my surprise, General Meyer agreed. He agreed it should be changed. He agreed that the Navy hadn't gotten a fair shake out there. He was a very charming man, J. C. Meyer, one of the most pleasant men I ever worked with, and a very intelligent man, well-

---

*General John C. Meyer, USAF, Commander in Chief Strategic Air Command, 1 May 1972-31 July 1974.

read--J. C. Meyer, former Vice Chief of the Air Force. So he suggested we form a study group and we put a Marine colonel in charge of this study, not an Air Force type. The group also included some Navy types and Air Force types. But we had one agreement, that Meyer and I wouldn't get involved in the study group. We'd give them a charter and let them go do it.

The study group came in with their recommendations, and they were reasonable. They allocated a certain number of positions to the Navy, and we would get another Navy admiral out there to head the intelligence organization. Lo and behold, Meyer agreed to the entire thing--the whole works. I went back to brief the Joint Chiefs of Staff. I thought the SAC-fanatic types were going to have kittens. They were absolutely flabbergasted at what Meyer was doing. Meyer even had to talk to the Chief of Staff of the Air Force about it. The Chief of Staff told him, "Well, if this is what you want to do, okay."

But SAC fanatics thought that somehow or other we were going to undermine the Strategic Air Command by being given some more responsible positions. It's quite a traumatic thing for them. But Meyer put the organization into place; we got some additional Navy people out there, got another rear admiral to head the intelligence organization. We still didn't have a proper role, in my view, but it was 100% better than it was under Power.

Other than that, not much went on in Omaha that I haven't described earlier. And, in addition, I had some time out there to go wandering around the countryside and look at things that I was interested in.

We had a very interesting man, Welko Gasch, on what we called the scientific advisory group for JSTPS. He was a designer, engineer for Northrop Aircraft. He and I talked at great length about the kind of an airplane we ought to have in the Navy. I went out to look at the F-17 and the F-16 while I was in Omaha. I had an airplane and lots of time. I began to form some ideas which later became the F-18. But I spent a lot of time thinking about naval aviation and looking at what was available, and talking to this particular individual.

I do have one other thing that I want to comment on having to do with JSTPS. We had this scientific advisory group, and we would have a meeting once a quarter and cover a given area of intelligence, usually technical intelligence, the status of our programs and the Russian programs. To do this we had to make contact with the Defense Intelligence Agency and the various intelligence organizations of each service that normally handle the specialties, such as surface-to-air missiles or surface-to-surface missiles. The Army handles their specialties, Air Force theirs, Navy theirs. We would go through DIA to get their help also the CIA, of course.

At all these SAG meetings once a quarter, scientific advisory group, these intelligence organizations would come in and give us their picture. My impressions were the following: the Defense Intelligence Agency, as you know, is just a recordkeeper, bookkeeper, administrative bureaucracy. But the services' intelligence units would do the technical work on their Soviet counterparts. The Army has one down at Huntsville. They're excellent, absolutely first-rate. I was very impressed with the Air Force, Navy, and Army. I was very impressed because that was my first exposure to it.

I didn't realize that we were following the Soviets that closely and were doing such a good job. The people doing this, of course, are knowledgeable people about our own systems, and then they look at the Russian ones. I never saw the CIA put on even a halfway satisfactory show for us. Maybe there's some good sections of the CIA, but we looked at lots of them. I was least impressed with the CIA from all the intelligence organizations that we worked with when I was at JSTPS. That surprised me. I expected the CIA to be the last word on all these areas. Not so.

Q: One major difference between this and the time you were there before is that Polaris was then just coming into its own and didn't have a track record. By now it did and Poseidon was coming along.* Did that make a difference in the relationship?

Admiral Lee: When Holloway was there, it didn't make a particle of difference. When Meyer came in, that was one of my arguments that we had a much greater role in the SIOP--Single Integrated Operational Plan--than we did before. Since half the weapons in the plan were Navy, we should have a commensurate role in putting it together.

But it didn't cut any ice with Holloway. With Meyer it made good sense. So that's why he agreed to reorganize, in effect, and put Navy people in the billets where they should be. We made about eight or ten billets on a rotation basis. Navy would have them one tour, Army would have one tour, Air Force would have one tour--that sort of thing, whereas SAC had had them year in and year out, and the Navy might have the deputy job.

That really about covers my time in JSTPS. It was a very pleasant tour, great athletic facilities. I was relieved by Vice Admiral G. E. Miller, former Commander Sixth Fleet.

In the spring of 1973, I came back to Washington and sat on a rear admirals' board. I'm going to talk a little bit about that later.

Q: Well, maybe this would be a good point to hit that.

---
*Poseidon was the next generation of submarine-launched ballistic missiles, capable of longer range than the Polaris.

Admiral Lee: During the course of my time as a rear admiral, I sat on one lieutenant commander to commander board in 1969. I sat on two rear admiral selection boards, selecting captains for rear admiral, one in the spring of 1973 and one in the spring of 1975. I sat on two plucking boards, which select rear admirals out of the Navy. I sat on one of them in 1974 and another one in 1976. The years I didn't sit on the selection boards, I sat on the plucking boards.

I would like to say this about the Navy's selection system. I think it's probably the best system that's ever been devised for a big organization. Why? Because that fitness report system tells a great story. If you look at one jacket on one individual, say, out of year group '60, or whatever, it doesn't tell you much. But in selection boards you treat entire year groups at one time.

When you do this on a comparison basis, looking at a whole year group at a time, the fitness report system and the Navy's recording system on officers is marvelous. We can immediately pick out the top 10% or 15%. They just stand out. You can also pick out the bottom 10% or 15%, people who have not carried their load through the years. If you looked at the individual records, not having looked at the whole year group, you wouldn't get that view. After you spend two or three weeks going through these records, you feel as though you get to know these people looking at them every day and briefing them. I came to believe that it was absolutely the best system that man can devise for selection and promotion. And, as you know, all promotions in the Navy come through selection boards through rear admiral. Above rear admirals, they're nominated by the President and confirmed by the Senate.

But the difficult part of a selection board is not picking the top 10% or 15%. For instance, if you've got a big zone and you've got to select 60%, the difficult part is differentiating from the 55% point to the 65% point. Other than that, it's easy. But in the last parts of a selection process, you might have 10 or 15 spots to fill and you have, say, 100 jackets to look at. That gets very difficult. In some cases, you pick people who are no better than the people passed over. But, by and large, the proper people get selected in my view.

Now every naval officer is looked at twice, by two boards, with no prejudice. So that if one year group is better than another, the preceding one or succeeding one, and, hence, some good people were not selected who maybe should have been selected for promotion, they'll be picked up the next time around. That's a good feature.

But I've heard any number of people explain in great detail why they weren't selected for admiral and why they weren't selected for captain or commander. Having sat on all these selection and plucking boards, I came to the conclusion that there was no specific reason why any one individual was not selected or why another one was selected. It's the total record. I've seen people selected who had bad fitness reports from, say, one particular captain in a 20-year career, or one particular commanding officer. But that was discounted because of his record on either side of that event.

The total record is looked at, and the total man is looked at. I never saw any good reason why a man was promoted, nor any specific reason why a man was not promoted. It's the total record, and you have nine members of a selection board, and they vote on how they view the man. I think when people say, "I wasn't selected because my wife's hair is red"--some reasons I've heard are that fanciful--they just haven't sat on a selection board and don't appreciate the system. It's a great system; it's a very fair system; and I hope the Navy continues it forever more.

Q: Well, I guess the one criticism from people who aren't selected is that the system tends to perpetuate itself. The people who are selected often look at the people who have the same qualities they do.

Admiral Lee: Yes. There is certainly some of that there.

Q: Well, we're getting to the end of the tape, Admiral. Do you want to have the next session devoted exclusively to the Air Systems Command?

Admiral Lee: If that's what you'd like, it's fine with me.

Interview Number 7 with Vice Admiral Kent L. Lee,
U.S. Navy (Retired)

Place: Logon Farm, Admiral Lee's home near Gordonsville, Virginia

Date: Monday, 21 December 1987

Interviewer: Paul Stillwell

Q: Admiral, today we're ready to embark on your final tour of active duty as Commander Naval Air Systems Command.

Admiral Lee: As I have said earlier, my wish in my final years in the Navy was to work in the material business, because I felt the Navy was in terrible shape in the sense that the maintenance man-hours per flight hour in our aircraft were just unbelievably high. We weren't buying and building maintainable aircraft. In other words, the equipment we were buying was just plain unreliable. I discussed this earlier, about my touring the hangar decks on Enterprise and the fact that I wanted to go into this area, where I felt I could make a contribution.

In late 1972, I talked to the Assistant Secretary of the Navy for Installations and Logistics, Charlie Ill, and I told him that I would be interested in the job of Commander Naval Air Systems Command, that I had some things I wanted to accomplish. I don't know what role Ill played in my transfer to NavAir. I assume he talked to Zumwalt or the Secretary.

At about the same time, Admiral Zumwalt, I believe, was looking for a place for Vice Admiral Jerry Miller, who was Commander Sixth Fleet. He sent Admiral Miller out to Omaha to relieve me in June of 1973. This was out to pasture for Miller, since Miller and Zumwalt were not getting along very well. Zumwalt, being the Chief of Naval Operations, had the upper hand.

I received orders to go to Naval Air Systems Command, to relieve an old friend of mine by the name of Tom McClellan. In years past the Commander Naval Air Systems Command was promoted to three stars and given either the Naval Air Force Atlantic Fleet or Naval Air Force Pacific Fleet. Tom was not offered either job and instead was offered another two-star job, so he elected to retire. I think the main reason was the Chief of Naval Material, Admiral Kidd, who, number one, didn't like aviators, and, number two, didn't like Tom McClellan.*

Anyway, Tom retired, and I became Commander Naval Air Systems Command. We had a very good turnover. Tom told me about all the projects, the problems, and the fact that the Grumman contract had just been restructured. The Grumman F-14 contract was a terrible problem for both Navy and Grumman for the previous three years, and finally the contract had been restructured. I didn't have to face that big problem on arrival at Naval Air Systems Command.

---
*Admiral Isaac C. Kidd, Jr., USN, was Chief of Naval Material from 1 December 1971 to 18 April 1975.

The very last item that Admiral McClellan gave me was a big package compiled by the inspector general. It had to do with Rear Admiral Snead, who was the program manager for the F-14, and McClellan wanted me to read this.* I read it, and my hair stood on end. Admiral McClellan told me that--and I will discuss this more later--that the decision had been made to wait until the F-14 program settled down, and then move Admiral Snead. I accepted that, but it was a very difficult several months before I decided that Admiral Snead had to be moved.

The Naval Air Systems Command was a very big organization, about 45,000 people, many facilities, seven overhaul and repair organizations scattered around the country, employing 3,000, 4,000, 5,000 people each. We had test facilities for engines, catapults, and airplanes. We had research and development facilities, labs, and industry. Within the Air Systems Command, at the time I took over, I believe we had 23 program managers. The command was divided into roughly eight divisions. Air-01 was programs. Program managers reported to a rear admiral, who happened to be Rear Admiral Feightner. We had an Air-02 for contracting, an Air-03 for research and development; an Air-04, Rear Admiral Faulders for logistics and fleet support who ran the NARFs.** We had an Air-05, Rear

---
*Rear Admiral Leonard A. Snead, USN.
**Rear Admiral Cyril T. Faulders, Jr., USN, Assistant Commander for Logistics and Fleet Support, Naval Air Systems Command; NARFs--naval air rework facilities.

Admiral Foxgrover, for engineering; and we had an Air-09, the deputy commander, who happened to be Admiral Wittman; and we had an Air-08, the comptroller.*

I think in Naval Air Systems Command at this particular time I had the finest set of assistants, officers, rear admirals and captains and civilians that I've ever run across. The legal department has a battery of lawyers. Most of them are specialists in procurement, and the head of this was one of the most able men I've known. His name is Harvey Wilcox, and he's now Deputy General Counsel of the Department of the Navy.

In addition to that, I had sat on a rear admiral selection board just before coming to Washington, and I had spotted two officers that I particularly wanted. One was Rear Admiral Foxgrover, who went to Air-05, and the other was Captain John Alvis, whom I felt sure would make rear admiral. He became F-14 program manager after coming to NavAir without a job initially. These officers were both highly qualified technically, had great records, and I felt they would make a great addition to Naval Air Systems Command.

One of the oddities in the Naval Air Systems Command is that the command is always headed by a line officer, a 1310. We have engineering duty officers in aviation.

---
*Rear Admiral James H. Foxgrover, USN, Assistant Commander for Material Acquisition, Naval Air Systems Command; Rear Admiral Narvin O. Wittman, USN, Vice Commander, Naval Air Systems Command.

They're called AEDOs. They've never headed the Naval Air Systems Command. In contrast the engineering duty officers normally headed the Naval Sea Systems Command up until very recently.

This is a good time to say something about the aeronautical engineering duty officers. I don't think Naval Air Systems Command could be run nearly as efficiently and as well as it's currently run without these AEDOs. I found them to be a highly talented, highly educated, highly intelligent group of people. Of the officers I've mentioned thus far, Faulders was an AEDO; Wittman was an AEDO; and then we had two program managers by the names of Jessen and Ekas, who later made rear admiral, who were also engineering duty officers.* But every once in a while officers in high places in the Department of the Navy try to get rid of the engineering duty specialists.

Having worked in the Naval Air Systems Command for two tours and in Washington for five tours, I think that would be a very great mistake. I think the engineering duty officers more than carry their weight. Without the continuity that they offer and the knowledge that they have gained over years and years and years in the procurement

---

*Captain George E. Jessen, USN; Captain Claude P. Ekas, Jr., USN.

business, and in the repair and overhaul business, and in every other aspect of running a big organization like Naval Air Systems Command, it would be difficult to get the same quality of 1310 officers in there to do the job. So I came away from my tour being a very great supporter of the AEDOs.

Q: Could there be an argument made for having an AEDO at the head of the Air Systems Command?

Admiral Lee: I think that the AEDOs should have a turn as head of the Naval Air Systems Command. I had in mind Rear Admiral Jessen, but came the time when he would have been eligible for the job, once again it went to a 1310 officer. I think the AEDs should be given a chance to be head of Naval Air Systems Command.

These division heads do most of the work with these various facilities that we have. The Commander Naval Air Systems Command oversees all of this. Also, you must understand that it's just not possible for the commander to know everything that's going on, with budgets in the billions and thousands of people. So the commander is normally spending his time with troubled projects, areas which are in difficulty for one reason or another.

Q: So it becomes management by exception.

Admiral Lee: Management by exception, if you want to call it that, because you spend very little time on those projects that run smoothly and aren't in trouble. That's one of the disadvantages of being Commander Naval Air Systems Command. When he goes to the Pentagon and the Congress, the commander is always working on a project which is in trouble. So the commander gets a smell about him. Out of the 23 projects that we had at that particular time, always there were three or four or five in one difficulty or another. The commander spends his time working on that until that's solved and then moves to another one, in addition to making the various decisions and administratively running the command.

The Commander Naval Air Systems Command reported to the Chief of Naval Material, who headed an organization set up in the mid-Sixties to sort of match an Air Force organization. The Naval Material Command organization, in my view, never contributed anything to the accomplishment of our mission. When I was at NavAir we had a Chief of Naval Material by the name of Isaac Kidd, who was not technically qualified but insisted on making a decision every hour, and it was a very difficult job working with him.

Also, the Commander Naval Air Systems Command has to work very closely with OP-05, which represents the CNO in matters involving aviation.* In addition, the Naval Air Systems Command also runs projects for all the other Ops in the Pentagon. For instance, OP-03 was the sponsor for the ship-to-ship missile.** There are lots of other projects at any given time, especially in the ASW area, which are not sponsored by OP-05. OP-05 fights the battles for the projects in the Pentagon. Mostly these are financial battles.

My first mission in Naval Air Systems Command was to work on reliability and maintainability. As I said earlier, I realized I couldn't do that in Air-04. The commander at that time was not interested, and I couldn't do the things that I wanted to do. It just wasn't possible because you'd have to instill this idea of reliability and maintainability into the project managers and make them insist on it.

It has to be contractual. The first thing I did was look around for some vehicle to measure our maintainability and reliability. We already had what was called a 3M system in the Navy.*** Every maintenance action on an airplane is reported in the 3M system. It's a computer system, and it's reported on a card and it names the part,

---

*OP-05--Deputy Chief of Naval Operations (Air Warfare).
**OP-03--Deputy Chief of Naval Operations (Surface Warfare).
***3M--maintenance and material management. For an early evaluation of the system, see Vice Admiral Bernard M. Strean, USN, "The Naval Aviation 3M Program--Success or Failure?" U.S. Naval Institute Proceedings, September 1970, pages 86-88.

it cites the trouble and describes what's done to it. This is all put in a computer. We had never really made any good use of this 3M system.

We set up an office headed up by Captain Frank Readdy, who was an aeronautical engineering duty officer and a very fine one, who didn't make admiral for a very peculiar reason.* He would have otherwise. His wife died when he was a senior commander or junior captain, and he had three or four children that he had to care for. He elected to stay in the Washington area and raise his family and not remarry. That made it just about impossible for him to make rear admiral, because he didn't get the jobs that ordinary candidates for rear admiral get.

But, anyway, he was the ideal man for this particular system. What we decided to do was to try to extract from the 3M system--which was up at Johnsville, Pennsylvania-- all the data fed in there, and just see how much information we could get on each type of airplane. For instance, for the F-14 we wanted to run a program that would tell us for the last six months what was the number-one trouble area in terms of parts, the maintenance. What was number two and what was number three? We would take a look at these trouble areas and go to work on them.

We found out, lo and behold, that the 3M system was a gold mine of information. After about six months' effort,

---
*Captain Francis J. Readdy, USN.

we produced a system called RISE, which published a monthly report on every aircraft type in the Navy inventory.* This monthly report included the maintenance man-hours per flight hour, the mean time between failures--the top ten, as we called it--trouble items, and any others that you wanted to look for. We just had absolutely all the information that we would ever need on each type of airplane. We printed these things up once a month and distributed them to the program managers. There's a program manager for each airplane. These program managers then would have to report to me, and to our management council, what they were doing on each of these top ten trouble items for each aircraft. The 3M system and RISE were unbelievably good.

Q: What would be an example of one of the trouble items?

Admiral Lee: I'll give you a typical example. We were changing fuel controls on the P-3 aircraft every 200-300 hours, and nobody really looked into why we had to change fuel controls that often. Through the RISE system we found out that the problem was in the O-rings in the fuel control. So then we ran a project to see if we could get improved O-rings. It was very inexpensive, and as these fuel controls went through the repair facilities, the new

---
*RISE--Readiness Improvement Status Evaluation.

O-rings could be put in. Then the fuel controls would last several hundred, or even several thousand hours.

Now that was one of our happier cases. Many others would require major money to fix them. We just had to watch those from month to month and do what we could. But we turned up literally hundreds of items that could be fixed on the way through repair work and overhaul and improve the reliability and the maintainability. The RISE system is still in existence today. We put it into effect in 1974. One of the things about it, though, which I didn't realize at the time, is that an airplane is hard to maintain if, in the initial design, they don't take maintainability into account, proper testing, and ease of replacing parts. As an example, it takes a crew about three days to pull an engine and put a new engine into an A-4 aircraft or most other aircraft, F-14, A-7. Not only that, once they put it in an aircraft, it has to be trimmed, or tuned up in the aircraft.

When we designed the F-18, our plan initially was to build an engine which, number one, could be tuned up in a test stand, because to tune up an engine in an aircraft you have to maneuver the aircraft into position on the hangar deck or flight deck, and direct the exhaust overboard and turn it up. That requires a lot of extra work. But an example of what we were trying to do: in the F-18 we said, number one, the engine should be tuned in a test cell after it comes out of overhaul or rework. When it's put in the airplane, it's ready to go. It doesn't have to be retuned. Number two, all those components that are mounted on engines should be mounted on a pad, such as the fuel pump, fuel control, generator. Just the engine itself should be pulled off, so it should take no more than two hours to replace an engine.

The F-18 was designed and built with those ground rules, and today the engine in the F-18 can be changed in less than two hours. It doesn't have to be tuned up once it's put in the airplane. That's the sort of thing that we were working on. But, of course, once an airplane has been built, such as the F-14, or the A-7, or the P-3, it's not possible to change that.

One of the problems that we had when I took over Naval Air Systems Command was Grumman. Grumman had gone very nearly bankrupt with the F-14 program. They had won the competition to build the F-14 by reducing their bid by $370 million dollars approximately. They had made a fixed-price bid for the research and development, and then a fixed-price bid for the first five or seven lots--the first seven years' worth of aircraft.

The research and development came out fairly well on, but it was in building the aircraft that it was costing them about twice as much to build it as they had anticipated. If they had not reduced their price by that

$370 million dollars, they would have been all right. There's good reason to believe that they didn't think that they would win the contract unless they reduced their price, which wasn't the case.

The contract had been restructured, and Grumman was no longer losing money on building F-14s, but they were in such bad financial shape that they lost their line of credit. Banks would no longer lend them money to build airplanes. So the Navy became Grumman's banker. There's a provision of law which allows the Department of Defense to declare this company's product necessary for the national defense, and the government then becomes the company's banker. The Assistant Secretary of the Navy for financial matters manages this, not the Naval Air Systems Command. About a year or two earlier Grumman had gotten this line of credit from the government.

The Congress didn't like this very much, because their idea of this line of credit was for small dollars to help small companies. Grumman was getting a line of credit of around a hundred million dollars, which was big money. The Congress passed an amendment to the law which said, "You have to come to us for anything over 25 million." That fall one of my first jobs was to go testify to the House Armed Services Committee and the Senate Armed Services Committee. Our position was that Grumman couldn't get a line of credit, so the Navy wanted to continue serving as

Grumman's banker. I studied the documents and discussed it with the people in the Assistant Secretary's office. I was nominated to be the Navy witness.

The hearings with the House Armed Services Committee went very well. The hearings for the Senate Armed Services Committee were scheduled for a few days later. Just before I went over to testify before the Senate Armed Services Committee, I learned that Grumman had been drawing down many more millions than it needed to operate. Most companies operate with a certain amount of cash on hand, and they invest this cash in the overnight market. Grumman was paying the government about 6% interest on the money it was borrowing, and most companies were getting 12% or 14% on the overnight market. Interest rates were fairly high in late 1973.

It turned out that Grumman had on hand $12 or $15 million of excess cash. The company was investing this in the overnight market, getting probably at least 12% interest, and paying the Navy 6% interest. Some Senate staffers found out about this, and I found out about it at about the same time, the morning of the hearings with the Senate Armed Services Committee. You can imagine how unhappy the senators were.

Q: And you also.

Admiral Lee: And so was I. I was absolutely livid. I discussed this with our financial people and with our lawyers, and it turned out that Grumman had done nothing illegal. Nothing in the agreement said that Grumman couldn't invest its treasury cash on an overnight basis at whatever the current interest rate was. As a matter of fact, this is standard procedure for most companies, businesses. However, this was a very different thing, because they were investing government money and making a profit on it. The senators were absolutely livid. We had a stormy session with the Senate Armed Services Committee. And Senator Symington said to me in the course of the hearing, this particular morning, "Admiral, we haven't charged you with fraud, yet."*

Senator Goldwater told me that Grumman would not get a penny.** If they went under, so be it. That concluded the hearing. You can imagine how unhappy I was with Grumman, having been set up in this fashion. So I learned, as Commander Naval Air Systems Command, that you have to be very careful in your dealings with industry, because they don't tell you everything that they know. You have to make doubly sure in almost every phase that you do have all the facts and you don't get whipsawed as I was in this case

---
*Senator Stuart Symington (Democrat-Missouri) had previously served as first Secretary of the Air Force when the Department of the Air Force was created in 1947.
**Senator Barry M. Goldwater (Republican-Arizona) had previously run for President in 1964 and was beaten soundly by Lyndon Johnson.

with Grumman. The other factor was that Naval Air Systems Command did not run this program. This was run by the Assistant Secretary of the Navy for Financial Management. His people had not wanted to go over, and so I was nominated.

But to end this little story, Grumman the very next week went out and was able to get a line of credit, which led me to believe that Grumman could have gotten this line of credit all along, that is, since the contract had been restructured. But they had a very good thing going then, getting 6% money from the Navy and able to invest their excess treasury cash overnight for 12%. Whereas, any line of credit that they set up with a bank they had to pay the prime rate or a little more, which was fairly high at this time, about 12%. Interest is not deductible on a government procurement contract. So that tells you a little bit about the procurement business from the government point of view.

Another very interesting thing came about in the fall of 1973. And it really was the genesis of the F-18. As I have mentioned earlier when I was in Air-04, when I was at OPA, and when I was in Omaha, I kept looking around for the solution to the Navy's problems of so many aircraft on the hangar deck, maintainability, reliability, having multipurpose aircraft. I was very intrigued with a visit I made to see the YF-16 and the YF-17 prototypes during this period I was in Omaha. I had many long conversations with the vice president of Northrop, who was in charge of this particular project.

In the fall of 1973 the Navy had what was called a VFAX study.* This study came to the conclusion that it was possible to build a multipurpose aircraft as we had had during World War II. The F-14, for instance, is a single-purpose aircraft. Its radar is hard-wired, and it's good only for air-to-air intercepts. It has no ground capability, either radar or for dropping of bombs. The A-7, on the other hand, has a radar which is only suitable for attack purposes. It's also hard-wired.

With the coming of computers, and with the coming of an inertial platform, and with programmable radars, the study concluded it was possible to build a multipurpose aircraft, an aircraft which, with the pushing of a button, would have a very good air-to-air radar and could fire missiles, all programmable, and guns. Then, with the pushing of another button, would shift that radar to the ground mode and would lock on ground targets, and the inertial platform would keep the airplane positioned in space so that you'd have an airplane which was equally as good as the F-14 in the air-to-air role and equally as good, if not better, than the A-7 in the attack or air-to-

---
*VFAX refers to an experimental (X), heavier-than-air (V), fighter (F) and attack (A) aircraft.

ground role with the items that I've just mentioned. These items were not too expensive, fairly reliable, and they were lightweight. We hadn't tried it before, but it looked to us like the way to go.

At about this same time the Congress and the Office of the Secretary of Defense were very unhappy with the F-14 program, very unhappy. The Navy was pushed very hard to find an alternative to the F-14. In the meantime, the Air Force had these two airplanes, YF-16 and YF-17, in prototype, and the Congress and the OSD decided that the Air Force should compete these and then build one, call it a lightweight fighter. We didn't really want a lightweight fighter. We didn't think that it would do our mission. What we liked was the VFAX.

So the Deputy Secretary of Defense, Clements, who is now governor of Texas, after many days of arguing, decided to let the Navy put out a procurement request for bid studies for a VFAX airplane.* We in Naval Air Systems Command put together a set of specifications which were really based on this VFAX study and which described the airplane we wanted. We had sent that out to industry, and meantime the Air Force was moving along to have a competition between the YF-16 and YF-17, now called the air combat fighter, when the Congress redirected our program.

---

*William P. Clements, Jr., was Deputy Secretary of Defense, 1973-77.

The Congress said that what we had to do was join forces with the Air Force and pick one of the lightweight fighters for our alternate airplane. Congress was going to severely restrict the numbers of F-14s we could buy.

Q: What was the congressional reasoning in redirecting that?

Admiral Lee: This might be a good time to describe what goes on in the Congress. Senators and representatives are usually not well informed about the various programs they're voting on. But nowadays they have hundreds and hundreds of staffers. These staffers are usually very well educated, they have enough time to probe around, and in many cases they try to run the Department of Defense from the Congress. They just have too many staffers in the Congress.

There was another factor. There was a man by the name of Chuck Myers over in the Department of Defense.* He was assistant deputy assistant for tactical warfare.

Q: Former carrier pilot.

Admiral Lee: Yes. He opposed our VFAX initiative, and he

---
*Charles E. Myers, Jr., served from October 1973 to November 1977 as Director of Air Warfare in the office of the Deputy Under Secretary of Defense for Tactical Warfare Programs.

lost. His idea of an airplane was a day fighter. He didn't believe in radars and all-weather fighters. But he was overruled by Mr. Clements and Mr. Schlesinger, and we got our VFAX.* But Myers had very close contact with some of the staffers on the Hill. These staffers got together with Myers, and they put language into the House and Senate conference bill which set aside $20 million for our joining the Air Force's air combat fighter program. There wasn't much of a way out of it, but that's how I believe it came about--Chuck Myers in the Department of Defense and staffers on the Hill.

We then joined forces with the Air Force, and the debate went on for some time as to whether or not we would have to pick the same airplane. It was decided that we could send our VFAX documents to both the YF-16 and YF-17 contractors. The YF-16 was built by General Dynamics, the YF-17 by Northrop. Since neither of these companies had ever built a carrier-suitable airplane, we also requested that they take partners. Northrop chose McDonnell Douglas for the YF-17, and General Dynamics chose LTV for the YF-16. We sent separate procurement documents different from the Air Force's. Our documents were exactly the same as we'd put out for the VFAX, exactly the same. We wanted both a fighter and an attack plane: programmable radar, inertial platform, computers.

---

*James R. Schlesinger was Secretary of Defense, 1973-75.

Q: So you weren't trying to stack the deck at all.

Admiral Lee: In addition, through these weeks of debate, it was decided that we could have separate competitions. The Air Force would have their competition between the YF-16 and YF-17; and we would have our competition. The hope was that we would both settle on one airplane or the other, the YF-16 or the YF-17. As luck would have it, the Air Force finished their competition and persuaded Mr. Schlesinger to let them go ahead and release their winner about a month or six weeks before we were ready. Our procurement documents were put on the street perhaps two months after the Air Force documents, so at the time the Air Force was ready to announce the winner for their selection, the contractors hadn't finished sending in their documents for our competition.

Mr. Schlesinger decided to let the Air Force announce that the YF-16 was the winner of the competition. He announced--and he also sent the Congress a letter to this effect--that the Navy's competition would continue, and that we would be allowed to pick whichever airplane was most satisfactory to the Navy, the YF-16 or the YF-17. We continued our competition for another six weeks, perhaps two months, because it took that long to get it all done.

As it turned out, our winner was the YF-17. The YF-16 we deemed to be unsatisfactory for carrier use. And, of course, when that happened, the roof fell in. Congress was unhappy; the staffers were unhappy; the contractors were unhappy. We were going to build separate airplanes, which was true. On top of that, Ling Temco Vought, which had assumed the lead on their bid for the naval air combat fighter, lodged a bid protest with General Accounting Office. As a result, we had to go to Congress and testify, which we did for weeks on end. Many times we had this bid protest over with General Accounting Office. I have a book of documents, which were put together after the bid protest was decided, which details the entire story of this F-18 competition, including the bid protest. Some sections of it might be of interest for this particular thing, which I will make available to you.

Anyway, LTV launched a very bitter bid protest, and its primary claim was that we had no choice other than to pick the F-16, since the Congress had told us to join forces with the Air Force. Our argument was that we had been given permission to pick whichever was best for the Navy, and the Congress had been notified and had not objected. The General Accounting Office ruled that what we had done was entirely legal in every aspect, and that the F-18 contract with McDonnell Douglas, which we had signed on the day we announced the winner, would stand and was legal. At about the same time Mr. Clements decided that we would call the F-17 derivative the F-18. So that's how the F-18 program got launched.

Q: What was the reason for changing the designation?

Admiral Lee: There was so much controversy associated with the YF-17 and YF-16 that Mr. Clements felt that it would give a new life to the F-18 to give it a new name--just that simple. But I think the F-18 has turned into a marvelous airplane. The reliability and maintainability are unbelievable, as compared to other airplanes, because we worked on them very hard, from initial specifications all the way through to the production aircraft. It's a very fine fighter plane, very maneuverable, has an excellent radar, outstanding engines, and it's also a very fine attack plane.

The only misgiving I have about the F-18 is the fact that it's too short-legged. But we were tied into that by having to take a derivative of the F-17. If the F-18 had about 2,000 or 3,000 more pounds of fuel, it would be a better airplane, because it has to carry that fuel externally. But I think it would be just about the ideal airplane which I've described earlier, not many of them built. The A-1 or AD Skyraider, I thought, was the all-time best design I ever ran across, and I think the F-18 is a close second with one exception, and that is fuel, if it just had a little more fuel.

Q: There has been an axiom, that it's a lot easier to take a Navy airplane and adapt it for Air Force use than vice versa.

Admiral Lee: Yes. They're different breeds of cat, although it's not as difficult as people say. I think this business of adapting Air Force airplanes to Navy purposes has really been put in the wrong light. When the Navy <u>wants</u> to take an Air Force airplane and adapt it for carrier use, it does so with a minimum of fanfare.

I'll give you an example: the F-86. We didn't have a fighter during the Korean War which would measure up to the F-86. Our Grumman fighters and our F7U Cutlass were just no match for it. They weren't good airplanes. So we took the F-86 and made it into a carrier plane, and we called it the FJ. It was a very fine airplane. And another part to that story is that the Air Force's F-86 was initially a Navy airplane. They made it into the F-86.

Q: So perhaps that's not a completely valid example.

Admiral Lee: It is a valid example, because the F-86 was not carrier-suitable. It was strictly an Air Force airplane, and we took it and made it carrier-suitable. We rebuilt it and put the strength points in it needed for a hook and the catapult launches. But, in my view, we can take almost any Air Force airplane which is a good airplane and make it into a carrier-suitable airplane. You'd have to start over again, but it's not that difficult, as I've just described. It became a political issue with the F-111 and later on with the F-15 when a good many people said that what we ought to do is buy the F-15 and cancel the F-14. Once again, that issue of carrier suitability came up. But in my view it wouldn't have been difficult to make the F-15 into a carrier-suitable airplane.

Q: Was there just too much leftover bad blood to prevent that from happening?

Admiral Lee: Yes, I think it's a matter of "not invented here." I think it could have been done, and it wouldn't have been all that expensive, although the F-15 was not the airplane we wanted. I think the airplane we really wanted and needed was the F-18, because what the F-18 does for us is something that's not appreciated by land-based aviators. That deck space on an aircraft carrier is very valuable. If you have an airplane which can be both a fighter and attack plane, you've got two for one. In my view, all the future tactical airplanes built for carriers ought to have that dual capability, because it's so easy to put in nowadays with the computers we have, inertial platforms, and programmable radars. All of our attack planes can have a very fine air-to-air fighter capability. And that just doubles the capability you have on an aircraft carrier of a given size.

Q: And you've got an attack plane that's less vulnerable to the enemy.

Admiral Lee: Yes, yes. But I think if we had been allowed to go our VFAX route initially, we would have had essentially the same airplane that we have for the F-18 except we would have had a little more fuel. I believe that's about the only difference we would have had. For the cycle time on aircraft carriers nowadays, F-18s have to carry fuel tanks. But A-4s were the same way. They always had to carry fuel tanks to meet carrier cycle times. And it's a perfectly satisfactory way to do business.

One of the unusual features of the F-18 program was that the pressure for the F-18 and the VFAX came not from the Navy but from the Department of Defense and from Congress. After I had looked at the VFAX and the possibilities there, I--and I believe all my assistants in the Naval Air Systems Command--became firmly convinced that the way to go was the VFAX. We concluded that we ought to buy a minimum number of F-14s and go this new route, which would be the future of naval aviation. I believe the entire group in Naval Air Systems Command, all the rear admirals and all the people who sat on the various selection committees, became firmly convinced that this was the way to go. So the Naval Air Systems Command was enthusiastic about the VFAX, which later became the F-18.

Now on the other side of the river, over in the Pentagon, OP-05, in the person of Admiral Houser and his assistants, wanted no part of the F-18--or the VFAX, for that matter.* They wanted to buy more F-14s and more A-7s. I believe the CNO, Admiral Holloway, also wanted to buy more F-14s. I don't believe Holloway ever believed in the F-18. But Holloway was enough of a politician that he was not willing to buck the Department of Defense, Mr. Clements, and Mr. Schlesinger, and even the Congress. So he didn't oppose the the F-18, but he was not an enthusiastic supporter.

I think Houser and the OP-05 crowd did everything they could to not have an F-18. But, as I say, we were pulling for it in the Naval Air Systems Command, so that led to some big divisions between Naval Air Systems Command and OP-05. We were enthusiastic for it, and they wanted no part of it, which was an interesting commentary. And, of course, with OP-05 against an airplane, it's almost never built because they have the ear of the CNO, and that's how things usually happen. In this particular case the

---
*Vice Admiral William D. Houser, USN, Deputy Chief of Naval Operations (Air Warfare), 5 August 1972-30 April 1976.

pressure, as I said earlier, came from Mr. Clements, Mr. Schlesinger, and the Congress. And we in NavAir were enthusiastically supporting them, so out came the F-18.

Q: You were mentioning the fall of 1973. That was the year that we airlifted a number of planes over to help Israelis out in their Yom Kippur War. Did your office get involved in that?

Admiral Lee: Yes, we got involved in both airplanes and in missiles. Something like this was going on almost every week in Naval Air Systems Command. It's a backbreaking job. During that Yom Kippur War, we shipped hundreds and hundreds of missiles, Sidewinders and Sparrows, and other types of ordnance to Israel.* We just took them right out of our war reserves and shipped them over. Also, we shipped airplanes. So we were involved in all of those events such as that and then had to make them up through purchases later.

I suppose I should talk a little about the Congress. The Commander Naval Air Systems Command testifies in the Congress about various items that come up that are of interest to the Congress such as the F-18, as I just described, or Grumman's banking problems. In addition to

---

*The AIM-9 Sidewinder and AIM-7 Sparrow are U.S. air-to-air guided missiles.

that, during budget time the Commander Naval Air Systems Command with OP-05 goes to four committees. We go to the Armed Services Committee, House; Armed Services Committee, Senate; and then the Appropriations Committee, House; and Appropriations Committee, Senate. This takes a lot of time for preparation and went on every year, testimony describing and justifying our budget for the next year.

In addition to that, while I was at Naval Air Systems Command I sat on one admiral promotion board and two admiral plucking boards. I previously described my views on the Navy's promotion system. I sat on one board in the spring of 1973 before coming to NavAir, admiral promotion board, captains to rear admiral, and another one in 1975. In the even years I sat on two plucking boards. Plucking boards are boards that decide which rear admirals will be retired. After three years in grade all rear admirals are looked at to be retired, and about half the rear admirals with three years' service each year are retired. That is the job of the so-called plucking board. I found the plucking boards were really not happy boards. It's one thing to be promoting captains to rear admiral; it's quite another to have 30 rear admirals up for retention and having to select out 15. I found that a very difficult, very difficult process.

Q: Were there any other factors besides fitness reports

that enter into those decisions?

Admiral Lee: You know, in promotion from captain to rear admiral, we spent days and days and weeks and weeks on fitness reports, because we looked at hundreds every year. In the plucking boards, we never looked at records. We knew them. The plucking boards were made up of one four-star and all the rest three-stars. We discussed them and voted, discussed them and voted. Never looked at records. We didn't need to.

Q: What kinds of things then would lead to a rear admiral being put on the retired list?

Admiral Lee: General reputation. Gotten into a problem. Had one type of social problem or another, a drinking problem, had not performed well in a duty assignment, had been fired from a duty assignment. But there were never enough of those to pluck. In the two boards I sat on, there were three or four obvious cases each time, and all the others were people who, in the opinion of the board, were not the best performers. So it's a very brutal process. The selection to rear admiral is very difficult, and then after three years, half of them go. So that those that are left are usually very competent people. It was very difficult, because the young rear admirals were on pins and needles waiting to hear if they were being plucked. I was very fortunate in that I missed that, since I was promoted to vice admiral before I came before a plucking board.

Q: Was it a deliberate decision to upgrade Naval Air Systems Command to a three-star billet in bringing you into the job?

Admiral Lee: I think it fitted in with Admiral Zumwalt's plans, and I think that was the reason. I think it was a good idea, but I was already a vice admiral, and I said I would like to have the job. The decision was made to let me keep three stars and take the job. I think Zumwalt thought it was a good idea to make Naval Air Systems Command into a three-star post, because shortly thereafter, in 1974, the Naval Sea Systems Command was created and made a three-star post. They've remained three. Even with a reduction in flag numbers, those two systems commands are three-star posts today. So I think it was a good move. It's a tremendously responsible job, and I think it deserved a three-star billet. There were a few three-star billets around the Navy which really weren't all that important.

I have a few areas I would like to cover in no particular sequence, which I think are interesting and sort of shed light on the things that went on in the Naval Air Systems Command.

Q: All right.

Admiral Lee: I said earlier I had 23 PMAs when I took over.* And we made a few new ones later on.

Each PMA has a certain number of dollars which are assigned to him for his project such as the F-14 is given all that F-14 money to spend as he needs it for his particular project. Every other PMA gets the same thing. They, in other words, have check-writing authority. They run their programs.

We had one program in Naval Air Systems Command which had to do with vertical takeoff and landing aircraft. The program was being done by Rockwell International, and it was a thrust augmentation aircraft. We had had a captain in charge of this program, but he left, and we gave the project to his assistant, who was a commander who had been passed over for captain. One morning I got a call from the Under Secretary of the Navy, David Potter.** He wanted to know about a contract we had signed with a Florida university having to do with large-scale integrated circuits. I said I didn't know about any contract with a

---

*PMAs--program managers air. Their counterparts in the Naval Sea Systems Command are PMSs, program managers ships.
**David S. Potter, Under Secretary of the Navy, 1974-76.

Lee #7 - 570

Florida university having to do with large-scale integrated circuits but I would look into it.

I started looking into it, and what I found I couldn't believe. This young PMA, with a retired colonel who was working as an influence man, contact man, had signed a contract with this Florida university for about $3 million. This $3 million was to be paid to the university over a period of, let's say, five years for work in large-scale integrated circuits. The problem was that this PMA had no money. He had gone around to all the other PMAs and had solicited token amounts such as $10,000 or $20,000 and had come up with the down payment, which I think was about $70,000 on this particular contract. There was no money in the budget for it; there was no way we were going to get $3 million for it; and, once again, I couldn't believe what had happened. Not only that, but the young PMA had gone to Florida and was quite a hero.

One of the Florida senators and the representative for that district were present at the university when the contract was announced, promising bigger and better things from the Navy. The more I looked at this, the more livid I got. So I called the Under Secretary back and told him the facts of the matter, one of our PMAs had gone off half-cocked and had done this. There was just absolutely no way that we wanted to do it in the first place, because we had had an all-day or two-day session on what we should do in the electronics area about a month before. Our decision had been not to put any money in this particular area, because there was plenty of work going on here, and it wasn't something that Naval Air Systems Command needed to do. We had decided that as a matter of policy.

Q: Had this PMA been aware of that decision?

Admiral Lee: I don't know that. Anyway, I explained all this to the Under Secretary, so he and I agreed we would scrape up enough money to ease them down slowly, maybe another $70,000, because they'd gone out and hired people to do this. That weekend I flew to Atlanta and met the school president who was there on, without a doubt, a fund-raising trip. Because he had a very nice suite of rooms in a hotel there with a bar set up. I had a Coke with him and then discussed it with him. After I had explained this to him, he was in a state of shock, much the way I was when I first found out about it.

I told him that what I had given him were the facts, but that if he wished he could send his professor up who had dreamed up this idea and got the contract. I would explain it to him and go over the books with him and show him that there were no line items, no budget items for this. I told him that PMA had merely scraped off money that was intended for the various projects and put this together, thinking he was doing a great thing.

To make a long story short, I fired the PMA. We gave the Florida university a certain amount of money to let them close out their program. But that, perhaps, was about as embarrassing an item as any PMA got me into.

Q: Did the Navy get any tangible results from that?

Admiral Lee: None. We got nothing.

There is another aspect to it. If we were going to do such a thing, we should have either had a competition or canvassed the academic world and gotten the best. But we decided not to do anything like this. I doubt very much if we had, we would have gone to a Florida university. But it wasn't something that I could do much about by the time I learned about it.

Another item which I found very interesting--when I got to Naval Air Systems Command, it appeared to me that we had too many test facilities. We had two huge pieces of real estate, one at Patuxent and one at Lakehurst.* We had other smaller facilities. Both places had thousands of acres, and both places were underutilized. We were only using about 20 or 30% of their potential. I put together a committee chaired by retired Vice Admiral Allen Shinn, a

---

*The Naval Air Test Center is at Patuxent River, Maryland, and the Naval Air Engineer Center at Lakehurst, New Jersey.

Lee #7 - 573

former Commander of Naval Air Systems Command, to see what we should do about this, knowing full well what they would come up with.* Because it was pretty obvious what we should do is consolidate either at Lakehurst or Patuxent. We wouldn't do that consolidation overnight, because Lakehurst had some very heavy installations, such as the catapult work and the arresting gear work. But over a period of time we wouldn't put anything new at Lakehurst, but would instead put new capital intensive installations at Patuxent.

As I expected, the study committee came up with the results that almost any logical man would follow, namely, slowly phase down Lakehurst and build up Patuxent. Try to concentrate all of our test activities for naval aviation at Patuxent. We had the test pilot school down there, and we had also moved the logistics center to Patuxent. The idea was to use the real estate we had to maximum efficiency.

As soon as the results of this study were known, the Lakehurst community was up in arms. We then had an exchange of letters and ideas and memorandums between the New Jersey congressman and our Secretary. This is sort of standard procedure, and I was fully prepared for this, because there's no way you can reduce a facility in one

------
*Rear Admiral Allen M. Shinn, USN, served as Commander Naval Air Systems Command from 1 May 1966 to 1 September 1966. Shinn retired in 1970 as a vice admiral.

state and increase one in another without flak. But after three or four months of discussing what we would do and how we would do it, we finally came to an agreement as to what we would do about Lakehurst and what we would do about Patuxent. We declared a truce. The congressman and I agreed that, all right, we're all settled now. What finally happened was that we weren't able to do what we really wanted to do, but we did some of it. That's the nature of the political animal we had.

One morning the congressman's aide called my aide and invited me to a New Jersey delegation breakfast. They had a breakfast once a month over in one of the dining rooms in the Capitol, and I was invited. It was portrayed as just a simple breakfast, to meet the delegation. So I showed up over there promptly, in uniform, for breakfast. And, lo and behold, when I got there, they had radio reporters, newspaper reporters, TV, and Lakehurst employees there. And the congressman got up and discussed Lakehurst a little bit and Patuxent, and then said that Admiral Lee would be glad to answer any questions you might have.

Q: You felt you'd really been sandbagged.

Admiral Lee: And I had been sandbagged, and I answered questions for perhaps an hour and a half, and was not very happy about it meantime. After I got through my question-

and-answer session, another congressman got up and made a speech. I finally did get a little breakfast. I came back to NavAir, and I called my aide and I said, "All right, let's play a game. Here's what I want you to do. I want you to call that congressman's aide that you've had contact with and say to him, 'What in hell's name did you do to Admiral Lee? I've never seen him so mad as when he came back from that breakfast. I just can't believe it. What did you do?'"

The aide was taken aback, but my aide then hung up after he'd described my anger and unhappiness about the whole thing, and about two weeks later I got a letter from the congressman, apologizing. But I played a little game with him too.

I'd like to talk about Grumman a little bit more, because we had some real problems with Grumman further down the road. During this time period, Grumman sold 75 or so airplanes to Iran. And, of course, the Naval Air Systems Command was charged with procuring these airplanes and setting up the Iranian airfields, and training the pilots--a really big job. That went on fairly well. I think we were doing our part of it fairly well, when all of a sudden out of the blue, it came to our attention that Grumman was paying an agent for the F-14 sale. The Shah had gotten wind of this and was very upset about it, because he had said, "No agents."*

It turned out that Grumman had already paid an agent, let's say, $50 million, and they owed this agent another $50 million. In the meantime, the Secretary of Defense for Iran, who was a general, came over, and in a room with me and some people from CNO and some people from OSD, this Secretary of Defense for Iran berated the two Grumman executives, called them crooks and every other name that you can imagine, about paying this agent. Iran wanted Grumman to give them the $50 million they'd already paid the agent, and also to give them the $50 million that they still owed the agent. Of course, Grumman had the contract with the agent.

Now the irony of this whole thing is that the Shah had a brother-in-law who was head of the Air Force. The agent's partner was the Shah's brother-in-law. So you see what a problem that gave Grumman. This was sort of standard procedure for Iran, the most corrupt government that I think the world has ever seen. But Grumman later worked out some agreement, some arrangement with Iran where they gave them some extra spare parts. And they had an out-of-court settlement with the agent. But that took up a fair amount of our time while we sorted out these pieces on the Grumman-Iran thing.

---
*Mohammed Reza Pahlavi was Shah of Iran from 1941 until his ouster in early 1979 when the Ayatollah Ruhollah Khomeini took power. The Shah was a long-time friend of the United States.

I had another very interesting exercise with Grumman. Grumman did, in my opinion, an unsatisfactory job in building the F-14. In making the airplane carrier-suitable and repairing both engine and airframe, we spent, certainly, a billion dollars on the first 250 Grumman airplanes in our own repair facilities, getting them ready. Grumman, of course, was going bankrupt at the time they were building these airplanes, and they weren't about to spend an extra nickel. For that reason I think that fixed R&D contracts are unsuitable for both the government and industry, because if industry underbid, they're not going to spend their own money to give you a good product. And regardless of the price, you want a good product. So what we had was a bankrupt Grumman and a lousy product. That's the result of that kind of contract.

In about 1975 Grumman came in with a claim. And, if I remember correctly, this claim was for something like $75 million.

Q: Claims were very popular then.

Admiral Lee: Claims were popular then. The president of Grumman came and presented this claim to me for about $75 million, and they put this claim in their annual report as one of their assets. This didn't sit too well with me, especially in view of the fact that we'd had to scrounge up several hundred million dollars to fix the F-14s. I didn't tell Grumman what we were going to do. I said we would look at it. I put together a team of the best people I could find in Naval Air Systems Command. We got out the contract and looked at the things that were wrong with the F-14 that should have been fixed by contract, and we put together a claim against Grumman for at least $75 million, roughly the same amount that Grumman was claiming from the Navy.

I called the president of Grumman down to Naval Air Systems Command and presented him this claim. I thought the man was going to jump out the window. After they had had two or three weeks to digest the claim, then we put together a negotiating committee which would negotiate with Grumman over their claim and over our claim. The net result was that our claim washed out their claim and vice versa. And Grumman essentially got nothing. But I believe that was a first in Naval Air Systems Command or Naval Ship Systems Command where we have presented a contractor with a claim.

But I have an interesting little sidelight on that. Some months later I was at a party. There are parties every night, receptions in Washington. You have to consciously avoid them if you're going to work a full day. But, anyway, one of Grumman's right-hand men, that I'd known for years, came up to me at this party--we'd both had a couple of drinks--and he said to me, "Why do you hate Grumman so?"

Of course, I smiled and denied any such thing. But I'm sure the question was because of that claim.

Q: Who was the Grumman president that you dealt with?

Admiral Lee: George Skurla.

Q: Grumman and a number of the other defense contractors hire retired senior naval officers. Are they a factor in these kinds of negotiations?

Admiral Lee: No, they're not a factor. They're not allowed to negotiate for Grumman. They're not allowed to sell, and they're not allowed to negotiate. All they can do is advise. As a matter of fact, Vice Admiral Townsend worked for Grumman at the time.* He was head of their international operations. But he was a very decent man, Admiral Townsend. He never overstepped the bounds.

Q: Just to pursue that Iran connection, wasn't the idea there that the extra production could bring down the unit cost for the U.S. Navy?

---
*Vice Admiral Robert L. Townsend, USN (Ret.)

Admiral Lee: Oh, yes. That was the idea--that the more airplanes you can build, the lower the unit costs. So, presumably, the Navy didn't have a part in selling these airplanes to Iran in the sense of marketing. That was done by Grumman. But once it was a government-to-government sale it was managed by Naval Air Systems Command, which is the way most of these foreign military sales are handled. Of course, we contracted for these airplanes for Iran with Grumman, just as we contracted for our own. But meantime Grumman had this agent who was a partner with the Shah's brother-in-law and who was head of the Air Force. There was never any direct connection, but the obvious is that that's how Grumman got the contract in the first place.

I've talked a little bit about the Chief of Naval Material. But I would like to talk about him a little more. I thought that the Naval Material Command was a completely unnecessary organization. As I said earlier, it was patterned after what the Air Force had done, and I don't think we should follow the Air Force's organization methods. But the systems commands, Naval Sea Systems Command and Naval Air Systems Command are self-contained. We have our own contracting facilities, and about the only thing that the CNM organization can do is look over our shoulder. They were of great nuisance value in one way or another, as all these bureaucratic organizations are. One of the greatest things that Secretary of the Navy Lehman did was abolish the Chief of Naval Material. I always wanted to become the Chief of Naval Material, because I wanted to abolish the organization.

We had an admiral by the name of Kidd who was Chief of Naval Material. Kidd was an aviator-hater. And with his seniors, he was a bootlicker and a flatterer and would tell them just what they wanted to hear. With his juniors he was overbearing, rude, harsh, absolutely the worst senior officer I have ever seen. He had no technical competence. People who worked with Kidd had a terrible time. His aide, while I was there, had a heart attack, died. He had a very fine Deputy Chief of Naval Material, who I thought was going to have a nervous breakdown. But, in short, I thought Admiral Kidd was an absolute disaster as Chief of Naval Material.

Q: What can you say about your personal dealings with him?

Admiral Lee: They were always difficult, always difficult. I tried to avoid Kidd whenever possible.

Q: Are there any specific things that you remember?

Admiral Lee: Every week there was some difficult thing. I can remember a typical Kidd event. One Saturday and Sunday I was called up by the Under Secretary of the Navy--who happened to be David Potter, very good man--and asked to go over to the Pentagon and help somebody in OSD put together some paperwork for congressional hearings for the following week. This wasn't unusual. I've forgotten what the paperwork was about, but it wasn't anything consequential. But the OSD people wanted to get it right, so he called on me. I called our lawyer, Harvey Wilcox, and our contracting officer. I believe that this had to do with the F-18, but I've forgotten. We went over to the Pentagon. I made a couple, three trips over there, and we went over this material with the man who was preparing it. He typed it up, and we read it and approved it, making sure that all the facts were proper, and that the testimony that was going to the Congress was accurate.

I called Kidd when I got back on Sunday afternoon, which he wanted us to do, and told him what I had done and that there wasn't anything of big consequence about it. He then ordered me to put it in writing and get it typed up and sent over to him, and he wanted to take it to the CNO, typical Kidd. So I sat down and wrote it up, and called the Naval Air Systems Command duty officer to come get it, type it up and take it out to Kidd. Kidd then would call the CNO, who happened to be Holloway at that time, and go see him and give him this little bit, which wasn't consequential at all, wasn't important. But that was a typical Kidd event. Things like that happened every week.

Q: So from what you're saying, his presence in the bureaucracy was very much counterproductive.

Admiral Lee: I thought it was very counterproductive. In short, I thought he was a disaster. We didn't need the organization in the first place. But to get one who was ignorant and not knowledgeable of technical things was a double disaster. And also an activist, and also very ambitious, and always stroking the secretaries. He's probably the best stroker of secretaries I've ever seen. I don't mean female secretaries either, the male type. Kidd's relief was a fellow by the name of Michaelis.*

Q: One of your predecessors in the Enterprise.

Admiral Lee: Highly qualified technically and one of the nicest guys you'll ever meet. An absolute prince. So you can imagine the difference between Kidd and Michaelis.

Now you asked me earlier to comment on the CNO selection in 1974. I do have some comments on that. The general opinion is that there were two final competitors, Admirals Kidd and Holloway. I believe that to be true. And there were other candidates. As a matter of fact--and I've never even told my wife this--Secretary Warner wanted

---

*Admiral Frederick H. Michaelis, USN, was Chief of Naval Material from 18 April 1975 to 1 August 1978.

to see me one day in the spring of 1974. I went over to see him. John Warner was Secretary of the Navy at the time, and he said that I had been suggested as a candidate for CNO. But he said to me that he felt sure that I wasn't interested in the job, and I could take a hint, so I said to him that, no, I really wasn't interested in the job.

I had a feeling at that particular time that Warner was pushing Ike Kidd. It's my understanding that Kidd and Holloway were asked to write a paper on their views on the Navy. They were the two finalists. I believe Clements and Warner were pushing for Kidd. Schlesinger made the final decision which, of course, had to then go on up to the President. I know Holloway wrote a paper; and I know Kidd wrote a paper. I believe these were sent eventually on up to Schlesinger. Holloway's a beautiful writer. In this paper of his, he described his Navy of the future, lots of V/STOL, which never came to pass.* Kidd was not a very good writer.

I believe through the paper writing that Schlesinger picked Holloway. Probably Schlesinger knew them both, interviewed them both, and Holloway is a very persuasive, very articulate guy. So is Kidd for that matter. There were other candidates, including Jerry Miller. I'm sure that he was nominated by Admiral Moorer, who was the Chairman of the Joint Chiefs. But I believe it came down

---

*V/STOL--vertical or short takeoff and landing aircraft.

to those two, and I believe Holloway got selected for the reasons I've just described.

Q: What would be Secretary Warner's purpose in mentioning that to you if he didn't have an interest in pushing you for it?

Admiral Lee: I think my nomination came down from the OSD crowd. In my years in the Naval Air Systems Command I did a lot of business with somebody in OSD. I had a lot of contacts down there. I believe that whoever was down at OSD suggested to Schlesinger or Clements that I should be a candidate too. Then this was put to Warner, is the way I saw it.

Q: And he was reacting to it.

Admiral Lee: Yes, and he was reacting to it. He had to go back and tell Clements and Schlesinger, "Yes, I talked to Lee and he's not interested."

Q: Since he put those words in your mouth.

Admiral Lee: I wasn't all that eager to be CNO, of course, but I got Warner's message fairly soon.

Q: Well, I think you probably would have been hard to sell, not having had a seagoing flag job.

Admiral Lee: I agree. I don't think I would have been a good seller at all. That's why I didn't pursue it.

In the summer of 1976, I'd been at Naval Air Systems Command three years, and that's a very tough job, as I said earlier. The reason that it's so tough is that you have so many projects, so many things going on, and the commander always has to take the projects that are in deep trouble and tries to straighten them out, and take them forward and get additional funding or whatever else is needed. So that this is very wearing in time. The F-18 was a very wearing competition.

So in the summer of 1976 I decided what I'd really like to do is retire. I had thought that I might be made the Chief of Naval Material, but when Michaelis got that job, I didn't think there was another job that I really wanted. So I said to Admiral Holloway that I'd been there three years, which was the normal length of the tour, and that unless he had other plans for me, why, I would be very happy to retire. Well, he didn't like that too much, but he said very little.

About a day or two later I was asked to come over and see Admiral Shear, who was the VCNO.* Hal Shear, who was

---

*Admiral Harold E. Shear, USN, was Vice Chief of Naval Operations from 30 June 1975 to 5 July 1977.

a submariner, very good man, said to me that they very much wanted me to stay on in NavAir, that we had a new OP-05 in, who was my old friend Forrest Petersen. Shear said he felt that we together could accomplish a lot for naval aviation, and that we didn't know what the future would bring next year. Something might turn up that I would like. Admiral Holloway had said after another year at the Naval Air Systems Command, I could have either AirLant or AirPac.

But I wasn't really interested. And, as I say, I was tired and worn out. I had had 36 years in the Navy, and also, the F-18 program had been signed, sealed, and delivered. I had talked to my wife, and I decided what I really wanted to do is retire. After another discussion with Shear, and another discussion with Holloway, they decided that I could retire, and I put in my papers. And then, much to my pleasure, Forrest Petersen left OP-05 and came over and relieved me.

One other final word. I had had five tours of duty in Washington, and I had seen what happens to retired senior military officers in Washington, and other people who were leaving government. They get into consulting jobs, and they become influence peddlers and intelligence specialists, because what industry wants is intelligence on new procurements. They want marketing intelligence. And they want influence brought to bear in various ways to get contracts. I decided that I wanted to get out of Washington.

I discussed it with my wife, and we decided to look in the Virginia-Maryland-West Virginia-Pennsylvania area for a farm. We decided we would try to find a farm which was suitable for our purposes, at least 150 acres with a house, and try some gentleman farming. If it worked, fine. And if it didn't, why, we could sell out and we could try something else. After retiring I also did a little consulting. I was called by several companies to do this or that for them, which I did. I became a director on one company's board. We bought a farm called Logon down in Albemarle County, moved down there, and have lived happily ever since.

But the real reason was to get out of Washington. I don't think Washington is a healthy place for senior people in government who retire. There's too much money floating around.

Q: Too many temptations.

Admiral Lee: Too many temptations. And if you're 90 or 100 miles out of town, those temptations are removed.

Q: Well, this placid environment is certainly far different from the hectic Washington arena.

Admiral Lee: It is that. About the most excitement we have is a cow having trouble having a calf down here.

Now if you have some questions, I think that about sums up my time at Naval Air Systems Command. I think it was a very rewarding tour. I think we did some good things for naval aviation. As I've said earlier, I had the finest team of officers and civilians, such as Harvey Wilcox the lawyer, some procurement people who were mostly civilians. I think I had the finest team that certainly I've ever seen, and I believe it was as good a team as NavAir and the old Bureau of Aeronautics ever had. I think we did some good things for naval aviation in the reliability and maintainability area and in various other projects we had going on at the time such as the cruise missile, the Harpoon missile, Sidewinder, Sparrow, the CH-53 helicopter, and two dozen other projects that we worked on during this period of time.*

Q: How does one individual maintain a span of control to keep abreast of all those developments?

Admiral Lee: It's not easy. However, after you work at it for about 12 hours a day for six months or so, you get to know the projects fairly well. You know where the problem

---
*The AGM-84/RGM-84/UGM-84 Harpoon is an antiship missile that can be launched by aircraft, surface ships, and submarines. The CH-53 Sea Stallion is a heavy assault helicopter developed specifically for the Marine Corps.

areas are. Plus you've got the world's experts on those particular projects right there. About 90% of the time the program managers know what the problems are; they know what ought to be done in terms of a solution; and the big chore for us was selling these solutions, because solutions always cost money. Sometimes there's just a schedule delay.

I'd say 90% of the time the program managers knew exactly what was going on; they had good solutions. But if you depart from the charted path in any one of those programs, you have to go through two dozen wickets to get it changed. Therein lies the problem. The Congress, the OSD crowd, and everybody are always watching your tests: missile test, if you have a failure; airplane test, you don't meet a milestone; production goals; R&D test.

Now many of these things are not important. As a matter of fact, most of them as individual events are not important. But they're of great importance in Washington, because there are so many people there who have nothing else to do but watch what the systems commands are doing in their various projects. But the project managers we had were very able. As I said twice before, I can't remember a project getting into trouble where the project manager didn't know it beforehand and didn't warn us and tell us beforehand. Also, nine times out of ten he would have the proper solution. But putting that solution into effect was the problem.

Q: Are there any general comparisons you would draw between aircraft programs and missile programs?

Admiral Lee: Yes, as a matter of fact. I think the most difficult programs to bring to a successful conclusion are missile programs. I was very concerned about our missile programs, and I did a study and I had a couple of fellows help me. I did a study of missile programs. The problem in missile programs is that it's fairly easy to build a missile in a laboratory with engineers which will do what you plan to have it do. But taking a missile into production and having the production missiles perform properly is a very difficult thing. Every missile program that we've run has run into that problem. The R & D missiles usually run well. Production missiles have bugs. It takes two or three years to get the bugs out.

Now one of the interesting things about the missile business is that the Air Force has spent billions in missiles. I don't believe they've had a successful one to this date, except possibly the AMRAAM, which they're now just bringing into production.* But the Air Force has used Navy missiles for the last 20, last 30 years--the Sidewinder, the Sparrow, the anti-radiation missiles, and there are several others which I've forgotten the names of right now. That is because the Naval Air Systems Command has been very successful in bringing missiles to production, good missiles. For that reason the Naval Air Systems Command was given the job of producing the surface-to-surface missile, which normally would have gone to the Ordnance Systems Command, the Ships Systems Command, the Harpoon. We put together a very fine missile for the Navy and for the world. It probably is sold to 20 different countries now.

The most difficult problem with missiles is the production transition. And _the_ most difficult phase is that transition from the laboratory to a production line for a missile.

Q: Are there any specifics you remember on Harpoon that you'd want to put on the record?

Admiral Lee: Harpoon had a marvelous record in R&D. Rear Admiral Ekas was the program manager. Had its own target,

---

*The AIM-120 AMRAAM is the advanced medium-range air-to-air missile intended as a replacement for the Sparrow.

on cost, had great hit reliability, hit percentage. But even Harpoon, with all of that, went through growing pains, when we tried to go from hand-built missiles to production. The Harpoon program ran into some troubles in the area I've just described. It was slowed down and delayed for about six months to a year and took additional money. Even Harpoon, built by McDonnell Douglas, which was probably the quality industry builder in this country, had difficulties. But we never really had any big problems, any fundamental problems with Harpoon. The program was delayed six months to a year in that transition period and the cost went up, which I considered kind of standard. But we got our lumps because of it.

Q: Did you get involved in Tomahawk at all?

Admiral Lee: Oh, yes. Tomahawk was a Naval Air Systems Command project too.* The project manager was Walter Locke, a very independent young man who worked on the Harpoon initially.** He was a very fine program manager. And, as a matter of fact, I was the chairman of the source selection council for that particular missile, Tomahawk.

---

*The Tomahawk is a long-range cruise missile designed for use against both ships and land targets. The land-attack version can carry either a conventional or nuclear warhead.
**Captain Walter M. Locke, USN.

Q: Any specifics you remember from that competition?

Admiral Lee: None. General Dynamics won it. We had some very good competitors, and it was almost a model project. Walter Locke ran a great project. But even Tomahawk had some problems in the transition stage. I thought Tomahawk was one of the most promising missiles that we ever put together. It's just amazing the accuracy you can get out of that kind of navigational and recording system.

Q: It's amazing how complex the weapon has to be as a result in order to do that.

Admiral Lee: Yes.

Q: And that drives up the cost enormously.

Admiral Lee: What people forget is that missile is a misnomer. Harpoon and Tomahawk and all of these other missiles you're talking about are really small airplanes. They have small jet engines; they have control surfaces; they have automatic pilots; they have radars which find targets and home in on them. They're very sophisticated, very complex machines.

Q: You mentioned that you were going to talk some more

about Admiral Snead. Is there more to say about him?

Admiral Lee: As I said earlier, Admiral McClellan gave me this package to read as his last act as Commander Naval Air Systems Command. I read it, and the following is what I found. Admiral Snead was the F-14 program manager and he had a civilian chief assistant by the name of William Dittmar. Dittmar was married and had three or four children, but he met a young lady that he wanted to bring into the F-14 project office as a secretary, which he eventually did. This young lady was Dittmar's mistress. He had a key to her apartment, and they had a very nice thing going for some months, maybe years.

But by and by Snead became attracted to this young secretary. After a period of months, Dittmar was out, and Snead had a key to the young lady's apartment. This made Dittmar very unhappy, and he and Snead had a falling-out. Snead then had Dittmar moved through the administrative machinery of NavAir to another office. I hadn't been in NavAir more than two weeks when Dittmar came up to see me. He had some letters that Snead had written this young lady. Dittmar had kept his keys to the apartment, and he'd gone in and gotten letters that Snead had written her, very incriminating letters, very descriptive. Not too long after that, Dittmar was observed chasing Snead through the parking lot with an automobile. In other words, it was just a mess, something that we couldn't put up with.

So I went to see Admiral Kidd and explained what the problem was, namely that I thought it was in Snead's best interest, in the Navy's best interest, and certainly in Naval Air Systems Command's best interest to move Snead. I had a meeting with Dave Bagley and a captain by the name of Horace Robertson who was representing the CNO, and I gave them the inspector general's package which McClellan had given me, plus these letters. We discussed the matter. Shortly after that, Snead was moved from Naval Air Systems Command to the Bureau of Naval Personnel awaiting further assignment.

I then decided that I would have our administrative people in NavAir observe Dittmar very closely, and if he didn't toe the line properly, we would bring charges against him, remove him in some fashion. There was another secretary in the F-14 office who was a problem, so I decided that we would move the two secretaries from the F-14 office. When they found out that they were being moved, the two decided that they would move themselves. So they left Naval Air Systems Command and got jobs elsewhere. Snead was at BuPers, and Dittmar never gave us cause for complaint the rest of my two and a half years at NavAir with him. He was a very good employee, and we had no case against him for anything. Of course, Snead was very unhappy about being moved out. But I think it should be a matter of record what went on.

Q: Well, it turned out also there was some difficulty finding a further assignment for him.

Admiral Lee: I'm not really familiar with those details, but, except that I know Ray Peet very well, and I believe Admiral Zumwalt tried to send Snead to Iran to be the Navy representative in Iran.* Ray Peet at that time was in charge of military sales for the Department of Defense. He vetoed Snead, which I think was a mistake. I think it would have been a good thing to send Snead to Iran. He would have done very well. But Ray Peet's ideas were a little different. He didn't want an aviator over there in the job, which I don't think was important. Ray Peet and Zumwalt were not at that time seeing eye to eye on a number of matters. So Snead lost out once again.

Q: Admiral Peet talked about that in his oral history. He said he had enough backing from Secretary Schlesinger that he was able to block the proposed move.

You talked about the difference of opinion between Admiral Houser when he was OP-05 and you were NavAir on the F/A-18. How does that team normally work, or could it be

---

*Vice Admiral Raymond E. Peet, USN, Deputy Assistant Secretary of Defense (Security Affairs) and Director, Defense Security Assistance Agency.

called a team, between OP-05 and the Naval Air Systems Command?

Admiral Lee: It should be a team. Naval Air Systems Command has a full-time job handling the procurement and all the other 1,001 tasks that they have. OP-05's job is to do the planning for naval aviation and to represent naval aviation in the Pentagon. When Connolly was there he not only ran OP-05, but from my observation, he also tried to run Naval Air Systems Command through Tom Walker. I let it be known when I first went to Naval Air Systems Command that I was having none of that, that I was going to run Naval Air Systems Command and let Houser run OP-05. But it should be as a team.

I thought when Petersen came we made a great team. But in the F-14, F-18 bit, Naval Air Systems Command, while I was there, and OP-05 had very different points of view. I think for perhaps the only time in history Naval Air Systems Command won, but not because of where we were or who we were. It was because the Congress and OSD had the final vote.

Q: So one thing then that you lost really by retiring when you did was the opportunity to really have a good teamwork relationship with OP-05.

Admiral Lee: Yes.

Q: What do you remember about working with Admiral Petersen during the brief period that you did?

Admiral Lee: Petersen was a great believer in the F-18. And Petersen's a very able man. I'm one of his greatest admirers. We had a number of meetings, discussions. Petersen and I would agree on how we ought to tackle some particular problem, and we would go do it. Very informal. But he agreed with me that the most important problem with naval aviation was maintainability and reliability. He felt the same way. He had about the same background as we had; whereas Houser thought we were wasting a lot of money, time and effort. So I think Petersen and I could have done some great things for naval aviation. But, as I said earlier, I was tired and I just thought that I'd done my bit, and I was ready to go.

Q: It's interesting that Admiral Houser had the perception that you were wasting money since the whole point was to spend money to save an even greater amount.

Admiral Lee: Yes.

Q: Among the other initiatives when you were trying to

improve reliability and maintainability, did you solicit the so-called beneficial suggestions from the field on how things could be improved?

Admiral Lee: Not formally. That had been done time and time again. The problem with that is that every command comes up with a different list. Say, for instance, you're looking at the F-14, and you ask AirLant to come up with a list of things we ought to work on. You ask AirPac to come up with a list; and you ask the Sixth Fleet and the Seventh Fleet. They all come up with different lists. And that had been one of the problems. "This command is having no problem with that." "This command is having nothing but a problem with topic eight." That's why we found out that the 3M system had a statistical record, no argument with it. You knew exactly how many fuel controls were changed last year in F-14s, or how many engines, or how many sections in the radar--a complete maintenance history.

The beauty of it was it wasn't on just one airplane; it was on our whole fleet, which is the picture you want. Because one squadron might have troubles because of the way they were operating the airplane or the way they were doing their maintenance. They might have troubles with fuel controls, for instance. And it might not be the fuel control; they might have changed the batch. We ran into that. So then you go off on a wild goose chase trying to fix fuel controls when, really, it was their maintenance causing it or their operating procedures. But the 3M system washed all of this out, an absolutely great system. Never been used until Frank Readdy put the RISE system in and extracted from the 3M system all these data, marvelous.

Q: I'm curious which you would nominate as your greatest legacy from that job, the F/A-18, or improved reliability and maintainability.

Admiral Lee: I'd say they're equal. The F/A-18, you see, is the first airplane we designed in the Navy from the very beginning where priority one was maintainability and reliability. We put a lot of money into it. It really paid off. Maintenance man-hours per flight hour and overall reliability of the F-18 now are just unbelievable compared to other airplanes, the reason being that we did it all up front. We made the spark plugs easy to change; we made the changing oil and the filter very easy; and we made troubleshooting very easy. It was designed that way.

Q: Did you sacrifice anything in performance to get those benefits?

Admiral Lee: We might have sacrificed a little. It's very possible, but that was not one of our concerns. Probably did sacrifice a little bit here and there. Maybe a little in weight, maybe a little in aerodynamics. But that was not a concern. Priority one was reliability and maintainability. We believed if we did that right, we could still get the performance we want.

Q: You shouldn't go too far in a tradeoff like that.

Admiral Lee: No. But, for instance, take the engine. I've described changing an engine in an F-14, an A-7, and an A-4. Takes a three-man crew three days roughly. They've got to tune it up--trim it, as it's called--afterwards. The reason being that it has so many connections to it and in some airplanes, like the A-4, you've got to take the airplane apart to get the engines out, take the tail apart and the fuselage. In the Harrier you have to take the wing off to get an engine out.*

In the F-18, we decided that the fuel control, the generator, the starter, the hydraulic pump, all these accessories which are normally bolted to an engine, would be put on a pad right by the engine, not be a part of the engine. So that the engine is only fastened in about four places like an automobile engine, four mounting brackets. You then only need disconnect maybe a dozen pipes and

---

*The AV-8 Harrier is a vertical and short takeoff airplane developed by the British and later manufactured in the United States by the McDonnell Douglas Corporation.

tubes. All the accessories remain right in the airplane on a pad--never been done before. You can change that engine, have a new one in and off again in less than two hours. It might have cost us a few pounds in weight by putting that pad there, the accessory pad, accessory drive pad. But I doubt it--I think the few pounds in weight that we have there we probably saved in the engine because you'd need those strong mounting points on the engine.

Q: It's interesting that that major change in a single aircraft probably had its origin when you were getting your hands greasy back 30 years earlier.

Admiral Lee: Probably was, probably did.

Q: There are a lot of avionics in today's modern aircraft. What was your relationship with Electronic Systems Command?

Admiral Lee: The Electronic Systems Command didn't do our avionics in aviation. Naval Air Systems Command did its own electronics. The Electronic Systems Command did other types, such as communications systems for the Polaris submarines. The electronics for ships and for aircraft are done by Naval Sea Systems Command and Naval Air Systems Command. But there are an awful lot of electronics in the Navy as a whole which are not done by Naval Sea Systems

Command and Naval Air Systems Command. Those things are done by Electronic Systems Command--communications stations, satellites, certain black projects, specific types of radar. So that we did our own electronics in Naval Air Systems Command--our own computers, our inertial nav systems, our own radars. We have sections in Naval Air Systems Command that specialize in this.

Q: You also do the ECM equipment?

Admiral Lee: Some ECM equipment. Now that's a specialized area which in some cases is done by Electronic Systems Command. There's a project manager who handles ECM equipment. At one time that project manager was in Naval Air Systems Command. He handled ECM equipment for everybody. When the Electronic Systems Command was set up, the ECM guy went there. But we do our own Tacan sets, our own radio sets, all of that in Naval Air Systems Command-- the R&D, the contracting, and repairing.

Q: There were a couple of new airplanes coming along the time you were there, the S-3 and the E-2C.* Did you get involved with their early years in the fleet?

---

*The Grumman E-2C Hawkeye is a look-down radar surveillance aircraft that gives the advantage of a much higher vantage point and thus greater range than shipboard radars.

Admiral Lee: Oh, yes. I hadn't mentioned any planes to speak of, other than the F-14 and F-18, but while I was there the S-3 came along, built by Lockheed. George Jessen was the program manager. I thought it was a great success and a great airplane. But the S-3 was about ready for production and about ready to go through the test process in 1973 when I took over NavAir. The E-2C, about the same story; P-3C about the same story.

Q: What do you as the systems commander do at that stage in an aircraft's development?

Admiral Lee: The program manager in NavAir is responsible for it from birth to death. He's responsible for following this airplane and making sure that it's properly funded, that the spare parts are where they ought to be, that the proper maintenance procedures are being carried out. He follows it going through Patuxent; he funds it; he follows its fleet introduction; he makes sure that the stations are properly equipped and funded. NavAir's responsible for these airplanes from cradle to grave in every aspect. And the person who's responsible is the program manager. That's why he's such a key guy.

Q: And since those programs were working well, you didn't have to get involved so much.

Admiral Lee: Yes. P-3C and the S-3 and the great majority of the programs that were completed or in various phases of development went to NavAir. I got the detailed briefing usually once a month on each program. If there were no problems and we had a good project manager, I didn't spend much time on it. There were enough projects in trouble to take up my time.

Q: One of the ironies of the S-3 was it was designed to fit in the old Essex-class CVSs, and by the time it came along those were gone.

Admiral Lee: Damn good plane.

Q: Could you talk, please, about the idea of foreign military sales in general as a concept. Do you think that's a good thing for the United States and the Navy to be involved in?

Admiral Lee: We took part in dozens of foreign sales of military equipment while I was at Naval Air Systems Command. And, certainly, all those foreign military sales to the Shah of Iran were a mistake. Now I think you could look at the foreign military sales that we made to Israel and say they were good. You could look at the ones to Iran and say they're bad. But we didn't make value judgments or moral judgments on these programs in NavAir. I think some were very good and some were very bad. What we tried to do is run them just as we ran our own programs, contracted for them in exactly the same way. We managed them the very same way, and we had foreign military sales with the Japanese; the Argentines; several NATO countries such as Harpoon, for instance; missiles--everybody was buying Sparrow and Sidewinder, especially Sidewinder; Israel; Saudi Arabia; Iran--really dozens of countries bought our equipment of one type or another.

Sometimes they bought used equipment, such as Singapore bought used A-4s. We sold the F-18 to Australia, and to Spain, and to Canada. I don't think you can categorically say that foreign military sales are good or bad. Certainly the sale of the F-18 to Canada, we think, is good, and to Spain and to Australia. I think the sales to Iran were certainly questionable, because 70% of the people in Iran in the days when we were working with Iran were illiterate. I've heard numbers higher than that, but the documents I was looking at said 70%. They just don't have a large educated middle class. You've got to have educated youngsters to maintain F-4s and F-14s and all the fancy equipment we sent to Iran. They didn't have this. Hence, I think it's a mistake to sell sophisticated equipment to a country that can't handle it. Yes, I think that's wrong. But other than that, our job was not to make judgments, and we didn't.

Q: You mentioned the problem with the agent's payments in Iran. Was there any involvement by NavAir in the Lockheed and Japanese payoff connection?

Admiral Lee: None. NavAir was not involved in any of these payoff connections. We got involved in the Grumman-Iran thing because the sale to Iran was an FMS sale, and this money that Grumman was paying the agent was coming to us, then to Grumman, and then to the agent.* But Grumman was taking this money right out of their profits, and they didn't make any more profits on Iran's F-14 than they were making on our F-14. They got no extra money from us for F-14s.

Q: You get into these cross-cultural problems where one culture expects the bribe and the other one says it's prohibited, and yet you try to do business between the two.

Admiral Lee: We had an Iranian lieutenant colonel come to Naval Air Systems Command to work in the F-14 office. Now in our FMS work for Iran and other countries, we contracted for the F-14s and for the parts and for the support

---

*FMS--foreign military sales.

equipment.

Our contract called for all of this equipment to be delivered to a freight forwarder. Iran used a freight forwarder in New Jersey. This lieutenant colonel came to report to NavAir to work in the F-14 office, to be a liaison, and one day the F-14 program manager came to see me--at that time Rear Admiral Alvis--and he said there was something he thought I ought to know.* He said that this lieutenant colonel had been in touch with the freight forwarders and that he had persuaded the freight forwarders to furnish his apartment there in Alexandria--rugs, furniture, refrigerator--which they had promptly done. I said to our project manager, "Well, I certainly thank you for telling me, but I don't see that there's a thing we can do about that. It seems to me that's between the freight forwarder and Iran." But that sort of thing went on in that culture.

Q: You mentioned the approach you'd had when you were a rear admiral on trying to overturn the results of a test and award a contract that shouldn't be. Did you get any kind of approaches like that when you were a systems commander?

---
*Rear Admiral John H. Alvis, USN. As a commander, Alvis had been executive officer of the Enterprise when Lee was commanding officer.

Admiral Lee: Never did, not once. I never was approached by anybody from the Pentagon, from the Office of the Secretary of Defense, or from Congress on pressure to alter or modify a competition in order to favor one bidder over another. Not once.

The only incident that I ever had of that nature I've previously described.

Q: Was the Lakehurst-Patuxent incident the only case where political considerations got involved?

Admiral Lee: No, I think political considerations are involved in almost all procurements in Washington. We had political considerations for the NARFs, whether or not we would close a NARF. We had an excess of one overhaul facility too many, we thought, and we did close the Quonset Point one. But political considerations enter into everything you do--buying F-14s, closing Lakehurst, the work you put at a NARF, the money that you request for facilities at a given NARF. Congressmen exercise great power in those appropriations committees. If they don't want you to have a facility at a given NARF, you're not going to get it.

But by the same token, if Congressman X gets a brand-new facility for his NARF in Pensacola, Congressman Y out in San Diego wants the same for his. This is the sort of thing that goes on. As I said, almost every aspect of our procurement and operations and facilities and bases are subject to politics of one type or another. I don't know that it's bad; I think it's the system we have. There are checks and balances there, because Congressman A is watching Congressman B. If Congressman B gets too much or steps out of line too far, he'll be brought back.

Q: Or else he'll want even more for himself.

Admiral Lee: Yes. Like the story that they tell about Mendel Rivers that if he put one more facility down at Charleston, his district is going to sink into the sea.

Q: It is amazing what all he got in down there.

You mentioned briefly Admiral Holloway and his interest in V/STOL. How much did V/STOL play a part in your time down there?

Admiral Lee: Very little. There was an interesting little item there. When I went to Naval Air Systems Command, when I relieved McClellan, this was in the Zumwalt years when what we wanted were new initiatives. And *the* new initiative in Naval Air Systems Command was the thrust-augmented wing airplane built by Rockwell International. The first year I was there I was called once a month, because the CNO wanted the latest data on the thrust-augmented wing. Now this thrust-augmented wing airplane was supposed to be magic. You direct some airflow over the wings and you get augmented lift, so it would be a very short takeoff and landing airplane. On a carrier it would be magic.

After I'd been at NavAir about six months, I decided I would really take a look at this thrust-augmented wing airplane, and I spent two, three days looking at it, going over the numbers and talking to our engineers. It turned out that it wasn't an airplane that NavAir sponsored. It was an airplane that Tom Davies, one of Zumwalt's right-hand men, sponsored.* We came to the conclusion in NavAir that even if the lift augmentation that they were advertising for this thrust-augmented airplane worked 100%, we still would have an unsatisfactory airplane. It wouldn't be useful for anything.

So the next time I was asked by the Pentagon, I said that I think the airplane only has a 10% chance of ever flying. There was a 90% chance that it's not going to amount to anything. And that wasn't the right answer. But in fact the thrust-augmented wing, after we spent maybe $300 million on it, was dropped. It was not a practical machine. I passed it on to Admiral Petersen, and I explained it all to him, and he was able to get it dropped

---
*Rear Admiral Thomas D. Davies, USN, Deputy Chief of Naval Material for Development.

while he was commander. Another example of non-technical people starting projects. Zumwalt was the direct cause of that--$300 million wasted, in my view.

Q: Who brought the Harrier program? That has taken on a much longer life.

Admiral Lee: I think the British are a very ingenious people. I put together a presentation one time for V/STOL. I started looking back through the records, and from World War II to the present--and this was done about 12 years ago--in this country and in the Free World we had built 50 or 60 V/STOL aircraft.

The only successful machine to come out of those 50 or 60 prototypes was the Harrier. The British built a marvelous airplane; it's very simple. Its simplicity is absolutely astounding. And it works. Although McDonnell Douglas made some improvements on it, it's not a great performer; it's subsonic; it won't carry a big load; and it's accident-prone in marginal weather, especially crosswinds. But other than that it's a fine little airplane. It has no weapon system in it. I think it's more of a toy than anything else. I think the Marine Corps made a great mistake in talking the U.S. Government into putting so much money into Harrier. I think Harrier was a good starting point. We should have put that money into building an improved Harrier, because they've got the right design. And the British are very innovative. I think the Harrier is a marvelous design. The only one out of 50 or 60 and several hundred million dollars, maybe several billion, that succeeded in about 35 or 40 years.

Q: There were a lot of carrier studies going on back in the Seventies looking at the sea control ship, and the mid-size CVV, and then eventually coming on to CVNs. Did you get involved in any of those?

Admiral Lee: No, I didn't. I observed them, but I tried to avoid those studies, because the sea control ship didn't make any sense to me. That was another Zumwalt idea. As soon as Zumwalt left, we dropped it. We had a sea control ship, these amphibious ships, LPHs and LPDs.* They're sea control ships. But Zumwalt had a different idea. He wanted V/STOLs, and helicopters, ASW, and he would call them sea control ships. But we just didn't have the airplanes to do what Admiral Zumwalt visualized. Admiral Holloway had a great plan for V/STOL, but as we discussed, after he became CNO, V/STOL faded away.

---

*LPHs and LPDs are amphibious warfare ships suitable for operating assault helicopters. The LPH is primarily for helicopter operations, while the LPD has a balance between helicopter and waterborne landing craft.

But the problem with V/STOL is that we looked at it at NavAir and the thrust-to-weight ratio on our engines was about seven or eight to one. You can get seven or eight pounds of thrust for one pound of weight. That's a great improvement over what we had several years ago. It used to be, maybe, one for one. But it appeared to us that you really couldn't build a good V/STOL airplane until you get the thrust-to-weight ratio up to about 15 to one, and then you might be able to. What you really have then is a very lightweight engine putting out a lot of power, which is what you need for a V/STOL. But I don't think V/STOL is going to be around as Zumwalt visualized them for a few years yet, because it's going to take a long time to work out the engineering. But the Harrier is the best by far. There's no competition. It's a great little airplane. I went flying in the Harrier.

Q: What do you remember of that experience?

Admiral Lee: I went to England for several reasons. One of the things I wanted to do was fly a two-seated Harrier over there. I went flying with one of the test pilots at the Harrier factory. We went out for about an hour and came back and made a vertical landing. What we did was a short takeoff, because we had a load of fuel, and then came back--we'd burned down all our fuel, and we made a vertical landing. But it was a two-seater with two sets of controls, so I flew it. It flew like a conventional airplane. The only thing different was the landing. And I, of course, in my one flight didn't make a vertical landing.

Q: A name I've heard in a number of contexts connected with NavAir is George Spangenberg. Did you have any dealing with him?

Admiral Lee: Oh, yes. George Spangenberg headed the evaluation group in NavAir for 20 years. The evaluation group is a very important, very key group. I'm trying to think of the man who replaced George Spangenberg who handled the evaluation of all the other competitions we had while I was there. George Spangenberg had retired when I got there.

Q: I see.

Admiral Lee: We used Spangenberg as a consultant. His replacement wasn't as articulate as George, but I thought he was equally good. He handled the F-18. He was a very fine man, GS-17 or something like that. Yes, George was a consultant with us, and George didn't like the F-18, but he liked the F-14. He was head of the evaluation section when the F-14 went through.

Q: He was in the midst of that TFX squabble also.

Admiral Lee: Yes.

Q: I remember the Proceedings carried a number of negative letters about the F-18 as it was coming along. For instance, there was a guy named Art Hanley that was very active in the debate, an air traffic controller.* Did you flinch whenever you read that stuff in the magazine?

Admiral Lee: No, but, Grumman fought the F-18 the entire time I was at NavAir, because they could see it taking business away from Grumman. They paid millions, I bet, in lobbyists to fight the F-18. The A-7 people were fighting the F-18. I've never seen anything like it. Industry was arrayed against it. They had their congressmen alerted. And then there were a whole bunch of people--the F-14 pilots--in OP-05 who didn't like the F-18. The F-18 was a very controversial airplane for a while. And, yes, we flinched. But I felt we had a world beater--if you'll pardon the expression, a world-class airplane except for fuel. And it's proved itself. The F-404 engine is one of

---

*See Arthur Hanley, "The F-18 Hornet: Did the Navy Get Stung?" U.S. Naval Institute Proceedings, April 1981, pages 116-118.

the best engines ever built, although they just had some problems with turbine blades, compressor blades, but they'll fix that.* That's not a big problem. First problem they had with that engine since '76, ten years. At 800 hours one of the compressor blades goes.

But the radar is one of the best ever. Everything about it is good. And it's going to be around a long time.

Q: Well, that's a legacy that you've left to the Navy of the 21st century.

Admiral Lee: It'll be there. A marvelous airplane.

Q: Well, is there any summing up you'd like to do, Admiral, on your entire career? You've certainly covered a wide span of issues during our talks together.

Admiral Lee: From working as a mechanic on an SBC to helping put together the F-18. No, I had a great 36 years in the Navy, and I'd do it all again.

Q: I'm certainly grateful for the time we've spent to record it. This is another legacy that you've provided. The transcript will be available from now on for people to read and to learn from. I've really enjoyed the pleasure

---

*The engine is the General Electric F404-GE-400 turbofan.

of getting to know you and coming to visit you on your farm.

You said at one point that you didn't make vice admiral by being a nice guy, but I think you're a nice guy, anyway. I would agree with George Wilson's assessment of you as a gentleman captain, now as a gentleman admiral. So thank you very much.

Admiral Lee: Well, I thank you, and I look forward to editing these papers.

Lee #8 - 620

Interview Number 8 with Vice Admiral Kent L. Lee,
U.S. Navy (Retired)

Place: Logon Farm, Admiral Lee's home near Gordonsville, Virginia

Date: Monday, 21 November 1988

Interviewer: Paul Stillwell

Q: Admiral Lee, this is a catchup session to fill in some of the blanks that I've perceived and you've perceived as a result of going through your transcript.

Admiral Lee: I do have a few things, but it might be better if we go with your list first, Paul.

Q: All right. I would like you, please, then to go back to about 1940 when you were an enlisted aviation mechanic. You said in retrospect that that was your most enjoyable tour of duty in the Navy, and I wonder what factors made it that way.

Admiral Lee: I went to the Naval Air Station Miami, which was an advanced training base for aviation cadets in, I believe, February of 1941. I went there as a seaman second from aviation machinist's mate school, and I stayed there until about the first of October 1942. When I left, I was an aviation machinist's mate second class. I left to become an aviation cadet and went to St. Mary's College preflight school.

It was a happy time, because there was enough work to go around. I worked in the maintenance division, and we maintained all these airplanes that the aviation cadets flew. I was learning every day. Besides that, as I've said earlier, we had a marvelous group of petty officers at Miami, many of whom later became limited duty officers--ensigns, lieutenants, lieutenant commanders--during World War II. I worked initially as a rigging specialist, which meant that I worked on the airframes of the airplanes.

About halfway through the tour I shifted over to engines at my request and worked on all those radial engines that we had prior to World War II, in airplanes such as the SBC, (SBC-3s and -4s), the F4B, the TBD, the Brewster F2A, the BT, the F3F, the F2F. It was a happy time, because I enjoyed what I was doing. We had a great group of people. Lieutenant Butts, who later made rear admiral, was my division officer for most of that time. We had a group of chief petty officers who were first-rate men, and a number of them were very fine mechanics.

When I went there, I was just 17 years old. When I left, I had just turned 19. In addition to that, Miami was a very attractive place. We were made to feel welcome around the area. We went to the beaches, went swimming. We had parties--beer parties, squadron parties. So it all was a very happy time. And, of course, these were very formative years for me. As I say, I was just 17, straight from the country, so this sophisticated world of Miami was something new and marvelous to me. I really don't have any unhappy memories of Miami.

Q: I've reread your transcript as you described your experiences as a boy who got great enjoyment out of making things and fixing things, and there was the allure of aviation. This tour at Miami combined both of those.

Admiral Lee: It really did. I fell in love with aviation as a boy after having a ride in a Ford Trimotor, I was able not only to work on those airplanes at Miami every day, six days a week, as soon as the war started; I was able to fly in them. I went flying in the SBC, the BT, and a couple of twin-engine planes over at the operations building. I got flight orders, as they say down there--actually, they were called flight skins, which meant I got flight pay every month. I had to fly four hours a month with these cadets. So I was both working on the airplanes and getting a chance to fly a little bit. So, yes, it was heaven.

Q: As a boy you had paid a hard-earned 60 cents to go up in the airplane. Now people were paying you to do that.

Admiral Lee: Yes, that was a double bonus.

Q: Are there any specific incidents or experiences from that tour of duty that you especially remember?

Admiral Lee: One day I was working on an airplane--as a check crew chief--and we finished checking an SBC and sent it out to go on a flight. We had a jackpad, which we inserted into the axle of an airplane to jack up the tires, to check the brakes and change a tire, if need be. We pushed this airplane out, turned it up, and signed it off as ready to go. I left the jackpad in the axle. The pilot took off, couldn't get the landing gear up, came back. Harry Dabb, who was the maintenance chief, met the airplane when it came in, spotted the jackpad, and brought it back to me. That's all he ever did about it, just handed me the jackpad. So yes, I remember that very well.

Q: Was it difficult to have to work on so many different types of airplanes, the ones you've enumerated?

Admiral Lee: Not really. There was a sameness about them. The landing gears were the same; the control surfaces were the same; and the engines were the same. And we had good publications and good mechanics to teach us. It's not very different from working on a Ford and a Chevrolet. The principles are all the same. Carburetors are alike, whether they're on Fords or Chevrolets. By working on these airplanes day in and day out, we got to know them pretty well.

Q: Did the pilots you flew with encourage you or inspire you to become a pilot yourself?

Admiral Lee: Yes. We never had any communication with pilots to speak of, because I was in the maintenance division, and the airplanes were fueled and handled out on the flight line in the operations division, where Spence Matthews worked. So I never really had conversations with these aviation cadets. But, yes, they were our heroes. All of us with any red blood wanted to be pilots too.

Q: What was the thing specifically that got you into being a pilot?

Admiral Lee: I wanted to be a pilot from the day I joined the Navy, but there was just no way to get into it at that particular time. There was one program, which was the naval aviation pilot program, for enlisted men. I intended to apply for that as soon as I became eligible, but you had to be at least second class petty officer and have a certain length of time in the Navy. I've forgotten the requirements, but, say, four years. At the time the aviation cadet program opened up for high school graduates, I still wasn't eligible for the naval aviation pilot program, the enlisted program. But the aviation cadet program in 1942 was changed from two years of college requirement to high school graduates requirement. That is how I became an aviation cadet. I applied because I was a high school graduate. I thought I was physically qualified to be a pilot, and I wanted to give it a try.

Q: You talked before about using the baseball stitch to repair fabric wings. What's a baseball stitch?

Admiral Lee: Many of those airplanes in those days had fabric-covered fuselages, and just about all the control surfaces were fabric. If a rock or a stone or some other object pierced the surface of this fabric, it had to be repaired, and we used the same stitch that is used on baseballs. What it does is allow you to put a firm stitch in and pull two pieces of cloth together. We would make a neat stitch, a strong stitch, and then after we'd done that to pull the torn pieces together, we would dope them, which forms a hard skin on the fabric, makes it impervious to wind and water.

Q: I've seen pictures of baseballs being assembled, and it uses two needles simultaneously in a sort of cross-stitch.

Was that it?

Admiral Lee: I imagine what you saw was a machine baseball stitch. I don't know. I never stitched a baseball, but we called it a baseball stitch. It's the same stitch. I've forgotten if we used two needles or one needle. Probably two.

Q: You talked about riding the escort carrier Midway from San Diego to Pearl Harbor after you were commissioned, and that was your first experience at sea. What was your reaction to that?

Admiral Lee: I was very interested in every aspect of it. Of course, I was on a little jeep carrier and it was loaded with planes being taken out to Pearl Harbor, and maybe farther out into the Western Pacific. They had 15 or 20 passengers, pilots, replacement pilots going west, or other officers with orders going west. I was very interested in the berthing arrangements; I was very interested in the wardroom; I was very interested in the sea and what shipboard life was like. I didn't get really seasick, but just a little bit woozy the first couple of days out of San Diego. I didn't fall in love with the sea in this one sea voyage, but I was happy enough aboard ship.

Q: What were your first impressions about Hawaii on getting there?

Admiral Lee: I thought Hawaii was a real lotus land. In 1944 Hawaii had developed hardly at all from prewar days. Down on Waikiki Beach there were only two big hotels--the Moana and Royal Hawaiian. They had banyan trees down there. There were these beautiful beaches. Hawaii had a very gentle climate, moderate climate, about the same climate all year; had fields of pineapples everywhere; had all Japanese and Hawaiian natives around. I thought it was a beautiful, picturesque country, and, as I said earlier, a real lotus land.

Q: What sort of opportunities for liberty for a newly commissioned pilot?

Admiral Lee: We had lots of opportunities for liberty. We went down to Waikiki and spent one or two weekends in a hotel down there. We only had to be available at this training squadron out at Barbers Point for the necessary ground school and flying in the SB2C. We had no assigned job, so there was plenty of time for liberty and sightseeing around the island of Oahu and in Honolulu.

Q: Did you get down to the notorious Hotel Street?

Admiral Lee: No, I never went to the notorious Hotel Street. I assume that's where all the girls were.

Q: I assume so from what I've heard.

Admiral Lee: No, I didn't get down there. It wasn't one of the things that we were looking for.

Q: My biggest surprise on going to Hawaii for the first time was to discover that pineapples grew in the ground. I'd always thought they grew in trees like coconuts.

Admiral Lee: Right on top of the ground.

Q: You mentioned the SB2Cs, and you said before that you had to make a specific effort to drop the nose and then flare. What do you mean by "flare"?

Admiral Lee: We're talking about landing an SB2C on an aircraft carrier. Some airplanes, like the F6F, when you cut the power, the nose will drop. You really then have to ease back on the stick to keep from hitting wheels first. Because in those days all airplanes were tail wheel types-- two big front main landing gear wheels and a tail wheel. In the SB2C, when you cut the power, the nose didn't drop.

You had to ease it over a little bit, namely, push the stick forward. As soon as you got the nose headed down, you had to pull back on the stick to flare it so that you wouldn't hit the two front wheels first and bounce. So the SB2C was a little bit tricky in carrier landing.

Q: Well, if you don't want to hit two wheels first, you try to get them all three down simultaneously?

Admiral Lee: The ideal carrier landing is to hit with three wheels all together. In the F6F, if you cut the power and do nothing with the stick, you will hit front wheels first because the nose will drop, so you cut the power and then you ease back on the stick to try to make a three-point landing. In the SB2C, if you cut the power and do nothing with the stick, you'll float up the deck--probably never touching down--and get a barrier. So on the SB2C you have to ease the nose down a little bit and then bring the stick back to make a three-point landing.

Q: When you made the switch from the SB2C to the F6F, did you have to consciously think about it for a while to make sure you did it the different way?

Admiral Lee: Yes, we did. We got two field carrier landing practice flights on Eniwetok. There we practiced making carrier landings with the F6F, so by the time we went back aboard ship, we didn't have any real problems. It was a much easier plane to land aboard ship than the SB2C. There were seven of us in this particular group who shifted from SB2Cs to F6F Hellcats, and none of us had any problems with carrier landings, because we all had anywhere from 50 to 100 landings by then.

Q: It would have been harder then going the other way, I take it.

Admiral Lee: Yes. I think going the other way would have been more difficult.

Q: You just briefly alluded to the business of having a rear seat man in the bomber. Could you talk more about that. What kind of a relationship did you have with that guy in the backseat?

Admiral Lee: Yes. Most pilots had a permanent rear seat gunner. Sometimes the relationship was very close, and at other times it wasn't. It depended on the two individuals. Many of them wanted to go to flight training and didn't qualify for one reason or another, and became rear seat gunners. They were an absolutely first-rate group of youngsters. They wanted to get out there and do their bit in the war. Unfortunately, in the SB2C, there really wasn't much of a role for them, because their aerial gunnery from the rear seat was not all that effective. Their opportunities for striking on land were not all that many either, because if any strafing was to be done, we usually did it with the forward guns which the pilot fired.

So that the Navy realized, after building the SB2C, that we really didn't need a rear gunner. With the next generation of dive-bomber, namely the AD Skyraider, we didn't have a rear seat man. Of course, for every pilot and airplane lost, we lost a rear seat gunner in the SB2C squadrons. But they were very much a part of the squadron. Relations were very good between pilots and gunners; as you can imagine, they formed a team. I think all of us have very fond memories of our gunners.

Q: What about in your own case? What kind of a relationship do you remember?

Admiral Lee: In my particular case, I joined VB-15 on June 20. I did not bring a gunner with me, so I don't think I ever had a permanently assigned gunner in VB-15. After about two months, I shifted over to VF-15, where we had no gunners.

Q: How much communication would there be between the two

of you during a flight?

Admiral Lee: There was constant communication. We had an intercom circuit, and the pilot and the gunner were constantly talking to each other. I was telling him what I was going to do, and he was scanning the skies to tell me if we were under attack. He also reported ack-ack.

Q: It must have been a type of relationship you enjoyed, because you opted specifically to go back into bombers after you'd been in the fighter squadron.

Admiral Lee: Yes, I enjoyed the relationship. It was a very good one.

Q: Later, after you'd been at Columbia, you went to the General Line School, I've since talked to one of the instructors there, now retired Rear Admiral Robert Erly.* What memories do you have of him for that period?

Admiral Lee: He was a commander at the General Line School when I went there in 1949 and '50.

I think Commander Erly taught gunnery and tactics, and he was a very good instructor. We got to know our

---

*Rear Admiral Robert B. Erly, USN (Ret.), has been interviewed as part of the Naval Institute's oral history program.

instructors at Line School quite well. Most of them were commanders, mostly surface line officers--1100s, a few aviators. And most of them were very good instructors. It was an excellent year. I don't remember specifically a great deal about Commander Erly, but I do remember he was a very good instructor. Very personable man.

Q: Then you encountered him later when you had the <u>Alamo</u>. Any memories from that period?

Admiral Lee: Yes. Captain Erly at that time was chief of staff to Commander Amphibious Force Pacific Fleet. All prospective commanding officers came through and met the admiral and the chief of staff and the operations officer. Captain Erly had about a one-and-a-half- to two-hour session with all prospective commanding officers. He covered all aspects of amphibious force operations, from ship handling to legal problems to relations with the squadron commander, to maintenance--a very good session, and, perhaps, one of the best introductory sessions I've ever had.

Q: Sounds as if it was useful.

Admiral Lee: He had a wealth of information, and he had it well marshalled, well outlined, and he went over all of these things with prospective commanding officers. He was the type man that you could have a discussion with and ask dumb questions and not feel intimidated. I thought he was a very fine chief of staff.

Q: It's interesting that he should have an influence on making a seagoing officer of you at two different points in your career.

Admiral Lee: Yes.

Q: You went to sea again after Newport on board the <u>Badoeng Strait</u>, and you mentioned that you were a staff watch officer. What duties were involved in those watches?

Admiral Lee: In the Korean War--as opposed to the Vietnam War--the flag ran the formation. The staff watch officer was on the bridge, and we kept a 24-hour watch on the bridge. The admiral was the officer in tactical command. We launched aircraft; we recovered aircraft; we positioned destroyers; we directed ships to refueling, to replenishing. We did all the things as a staff watch officer that I did as a captain later on, since I was the officer in the tactical command in the Vietnam era. So that it was a very useful training experience for me.

Q: Was your Newport training useful in being able to run a formation?

Admiral Lee: I thought the Newport training was invaluable, because we had gone through all the tactical publications in Newport. I learned to use the maneuvering board; I had learned the signal book; I'd learned navigation of the various types; and I'd learned about the line Navy. Because of my year at Newport, there were no surprises when I went to Badoeng Strait. I knew just about all that I thought a young officer needed to know to become a staff watch officer.

Q: You pulled out the jackpad incident from Miami. I wonder if now you have some specific incidents you remember from those watches on board the CVE?

Admiral Lee: I thought we ran a good show. I can remember coming down on the western side of Korea after the Inchon landings, and the night we made departure I had the midwatch, the midnight to 4:00 A.M. watch. If you look at the chart, there are some islands on the western side of Korea. I remember my big decision was on which side of those islands to go and how much clearance I should give them for the screen. And I can still vividly remember seeing those islands and seeing our formation on the radar as we came down from Inchon. But I don't remember any incidents where we had a problem such as a collision or an aircraft accident or any problems with the formation in those months.

Q: It sounds as if you learned quickly.

Admiral Lee: Yes, I think I had to learn quickly.

Q: I'd be interested in more details on your recollections on the Inchon event itself, what you were doing and what you remember hearing and seeing.

Admiral Lee: The landings took place at high tide--slack tide because the tidal range on the western coast in the Inchon area is so large that tides were very important. We launched airplanes from sunup to sundown for the two or three days we were in the Inchon area and were following very closely the landings, and getting, of course, daily reports through the communications center on how we were doing. We also had reports from our F4U pilots, the Marine squadron aboard Badoeng Strait and aboard Sicily, on their air support of the troops ashore. So that it was a very exciting time.

We were on pins and needles to see if the landings

would succeed. And, of course, they succeeded beyond all expectations--one of MacArthur's greatest triumphs. They went so well, in fact, that we found it hard to believe on <u>Badoeng Strait</u> that the landings went without a hitch, and that our troops went ashore almost unopposed, and took the North Koreans completely by surprise. I can remember how elated we were with the success of the landings.

Q: That was a risky proposition, so I can understand the apprehension.

Admiral Lee: It was very risky. I can remember Admiral Ruble shaking his head. But then the more he thought about it, he thought that if they succeeded, it would be a marvelous exercise. As I said a moment ago, the landings at Inchon succeeded beyond anyone's expectations, not only getting ashore almost unopposed, but getting a sizable force ashore--that force having plenty of air support. Because there was no air support from Korea itself, it all came from Japan or from our carriers. Then our troops were to trap that large North Korean army to the south of Inchon. It was a very happy time when those landings succeeded.

Q: Who had control of the F4Us once they were in the air?

Lee #8 - 638

Admiral Lee: We on <u>Badoeng Strait</u> and on Carrier Division 15 didn't have control of the airplanes ashore. We sent them to the controllers, who were stationed with the landing force. They designated the targets for our airplanes. But it worked very well. We didn't have any problems with air control. I think some of our pilots, rather than being used directly in support of the landing troops in, say, the front lines, were used to attack targets of opportunity in front of the landing troops-- anything that was moving: trucks, trains, troop groups.

Q: You talked also during that tour of duty about the helicopter trip that you and Admiral Ruble made to Nagasaki. This is then five years after the atomic bomb was dropped there. What do you remember from that aerial view?

Admiral Lee: Admiral Ruble had a very inquiring mind. He was a bright man and technically trained. I think he had a master's degree in aeronautical engineering. He was very interested in Nagasaki, in the atomic bomb. Since we had a helicopter on <u>Badoeng Strait</u>, almost our first trip into Sasebo, he and I took a helicopter to tour Nagasaki. He really took the helicopter and invited me to come along, since I was his aide and flag lieutenant, and we had a very good personal relationship. We probably spent 20 minutes flying all around the area. Nagasaki in 1950 had not been rebuilt. There was just complete devastation with some smokestacks, wrecks of building. It looked to me like there was complete devastation for 40 or 50 square miles. For several miles in every direction there was no life, no buildings, no rebuilding, and just wrecks of buildings. That just about explains it. I daresay the total distance across this devastation was probably six or eight miles.

Q: As a professional naval officer, you can have a technical view on the kind of weapon to create that destruction. As a human being, what sort of an emotional reaction do you have?

Admiral Lee: It was awesome to imagine one bomb causing that damage, that devastation, and killing all those thousands of people. It's unbelievable when you look at it. You just wonder what's next in the way of weapons. You hope that we don't have to use them again, or that they're not used again. It was an awesome spectacle, really, really heart-stopping.

Q: I imagine that mental picture came to your mind later when you were at Omaha and doing the targeting.

Admiral Lee: Yes.

The mental picture that came to mind in Omaha was the absolutely gross overkill of our weapons planning today. In Nagasaki, if I remember correctly, we only dropped a 20-kiloton weapon, and it didn't hit the center of the city, if I remember correctly also. Yet the devastation was complete and large, large areas. In today's targeting we would hardly consider using a 20-KT weapon. We're thinking in terms of megatons today, in hundreds of kilotons. So that I think our sense of damage expectancy today is out of all proportion to the size of the weapons, when you consider what damage was done by a 20-KT weapon on Nagasaki. Those were the thoughts I had in Omaha, that we had lost our perspective.

Q: Did you ever bring that into the discussions in Omaha?

Admiral Lee: Many times. But as I've described in other parts of the interview, I didn't have much success in Omaha, either my first tour or my second tour, in changing the thinking and changing the ways of the SAC types. Their ideas were too fixed. They were too set in their ways in Omaha.

Q: Had you been able to change them, in what direction would you have done so?

Admiral Lee: Probably the most important point is that I would have set up a sizable reserve force. In Omaha, both in my first tour and in my second tour, we had no reserves. Our reserves were only what was left over. We had overkill beyond imagination and no reserves. That to me was incomprehensible. So maybe I would have kept at least a third of our weapons in a reserve to prepare for contingencies, to prepare for third parties coming in. We had none of that. Number two, I didn't think that 10- and 20-megaton weapons were worthwhile. I thought it was overkill. I think with good accuracy, a weapon of no more than 200 or 300 kilotons is adequate. It seems to me that with more than that you reach the point of diminishing returns; you don't get adequate damage for the additional size of the weapon.

Also, this continual push by SAC, Strategic Air Command, and the Air Force for more weapons and more weapons, I would have turned that off. In my view, we can have a credible deterrent with far fewer than 12,000 weapons to target on Russia. Since we kept building our forces larger and larger, the Russians for political reasons kept building theirs larger and larger. Now it's politically very difficult to reduce the numbers to less than the 10,000 or 12,000 we currently have, because it would look as though we had less than the Russians.

But if we had started in 1960, say, and decided that

for every new weapon we bring in, we're going to retire one, and had kept the force for political reasons, and for reasons of cost--at, say, 6,000 or 8,000 weapons--no more than that, then certainly the Russians wouldn't have built beyond that. But we could have divided up our weapons among ICBMs, bombers, and the submarine force, and other weapons such as cruise missiles on ships. By doing so that we could have had, perhaps, half the size of a nuclear force as we have today, and have a deterrent equally as good in my view.

Q: The political point you make is an important one, because in that presidential campaign of 1960 the term "missile gap" was thrown around. And so it acquired this aura that the United States had to keep building more and more.

Admiral Lee: Of course, as McNamara said to President Kennedy after he'd been properly briefed, there was no missile gap. That was a fairy tale.

Q: Right.

Admiral Lee: But it's politically very important to appear powerful. The more weapons we have, the more powerful we appear. So the Russians feel that they must have as many weapons as we have. Perhaps if we had stopped at a lower level, say, 6,000 rather than 12,000 and had them divided up in some reasonable manner, why, then the Russians would have stopped at 6,000, too. But I think they felt that they had to build to the point where they had parity, as they call it. But I think the numbers we have today are just unbelievable.

Q: Just as an aside, what's your view on the Strategic Defense Initiative?

Admiral Lee: I think the Strategic Defense Initiative is an impossibility. I think we're wasting billions of dollars in it, and for these reasons: we have been building a missile defense system for a long time. The Army has been getting several hundred million dollars, a billion dollars a year a long time before SDI came in to build a missile defense system. We believed then--and we believe today--that we could build a missile defense system which would shoot down a fair number of incoming warheads, warheads fired by ICBMs from Russia, because we know where the ICBMs are located, and we know the trajectory the warheads will have to take to hit the United States. So we believe we can position our defense missiles favorably, and with our radars, pick up these warheads and shoot down a fair number of them coming in. The one problem there is that the Russians can put up more decoys than warheads. Then we'd have to have a huge defense system to shoot down the bulk of the warheads. But that, I believe, is technically possible. The technology is with us and we could do it. I'm not sure it would be worth it, but we could do it.

The rest of it, I think, is not technically possible. We're talking about cruise missiles which come in at very low levels, and can be launched from the Gulf of Mexico or the Southern California area. We're talking about low-trajectory ballistic missiles; we're talking about bombers. We're also talking about submarines launching, not only low-trajectory ballistic missiles, but other types of ballistic missiles from all around the coast. When you add all of this in, I think it's a physical impossibility and a technical impossibility to build an SDI system which will knock down the bulk of the incoming warheads if the Russians mount a determined campaign to build, and man, and launch such weapons. I felt this way all along, and I have read any number of articles by very good scientists who have looked into this, and that is essentially their view also. So I think SDI is a pipe dream. I think it's a waste of money.

Now there's another aspect to it, and the one aspect which I don't understand is why the Russians are so violently opposed to SDI. Is it for political reasons, or is it because they think we might succeed? Or is it because if we mount a big SDI effort, do they feel they have to mount one? I don't understand the Russian reaction.

The second point I wanted to make: I think we should put together a good R&D effort here so that we aren't left at the starting gate. I think we should do some research in SDI and in all forms of defense. We should know what the technical possibilities are and be prepared to exploit them if we come upon some system that we think will work. Today I don't think we have the technology to do it is what I'm saying. And even if we did have the technology, I think the cost would be astronomical. It would bankrupt us.

Q: And then we would force the Soviets to find things to counter that.

Admiral Lee: Yes. So, no, I'm not a big believer in SDI. I think President Reagan was sold a bill of goods. Is that enough?

Q: Yes. Jumping back from there to the jeep carriers--you went from CarDiv 15 to 17, and we skipped over that very quickly. I wonder if you have any specific memories of 17.

Admiral Lee: CarDiv 17 was formed in San Diego in, perhaps, March 1951 to replace CarDiv 15, which was to be kept out in the Korean area for the time being. I came back from 15 and joined 17 on a temporary basis as aide and flag lieutenant. Captain Joseph L. Kane was Commander Carrier Division 17. He was a senior captain and hoped to make admiral with this command. My job there was to help the staff get organized, and that's what I did. And by and by most of us who came back from 15 joined Carrier Division 17 for a brief stay.

My only unhappy experience in Carrier Division 17 was that Captain H. T. Dietrich, the former chief of staff who had not gotten along with Admiral Ruble, was the temporary chief of staff of CarDiv 17. That gave me some bad moments, but as it turned out, Captain Dietrich never mentioned his problems with Ruble in CarDiv 15, and I never mentioned them.

The two months that I was with Carrier Division 17 on temporary duty, helping them to get organized and breaking in a new flag lieutenant and aide, getting their quarters organized, the mess organized, went very quickly. In the meantime I had lined up a job in an AD squadron, Skyraider squadron, which had just returned from a Korean tour and was going back for another tour after retraining. The Carrier Division 17 tour was an interlude, not too important, and I didn't really learn anything.

Q: In what ways was your relationship uncomfortable with Captain Dietrich? He could hardly hold you responsible for your former boss.

Admiral Lee: It was uncomfortable in the sense that I knew what had gone on, and he knew that I knew what had gone on. I knew that he, in effect, had been fired, and that his relations were stormy ones with Admiral Ruble. I was a witness to it all. Since I was a young--27 years old--I think it was perfectly normal and natural to be uneasy.

Q: But nothing that really became overt, I take it.

Admiral Lee: No. Nothing never overt on his part and certainly nothing on mine.

Q: Was this staff being worked up for the Korean role, or was there any ASW consideration in it also?

Admiral Lee: It was to be an ASW staff, just as Carrier Division 15 was an ASW staff. If I remember correctly, we went to sea on one jeep carrier during that two-month period. I've forgotten what it was. I can remember that I really couldn't wait to get to that Skyraider squadron to begin flying and training. And, of course, I was getting organized and settled in the Coronado area, getting caught up on flight time. I went flying with Captain Kane several times. He was a very nice man; I had a good relation with him.

Q: Any specifics you remember about him?

Admiral Lee: None really. Very nice man. He hoped to make admiral the next selection. He wasn't selected, and he was, of course, very disappointed about that, as most people are who have every expectation to be selected.

Q: I can see why he would think he would be since he was put into an admiral's billet.

Admiral Lee: Yes, he was.

Q: You talked before about VA-115, and confined it almost exclusively to that squadron. I wonder if you could talk about the bigger picture, your relationships with other squadrons and with the air group commander.

Admiral Lee: We had an air group commander by the name of Jacob Onstott, and he flew Skyraiders with us.* He was an ex-aviation cadet and a very nice man. Not the world's

---

*Commander Jacob W. Onstott, USN.

best aviator, but he didn't have any real problems. He was able to get the Skyraider on and off the carrier without too much trouble.

In that air group we had one F9F squadron, jet squadron, and I believe we had one Skyraider squadron and two or three F4U squadrons. In addition to that, we had an F4U-5N squadron--night fighter squadron. It was a typical air group for those years. The one big difference in Korea from World War II was that we almost never flew as a group. There was no air opposition to speak of in Korea, and the jet fighters tried to go over and hit a MiG.* They had short cycle times, so that was a problem. But the F4Us and the Skyraiders went independently. So we did very little flying with the F4Us and none with the jets.

I thought the most interesting group we had aboard was the F4U-5N squadron, headed by a Lieutenant Commander Slim Russell. Very fine aviator. Didn't see very well, but a good aviator. He had a young ensign straight out of flight training by the name of Fred Dunning who was a marvelous aviator. And, of course, flying those F4U-5Ns at night over Korea and getting them back aboard ship was the challenge of a lifetime. The upper levels of the bridge were always filled to watch those F4U-5Ns come in. I think all of those pilots banged up one or more F4U-5Ns apiece.

---

*MiG is the designation for a number of Soviet fighter aircraft. The contraction is from the names of aircraft designers Artem Mikoyan and Mikhail Gurevich.

Q: Were the F4Us from the big carriers used mostly in an air-to-ground role?

Admiral Lee: Yes, F4Us and Skyraiders were interchangeable. F4Us carried a load of ammunition and a load of bombs. So did the Skyraiders. Even the F9Fs carried a 250-pound bomb. That's about all they could carry, and a load of fuel.

Q: Maybe the F4U was a predecessor of the F-18 in being versatile that way.

Admiral Lee: The F4U was a good airplane. I didn't have a lot of experience with it, although I did fly it. But it was a good, it was a good air-to-air weapon, and it was a good air-to-ground airplane.

Q: What are your memories from those few times you flew it?

Admiral Lee: I was very interested in flying the F4U, because I had flown the F6F. The F6F Hellcat was a big, clumsy airplane with a very high wing loading. The F4U had more wing area, but it had the same engine as the F6F. That was a Pratt & Whitney R2800. The F4U was more maneuverable. And the later F4U, which we had on the <u>Philippine Sea</u>, was a very good carrier plane and would carry a bigger bomb load than the F6F. I thought the F4U was more maneuverable, carried a bigger load, faster, had a better climbing ability. It was just a better airplane all around than the F6F Hellcat. And we would have been better off with F4Us in World War II, except that the first F4Us were not very good carrier planes. They later corrected that defect.

Q: That long nose made it difficult to see when you were landing.

Admiral Lee: I never landed one on a carrier, but most of them tried to be coming out of their turn into the carrier just as they got the cut. Because with the long, long stretch up the groove, you lost sight of the LSO. But it was a very good carrier plane. I didn't have enough experience with it to really tell you what kind of a gun platform it was, but I understand it was very good. I also understand it was a very good glide bomber.

Q: It's interesting that the F4U had greater longevity, but the F6F was in just the right place at the right time in '44 to do a lot of damage.

Admiral Lee: Yes, it was. The F6F did yeoman service in World War II.

Q: We talked about what you felt about the Essex-class carriers and how good they were. Every ship has its quirks and its own personality. What do you remember about that of the Philippine Sea?

Admiral Lee: You know, one of the amazing things about the Essex-class carrier is that it had no failures, to my knowledge. It had a good set of engines, four propellers, 600-pound steam plants. They would run forever. It was a smooth running ship; it was a very maneuverable ship; it had good elevators, good flight deck, good hangar deck, good accommodations. The Essex-class carrier was one of the great ship designs, as I've said earlier. I think ships are like airplanes. You don't often get a first-rate design. There are always failures. If the Essex-class carrier had a failure, I don't know what it was. Everything about it, I thought, was good. I was on the Essex in World War II, and then the Philippine Sea and the Intrepid post-World War II for cruises.

Q: Well, its only fault was that it couldn't grow as the planes grew.

Admiral Lee: Yes.

Q: Any specific memories on Philippine Sea as a ship?

Admiral Lee: I thought the Philippine Sea was a very happy ship. Our captain was a Captain Smith who made rear admiral.* He was a typical low-key man. It seems to me that the captains who make admiral are very often low-key people. He was not an excitable man. He ran a good ship. I thought he stayed abreast of the ship, stayed abreast of what was going on with our part of the Korean War. It was a comfortable ship and a comfortable command. Good relations between the ship and air wing, a good wardroom, a good executive officer whose name was Marshall White.** Good air officer. Philippine Sea was a very good ship.

Q: You had a much different role in that squadron than you did when you were in the squadrons in the Essex. Now you were the number-three man. What did that entail?

Admiral Lee: I was operations officer of VA-115, which meant that I was in charge of training, flight scheduling, everything to do with operations. I was in charge, in a sense, of safety, disciplining of pilots, making sure that everything we did was properly done from dive-bombing to

---
*Captain Allen Smith, Jr., USN.
**Commander Marshall W. White, USN.

every other aspect. I had a commanding officer by the name of Charlie Carr, who was a Naval Academy graduate of 1941. We had an executive officer by the name of Jack Sands, lieutenant commander, ex-aviation cadet. They were both very good people. Sands had a little bit of a drinking problem, and I think got passed over for captain. Charlie Carr made captain but didn't make admiral.

But we had a brash young pilot in VA-115 by the name of Abie Price.* He had had a previous tour in Korea when I joined the squadron. He was a personable young man but he would do such things as flat-hat. And while we were in the San Diego area, he took a Skyraider over towards El Centro, California, and did some flat-hatting and got caught. He was buzzing a car that his parents were driving over there. The commanding officer sent me over to investigate it. I went over and investigated and got all the facts, and made a report to the commanding officer that we properly discipline Abie Price. Price was properly disciplined but probably not severely enough, because several years later, Abie Price was in an A-4 jet squadron. One day, over at an outlying field, he landed this A-4 and gave a camera to a man on the ground and said, "I'm going to take off and come in, and I want you to take a picture of me."

He came in, made a very low pass, took off again and

---
*Ensign Allen B. Price, USN.

and crashed and killed himself. But that was Abie Price. I guess my feeling is that we made a great mistake in not taking his wings in the first place, because what he did was a complete violation of rules and regulations when he was in the VA-115. I guess the moral of this story is that adequate punishment should always be meted out. Because here if we had, perhaps, taken a little sterner action, he wouldn't have killed himself at a later time.

But I enjoyed the operations officer job, good job.

Q: How demanding was it in addition to your flying role?

Admiral Lee: It really wasn't all that demanding once we got aboard ship. But in the training phase in San Diego, it was quite demanding--flight schedules, going to El Centro, a syllabus for each pilot. But I had lots of help, and it wasn't all that challenging, and I enjoyed flying the Skyraider. So it wasn't a job that I felt particularly stretched.

Q: I imagine the Mini influence came through during the training.

Admiral Lee: Yes, I probably was a little harder to get along with than most operations officers, because I wanted

---
*Ensign Allen B. Price, USN.

things done properly--schedules met on time, briefings on time, proper safety. We never lost any pilots in training; and we lost only one pilot during the Korean War. I think the kind of training we had and the kind of safety program we had, and the maintenance all paid off. The squadrons that lose a lot of pilots have a lot of accidents that can usually be traced back to the kind of training program and safety program they had. We had a very good one, as evidenced by our record.

Q: How much as ops officer did you get involved in the strike planning for Korea?

Admiral Lee: Initially we did a great deal of work in making sure we were doing it right. But after the first two or three weeks, since all strikes were alike, I really had very little role in it except planning my own flights. We would get the intelligence information and get our target assignments, and then the flight would go off and do its own planning. So I really didn't get that involved on a squadron basis for Korea. It wasn't that complicated a war by the time I got there. It was sort of cut-and-dried, standard missions every day.

Q: On the other hand if everything becomes pretty routine, then complacency becomes an enemy.

Admiral Lee: Yes, it does.

Q: How did you fight that?

Admiral Lee: We tried not to be complacent. The way not to be complacent is for the senior officers to toe the line themselves in every aspect, such as dive-bombing runs. Some squadrons lost a lot of planes in Korea by flying their bombs into the targets almost, into those railroad tunnels. Some squadrons lost 10 or 12 planes that way. We absolutely would ground a pilot who did that. It was foolish. There wasn't a railroad tunnel worth a Skyraider. Commander Carr backed me up: "We don't do that sort of thing, and anybody who does won't be flying in this squadron."

But a lot of squadrons tried to be heroes. There was a one Commander Gray who had a big record in this regard.* There was some foolish flying done in Korea. We didn't do that. We tried to be logical about it, and sensible and safe, and yet get the job done.

Q: Was any target in Korea worth a Skyraider?

---

*Commander Paul N. Gray, USN, was commanding officer of VF-54, a Skyraider squadron in the carrier Essex (CV-9). For details on the damage incurred by Gray's aircraft, see Malcolm W. Cagle and Frank A. Manson, The Sea War in Korea (Annapolis: U.S. Naval Institute, 1957), pages 422-423.

Admiral Lee: I didn't see one, not while I was there. If the enemy army is pushing our army to the south and beating the daylights out of them, yes, it's worth taking chances. But when we got there, the front had stabilized, and it was sort of a war of attrition, just trying to keep them from supplying their forces along the front. We kept up pressure day in and day out, so I suppose that was our biggest problem, keeping complacency away.

Q: That's where you do a lot of talking in the ready room, too, probably.

Admiral Lee: And attention to detail. That's where it pays off. The senior officers paying attention to detail, and themselves being disciplined enough to pay attention to detail so far as their own personal habits are concerned.

Q: Setting the example.

Admiral Lee: Setting the example.

I thought we did a pretty good job in that regard, judging by our record. We lost one pilot to what I believe was small arms fire. He wasn't lost because he was violating the safety rules and regulations or using poor procedures. His was the luck of the draw.

Q: Was weather a factor at all in those operations?

Admiral Lee: Not really. If the weather was all that bad, we didn't fly, or we went to another target. Because we had a strictly visual system. We had to have good weather; the target had to be visible in order to attack.

Q: Jets were still quite new in the fleet then. Was there any problem running the flight deck with the mixture of propellers and jets?

Admiral Lee: Yes, there was a little bit of a problem. The Skyraiders and F4Us normally went on a three-hour flight--maybe it was two and a half. But the jets could only fly about an hour and 15 minutes or an hour and a half. They would take off first, go over and make their attack, and come right back to the ship and land. We would take off and be gone about three hours, come back. So that we never really operated with the jets. There was a lot of kidding around the wardroom and in the ready rooms. The Skyraider and F4U pilots were always ribbing the F9Fs carrying their deadly 250-pound bomb.

Q: What kind of an ordnance load did you have?

Admiral Lee: Oh, Lord, the Skyraider could carry everything. We could carry rockets; we had 20-millimeter cannon; we could carry any kind of bomb; we could carry 8,000 or 9,000 pounds of bombs. The Skyraider was a real workhorse. We normally carried 6,000 or 7,000 pounds. It depended on the target. We carried an awful lot of 500-pound bombs and a fair number of rockets. We used our cannon frequently. There wasn't anything the Skyraider couldn't carry.

Q: I've seen a picture in a book about the Korean War that showed literally a kitchen sink strapped onto a plane so that they could drop that, too.

Admiral Lee: It would drop it.

Q: Well, moving from there to your time at the weapons employment course at Sandia, what do you remember about that specifically? Was it a hands-on type course?

Admiral Lee: No, the weapons employment course at Sandia was an academic course. It was the first course set up by the services to train staff officers to use atomic weapons.

Initially the services went together and set up the school at Sandia under the auspices of a joint command.

Admiral Lee: We had a rear admiral--sometimes a vice admiral--or a lieutenant general who headed this command. The command itself was in Washington, but Sandia worked for it. The services, through this joint agency, set up this school. The weapons employment course, I think, lasted six or seven weeks. Its purpose was to train staff officers of the Army, Navy, and Air Force for the employment of nuclear weapons.

Down there at Sandia we first went through a little course in physics of bombs, then the bombs themselves and how they worked. We went through the fusing, air burst, ground burst, and then what went in the damage criteria. After we'd studied all the damage criteria from thermal to an air blast, to a radiation--nuclear radiation--we then went into various employment situations.

Say you want to drop a bomb on Moscow, or say your division is engaged with another division and you want to hit behind them. You'd pick the size weapon and whether you want a ground burst or an air burst. We were given a lot of problems like that. We'd come up with a solution, and then there would be a staff solution.

The services themselves later on set up their own schools, one on the East Coast and one on the West Coast. I taught in the one on the East Coast from 1956 to 1958. This particular course at Sandia was in the summer of '53. I thought it was a very good course, and it fit in very well with the graduate program we had.

Q: So you probably drew a great deal on that when you taught the course yourself.

Admiral Lee: Yes.

Q: When you sent back your transcript, you mentioned that you'd been involved in seeing the atomic bomb test in Nevada.

Admiral Lee: I discussed this with my wife, and we decided it was in the fall of 1953.

In '52, '53, '54, the Atomic Energy Commission had a series of atomic bomb tests in the Nevada desert. It was decided by the AEC, since we were taking this nuclear engineering course at Monterey, that it would be a good thing for us to go witness an atomic explosion. So my entire class of about 15 students was sent out to Las Vegas. We were flown to Las Vegas and then went by bus out to the atomic weapons site. We were housed there overnight in a barracks type affair and then given briefings.

The next day, the day of the atomic bomb blast, we were taken to see various structures that were to be near ground zero. There were buildings; there were trucks; there were tanks; there were a number of structures--some wooden structures, some concrete. We were given a look at those before the blast. After we'd had a look at that, we were led to some trenches. These trenches were, perhaps, ten miles away. This weapon was dropped by air, and there was a ground zero. It came pretty close to ground zero. But just before the blast, we were given glasses and told to stoop down in the trench and not to look. But the bomb was dropped; it went off on schedule and just about at ground zero.

Then we were given an all-clear and could look at the mushroom cloud going up. That's when we looked up, and then afterwards were allowed to tour the areas around ground zero and see what damage had been done the structures. As I understand it, this was about a 20-KT bomb. We were allowed to see the structures, the vehicles--trucks, tanks, automobiles--and see what damage had taken place at various distances from ground zero. They had plotted where the planned ground zero was and then where the actual ground zero was. So it was a very interesting day, and I thought something that should be in here.

Q: What do you remember of the damage that you saw?

Admiral Lee: The damage was quite severe, as you would expect. The vehicles were overturned and wrecked; the structures that they had placed in certain distances from ground zero were destroyed. Then there were enough structures farther on down so that you could see how far the damage went. It was a very good exhibition of the power of an atomic bomb and I thought good for our class.

Q: Was there any concern about being exposed to radiation?

Admiral Lee: There was no concern at that time. Now later on there's been great concern. All people who were involved in those tests in Nevada have been asked to come forward and sign up, because apparently a number of people who were involved in those tests have developed cancer prematurely.

I didn't sign up. I don't know if my classmates signed up or not. I haven't followed up on what the statistics of cancer have been in the group of people who were out there. But since I only witnessed one test, and I was about 60 years old at the time they called for signing up, I didn't sign up. I just thought that since I'm already getting government retirement pay so what more can they do for me?

Q: We talked before about your time in VX-3. You said that Bob Dosé was a particularly good aviator. What qualities did you admire in him as a pure flier?

Admiral Lee: You know, since our discussion, I've thought about this. A good flier's like a natural athlete. If you ever see a natural athlete--Joe DiMaggio was one, and there're many others--they always seem to make the right move, whether it's throwing the ball or hitting the ball or moving the ball. Whether the ball is a football or a baseball, they're graceful. Whatever they do, it just seems to come naturally. There are also aviators like that. They just never seem to make a mistake. Their landings, their takeoffs, their gunnery runs--always seem to be just right. Bob Dosé was like that.

I've known in my career, perhaps, a half a dozen of what I would call natural pilots like this: people like Don Engen, Bob Dosé, Whitey Feightner, a fellow by the name of Marlar Stewart. There aren't many. Whatever they did in an airplane, it couldn't be done better. Make smooth turns on approaches to the carrier, perfect landings. Gunnery runs were always very good. Bombing first rate. So that's what I'm talking about. Bob Dosé was one of those people. Now I was not one of those natural athlete pilots. I'd say I was a better than average pilot, but not in the class with Bob Dosé and Whitey Feightner.

Q: Would you see a correlation between athletic ability and this natural flying skill?

Admiral Lee: No. I've thought about that. Some of these people that I've described as being natural aviators were not very good athletes. Bob Dosé wasn't a good athlete.

By the same token, you've seen people who handled an automobile beautifully. Not necessarily good athletes. They just had an affinity for it. That's what I'm talking about.

Q: It's good when a person who has an ability like that finds his niche.

Admiral Lee: Yes.

Q: Some people never find their niche.

Admiral Lee: Yes. So true.

Q: You talked admiringly, also, in a different context about Captain Masterton of the <u>Intrepid</u>. What do you remember about him as an operator?

Admiral Lee: Captain Masterton was another one of those low-key captains. He didn't blow up if somebody made a mistake. He ran a good ship; he always did his homework; and he always seemed to make the right moves in an operation. He was a good ship handler. He was always at the right place at the right time, and he was always approachable. He was always willing to listen to any suggestions anybody had. Sort of my ideal as a ship's captain, Captain Masterton.

Q: Would you say you modeled yourself after him when you became a ship's captain?

Admiral Lee: Yes, probably, but I think I modeled myself more on Commander Mini than Captain Masterton. Masterton was not an attention-to-detail man. He sort of left that for other people. But, even so, he was a very successful commanding officer. In my own case, I wasn't content to leave the details to other people. I wanted to make sure that the details were done and done properly, which was the Jim Mini style. Both very successful men, good leaders.

Q: I think, though, that you'd probably be put more in the low-key category than the excitable, also.

Admiral Lee: Yes, yes. I'm not the excitable type. That's the worst attribute a captain can have, I think.

Q: The screamer.

Admiral Lee: The screamer. Absolute worst.

Q: What do you remember about Jack James, the air group commander in the Intrepid?

Admiral Lee: We went almost overnight from Roosevelt to Intrepid, because we had an extra A-4 squadron and Intrepid needed one. Jack James was a stern taskmaster but a very good group commander. He ran a good air group, and I have a fondness for Jack James, because he had had this group together for several months, and they'd been on one or two cruises on Intrepid. Then we came along, newcomers, new boys. Jack James made us feel very welcome and made us a part of the group, which was important, because we could have been treated as outcasts. That didn't happen. He flew with us some. I would give Jack James very high marks as a group commander.

Q: I think that was smart on his part, because that made you give all the more for him.

Admiral Lee: Yes. We had a very successful cruise. We didn't lose any planes; didn't lose any pilots; had an operational readiness inspection and got the top grade in Jack James's air group, I think they were taken aback at that. VA-46 had the best volleyball team. That cruise was the best thing that ever happened to me personally. I think it was a good thing for VA-46. So, all in all, I have very fond memories of Jack James, and I'd give him very high marks as a group commander and as a naval officer. Good man.

Q: What kind of missions were you flying in that squadron when you were deployed to the Med?

Admiral Lee: Back in those days, the A-4s and every other naval aviation squadron, on which we could hang an atomic weapon, was given an atomic weapon mission. Our number one job in the Med was to plan to hit targets in Russia from various launch points. We each were given two or three targets to plan, depending on the launch point. So on many of our missions in the Med we would practice as much as we could. We could fly low level over Spain and Greece and Turkey. We practiced those atomic weapon missions. Other times we bombed the sled. At night about all we could do was navigational flights. We'd take off and go out to some point and come back--night formation flying. We did a fair amount of night flying.

A cruise in the Mediterranean in those days was not all that demanding in terms of the things you did. There wasn't much you could do. We did have some targets in North Africa that we practiced on once or twice. But we served as targets for F4Ds, for instance. We would be sent out and would come back as the enemy. Or we served as targets for radar of one type or another. We would serve as some other ship's air target, some destroyer that wanted to practice vectoring aircraft, that sort of thing. No really demanding missions, but I think an interesting assortment for six months or so we were in the Mediterranean.

Q: Do you have any specific memories about the Intrepid as ship?

Admiral Lee: Yes, Intrepid was another Essex-class carrier, one modified with an angled deck and steam catapults, and also a very fine ship. I thought Captain Masterton had about the happiest ship, most congenial department heads, that I've been aboard. I was the squadron commander, a commander at this particular time, and we had numerous dinners with Captain Masterton in the captain's quarters during the course of the cruise, and always had a drink with him ashore. So it was a very happy ship and a happy cruise. We lost only a few pilots. The other A-4 squadron lost a commanding officer. I think I previously mentioned this. His father was a former comptroller of the Department of Defense.

Lee #8 - 671

Q: McNeil.

Admiral Lee: McNeil. We lost Jim McNeil, VA-66. I was the senior member of the accident board.

Q: I would think that being on one of those accident boards is not a pleasant duty.

Admiral Lee: No, it isn't. But it's necessary. It's amazing what you can develop. You study all the details, piece it all together. But Jim McNeil, we think, simply flew into the water on one of these night carrier approaches. Best explanation.

Q: You talked about the low-level flight profiles. What are the differences in navigation at low level versus high level?

Admiral Lee: At high level you can see if you have the visibility. You navigate high level two ways: either with radio aids or DR-ing, one or the other. At low level you don't have any radio aids, so you DR from recognizable, visible point to recognizable visible point. It's absolutely necessary that you stay with it. If you ever get lost, the only thing to do is to climb, because you'll never pick it up again. But if you go from bridge to railroad, to highway, to town, staying with it all the way--having it marked off on your chart--low-level navigation is very easy. You have these charts laid out and you just follow it, point to point, and you get the time it takes. But if you ever look away for a few minutes and then come back and try to pick it up, chances are you never will.

In high level, you DR on navigational aids, and if you have good visibility, you can see for dozens of miles and pick up rivers, and towns, points. So high-level navigation, if the visibility is good, is a piece of cake, as they say. Low level you could get into trouble very quickly.

Q: Moving from there then to the Enterprise, I'd be interested more in the specifics of your role as CAG. You talked before more in terms of the ship's mission. What did you do in commanding the air group?

Admiral Lee: With Enterprise when I was group commander, I had Air Group Six, same group as Jack James had on Intrepid, same group.

My role was as a department head. I went to the department heads' meetings every night with the executive officer. My role was to pass along information to make sure that the squadrons were following ship regulations, following proper safety procedures, the commanding officers were toeing the line. I flew the A-4 and the Skyraider. I also checked out in the F-4 and the A-5 and the F-8. I carrier qualified in the F-8.

But I'd say my role, the group commander role, was more administrative aboard ship than otherwise. The fighter squadrons have their own tactics and sort of do their own thing. The attack squadrons have their own tactics and plan their own operations. So the group commander sort of sits back and watches all this, because the men in the squadrons are professionals in what they do. So that a group commander aboard ship is largely an administrator. He talks to the captain, talks to the executive officer, helps plan the overall operation, makes sure that our heads are clean. But on Enterprise we had an extra bonus there. We had two tough hombrés, as I mentioned earlier, in Vince dePoix as captain, who was not a gentle man and not an easygoing individual. He was a martinet. Then we had Max Harnish, the executive officer, whose attention to detail went beyond all reason, I thought. He was also something of a martinet.

I perhaps spent a third of my time on Enterprise running interference for the air group. Whether it was somebody's head wasn't properly cleaned, or some young pilot who came back aboard last night three sheets in the wind, or somebody's white hat wasn't squared on a hangar deck, or somebody was working on airplanes in dungarees when we had some guests aboard. It was a difficult cruise in that sense. These people were intent on spit and polish, and not so much on flying airplanes.

We had an admiral aboard, John T. Hayward, who really didn't pay too much attention to any of it. As I've said earlier, I always thought John T. Hayward was a political admiral, and he also had the reputation of being a sort of a whiz kid. But I got to know him fairly well then and later, and I always felt that John T. Hayward was highly overrated. I never thought he was much of a whiz kid, and I had many conversations with him. He was a personality kid. I never felt that he had read very much. I never felt that he was really all that qualified technically. So John T. Hayward was not one of the people that I wanted to emulate. But he was for a long time a fair-haired boy in the Navy. Maybe you know John T. Hayward.

Q: I've talked to him. I found him an extremely likable person, but I don't have any basis for judging him technically.

Admiral Lee: Very likable. He's a real charmer.

Q: You're describing a number of irritants, and yet before you talked of this as a very enjoyable job. What made it so?

Admiral Lee: I've described these irritants, but being a group commander is a great job, and we had some very fine squadron commanders, some wonderful airplanes. But I really shouldn't dwell too much on the irritants. It was a great ship. We had a good air group, very fine. The best. We had a couple or three very fine cruises. First cruise to the Mediterranean. We were down off Cuba during the missile crisis. Then I went back for a second cruise to the Mediterranean, a short cruise before I was relieved by Jack Christiansen and went to join Rickover's shop. So there's no better flying job in naval aviation than a group commander job. But, as I say, it was tiresome in the sense I've described. Being the group commander on Enterprise when she was brand new was also a big thrill. Enterprise was such a great ship. She was so much the center of public attention wherever she went. So I was very proud to be a group commander on Enterprise.

Q: A lot of prestige associated.

Admiral Lee: A lot of prestige. So, yes, it was a very fine cruise.

Q: How large a staff did you have?

Admiral Lee: The group commander had about five or six officers: an intelligence officer, an operations officer, a maintenance officer. I had some good people. The senior LSO was on my staff.

Q: How often did you have interaction with the squadrons?

Admiral Lee: Daily. I saw the commanding officers every day. I spent a fair amount of time in the ready rooms. I would go to movies in the ready rooms. I flew with two A-4 squadrons and a Skyraider squadron. So I was a part of the air group, and I spent the bulk of my time with them.

Q: Is there any sense of disappointment on that kind of tour that it's going to be your last shot at flying?

Admiral Lee: No, I think you look at it in a different light. You look at it in the sense that your cup is half full rather than half empty. You consider yourself very lucky getting a group commander job. You want to enjoy every minute of it, because, normally, the squadron commander tour is about the last flying job in carrier aviation. There aren't that many groups.

Q: So this is some more icing on the cake.

Admiral Lee: Yes. That it was. It sure beat being executive officer or operations officer on an aircraft carrier, I thought.

Q: We talked somewhat about the planning process for possible strikes on Cuba. I'm wondering where the inputs came from in making those plans.

Admiral Lee: The photos of the missile sites in Cuba were flown to the ship, and they were taken by the U-2s and RF-8s. We had a very good set of photos of Cuba. We probably had those before we got down there. The recon planes would go and take those pictures and come back and immediately develop them. When the word was given, they'd send them to us annotated, so that we had all these photographs. Then the mission planning was up to us. We decided what weapons and what tactics, right in Enterprise. We did the planning, given the information. We were assigned various missile sites. There were two or three carriers down there, depending on the time. We did what I thought was some pretty good planning.

Q: You carved it up among the different carriers, who would get what?

Admiral Lee: I don't know this to be true, but I think each carrier was given all the photos. I think each carrier made plans to hit most of the sites. If the time came, why, a carrier would be designated to hit a certain site, and then we would pull those plans out and go. That's the way I think it was done, so that we would be prepared for any eventuality.

Q: You certainly don't want people falling all over each other either.

Admiral Lee: No. But we did a lot of detailed planning and replanning, and thinking, and studying how to evade the missiles. That's what we spent most of our time doing. Russian missile sights had never been attacked before. And luckily we didn't have to do it.

Q: One of the criticisms of Vietnam is that there were too many rudder orders from Washington on conducting air strikes. Did you get any of that during the Cuban planning?

Admiral Lee: No. We didn't get any of that in Vietnam in the sense that, "These are the tactics you're going to use." We got a lot of it in terms of, "These are the targets you can hit."

In Cuba we got that kind of steerage; namely, "If we hit them at all, these are the ones you can hit." But the tactics that were used in both Vietnam and Cuba were left up to squadrons--how you go about hitting.

Q: Do you remember any specifics on the tactics for the Cuban scenario?

Admiral Lee: Yes, we planned to go in low level, very high speed, pop up to 8,000 or 10,000 feet, dive on the target, drop bombs, and then go away low level.

Q: Did you have any concern about an enemy air threat?

Admiral Lee: Yes, we had concern about enemy air threat, and we would have planned to have F-4s and F-8s in the air to take care of the air threat. The A-4s and the Skyraiders would have done the attacking, because that's what we had on board.

Q: I think you said you took off the A-5s for that.

Admiral Lee: A-5s were taken off. We got an extra A-4 squadron, a Marine squadron. The A-5 was the most useless airplane, next to the F7U, that we ever bought, as I say again.

Q: Did you have any ECM planning for possible strike?

Admiral Lee: No, we didn't. We didn't really have any ECM to speak of at that time. That was developed later on. We were going in and hitting them, hope we could get away.

Q: Sounds like speed was one of the main things you were counting on.

Admiral Lee: Speed and surprise. In retrospect, I think we could have done a good job. Because the tactics we were using, they couldn't have hit us.

Q: I talked to one of the pilots that flew those recon missions, and it was essentially the same thing--fast and low level.

Admiral Lee: We got some good pictures.

Q: How much involvement did you have with Admiral Hayward and Captain de Poix on the strike planning?

Admiral Lee: I had absolutely none with Captain de Poix. He didn't take part in the strike planning. I don't ever remember Admiral Hayward being involved. He might have discussed it with his staff officers, but I don't remember that he was personally involved.

Q: So you were the guy?

Admiral Lee: The squadron commanders and I did our own planning, yes. We discussed it, and they did the planning. I'd say primarily the squadron commanders. They knew the weapons; they knew the airplanes; and it was their neck. I think the best planning you'll ever get is from the man who's going to do the mission. He's off looking at the publications and assessing the risk. It was primarily the squadron commanders and their operations officers.

Q: Did any of those plans get written down at the time?

Admiral Lee: No record was kept of it. We had all these detailed plans for striking these missile sites, but after it was all called off, I imagine they were destroyed.

Q: So it's whatever is in the heads of the people who were there.

Admiral Lee: That's about it.

Q: In that case, is there anything else you have to say

about it?

Admiral Lee: No, I don't. It was a long two months down there.

Q: How frequently did you get updated on recon photos and intelligence as these two months went along?

Admiral Lee: I thought almost daily. We got a continuous stream of photographs, pictures. I thought the intelligence was excellent.

Q: Did the antiaircraft threat seem to be changing as time passed?

Admiral Lee: Not much. Didn't seem to. I think very little went on in Cuba during that period. I believe our people were taking almost daily pictures to make sure, but we didn't see any changes to speak of.

Q: Do you get any sense of complacency in that kind of an atmosphere, that you put people up on the step and then nothing happens?

Admiral Lee: It's hard to stay on step and be very alert for two months, but that's what we did. I think we could have done a good job. In retrospect, no doubt about it. But we had untried airplanes, untried weapons, untried pilots. They later did very well in Vietnam, and I think we would have done well.

Q: In an earlier interview you provided a graphic picture of ejecting from your airplane, hitting the water, and taking off your parachute the 26th of October. Young pilots sometimes have a psychological problem then getting back into the cockpit. Were you too senior for that?

Admiral Lee: I didn't have any problem. That happened in October 1962, so I was 39 years old. I don't remember that it was an issue. That sort of thing, I guess, fades out with the years.

Q: Any of the ship's officers or enlisted men you especially remember?

Admiral Lee: I don't really have any thoughts along those lines. Good ship, good set of officers.

Q: I think for a showcase ship like that you'd practically have hand-picked officers.

Admiral Lee: Yes, they had a first-rate ship.

Q: Moving you ashore again, you talked about the F-111 business and George Jessen being called in. What did he do specifically?

Admiral Lee: Well, in that particular period, the Assistant Secretary of the Navy research and development was Bob Frosch. He was a Ph.D. in theoretical physics, and he was the point man for the F-111 for the Secretary of the Navy. Now, actually, all these technical arguments that they had with McNamara were developed over in Naval Air Systems Command about the center of gravity, the weight, and approach speed. This went on for months. I've forgotten how the recommendation came about, but it was decided that what Frosch needed was one officer who was technically competent to handle the F-111 items for him. He could come in and explain them to him if Frosch had to go down to a meeting with McNamara, to explain why the Navy was opposing the F-111 on various grounds.

I recommended George Jessen, because I knew George from Air Wing Six. He was in the A-5 squadron and had become an AED, engineering duty officer, was an aeronautical engineer, and I thought absolutely a first-rate officer. I had written a concurrent report on him when I was group commander on _Enterprise_. He was one of the bright young officers, I thought. He was a young lieutenant commander, and I told Dr. Frosch that I thought Jessen was just the man for it. Very articulate, technically qualified, and well spoken and presentable, and wouldn't ever embarrass him. Jessen was very conscious of what could be done and couldn't be done--which is very important in an aide. He has to make sure that the secretary understands the pros and cons of the various arguments and what the political positions are.

I recommended George Jessen for this job, and Dr. Frosch interviewed him and decided George Jessen was a good choice. As a matter of fact, he and George Jessen became great friends. George Jessen is a very likable guy. Not the personality kid that Jerry Miller is, but a very competent man. He later was the S-3 program manager when I had Naval Air Systems Command. I kept my fingers on George for many years, he said.

So that was his role with Dr. Frosch. He did a fine job.

Q: So he lived up to your expectations?

Admiral Lee: Yes, and then some. George always did. He's the kind of a guy you want working for you, because he makes you look good. He had more talent than I did along those lines.

Q: Getting you back to sea again. Commander Paul Peck was your air wing commander on *Enterprise*. What do you remember about him?

Admiral Lee: He was a very fine wing commander. He later made rear admiral. But I had the highest regard for Paul. I think he flew the F-4 and maybe the A-4. He ran a good air wing. He and I had excellent relations. I gave Paul the highest recommendations, first-rate man, very fine aviator. Very good leader. Should have made admiral, and he did.

Q: You mentioned that Ambassador Alexis Johnson came out to your ship when you were going to Sasebo. What was the substance of what he told you?

Admiral Lee: He just explained the Japanese sensitivity to nuclear weapons, and how it was very important that we make a good impression on the Japanese, and not have any incidents. Since this was politically sensitive in Japan, there would be demonstrations. These demonstrations were not directed against us as such, but were directed against the political leaders of Japan who were allowing us to come in. We understood that, but we thought it very nice that he would come out and explain this to us. We had a very nice day with Johnson.

Q: Was there any Japanese measuring of radiation levels around the ship?

Admiral Lee: Yes, they did have some people out in boats, and we had lots of demonstrators out in boats. But the Japanese had a patrol in Sasebo Harbor, and they kept the demonstrators and demonstrators' boats at a certain distance, so that that didn't turn into a problem either.

Q: You talked about photo recon for Cuba. Do you have any recollection about the running of recce planes from Enterprise in the Vietnam scenario?

Admiral Lee: Yes, we ran a lot of recce planes from Enterprise. We had the RA-5C. The RA-5C had some good cameras that took excellent pictures, but the RA-5C was designed to do much more than take pictures. You can take good pictures with F-4 or an F-8. The RA-5C had an inertial platform, and, supposedly, it would go in and make one sweep and have about five different sensors, and come back and feed this information into the integrated operational intelligence center, called the IOIC. Then all you had to do was push the right buttons and you'd get a picture of the radars and where they were, and all that sort of thing.

The concept was marvelous, magic. It never worked. Never worked. Not once. One of the things I looked into during my training period, when I was aboard and Holloway was captain, was the RA-5C. I had opposed the A3J and I had opposed the RA-5C. But I lost. I was back in assistant secretary R&D's office. But I lost. So I went to Enterprise to see what the RA-5C had done. The RA-5C had taken some good pictures. Period. None of the other worked. Not one time--for two tours with Holloway and two tours for me. So the RA-5C was a disaster, I thought, in every way.

Q: You talked briefly before about what you would do during bombing halts. If you could go more into that, please. What occupied the ship when you weren't bombing North Vietnam.

Admiral Lee: There were various trails that the enemy used in South Vietnam. I don't remember exactly. It may be that there were some periods when we didn't go into North Vietnam at all. That may be. I've forgotten. But when we were not allowed to go into North Vietnam, we pursued the North Vietnamese along their trails in South Vietnam. We tried to mine the various rivers they used. We tried to knock out their bridges, and hit their transportation, and hit their troop concentrations in South Vietnam, and especially up along the DMZ. We just saturated the DMZ area, so it was harassing work all the way down. It was trying to prevent them from getting men and supplies down. Of course, it was a failing operation, but that, essentially, is what we tried to do.

Q: Did you have any capability for providing close air support of ground troops?

Admiral Lee: Oh, yes. We could supply as much close air support of ground troops as they wanted. We had good capability. We had pilots who were trained to do it. We had the A-4 and A-7 airplanes, which could make good ground attacks. So we had however much close air support capability they wished. We could provide it day or night.

Q: Were there any hassles during these bombing halts with land-based planes in the South that would normally cover these areas?

Admiral Lee: No hassles with <u>Enterprise</u>, but the Seventh Fleet had a liaison officer over in South Vietnam, and he handled this for us. The targets were handed out from South Vietnam. The liaison officer worked out all these details, and came out to see us periodically. But we didn't really get involved in that. This was worked out and given to us.

Q: You sort of hinted before at your communications capability, that the President of the United States could call you on the phone; what sorts of comms does a carrier like that have?

Admiral Lee: We had teletype machines. The various messages that went to and fro, went into these machines and came out as printed copy. Then for voice communications, we had a single sideband. I think we had several single sideband systems, and any voice communications we had went to Hawaii, I believe, single sideband. From Hawaii we probably went by landline to Washington. And probably from Hawaii out to Enterprise by single sideband.

Q: What do you remember about the phased-array radars?

Admiral Lee: The phased-array radars were SPS-32 and SPS-33 which were on Enterprise when I was group commander. We still had them when I was the captain, and I thought the phased-array radars were marvelous. We had one phased-array radar which was good for distance and another one which was good for altitudes. The four faces of the Enterprise island structure were phased-array radars. Each one of the radars had about half each face. We didn't have a lot of trouble with them. We kept them running most of the time. They really were four independent systems. Face one would be independent from face two and so forth. So you could lose one face and still operate the other three. Good systems.

Q: Did you work with the PIRAZ ships and NTDS during the strikes?

Admiral Lee: Yes. Everybody worked with the PIRAZ ship and NTDS every day. If I remember correctly, our pilots checked in and out with the PIRAZ communication ships when we were hitting targets in North Vietnam.

Q: Did you have occasion to go to emcon?*

Admiral Lee: I don't ever remember going to emcon. We might have, but I don't remember.

Q: Without an air threat, there wasn't probably all that much need to. I think we've sort of gotten so dependent on it now, we'd probably be in trouble if we had to go to emcon.

---

*Emcon--emission control, which means either minimizing or eliminating electronic emissions to avoid giving electronic notice to the enemy of the ship's presence.

Admiral Lee: Wouldn't we, though!

Q: You said before that being commanding officer of a ship is the best job in the world. Why do you feel that way?

Admiral Lee: Commanding officer of a ship has so much authority and power and prestige in his own right. I don't think there's another job in the world today comparable to being commanding officer of a ship. You have the responsibility and you have the authority. The captain of a ship today is, perhaps, the last king on earth. The King of England has no power. The captain of a ship, even today, has lots of power, lots of authority, lots of responsibility, and lots of prestige. It's a very good job. There's nothing else comparable to it, I don't think.

Q: Better than being CAG, I take it.

Admiral Lee: They're different. But, of course, the nice thing is to be a CAG and then a commanding officer of a ship.

Q: The best of both worlds.

Admiral Lee: You have them both.

Q: During one of our previous interviews, you alluded to some contact you had with Vice Admiral Tom Connolly following his retirement, but you didn't really discuss it.

Admiral Lee: The only contact I had with Admiral Connolly was when he came into my office one day having to do with an ejection seat contract. He was representing an ejection seat company. He came with the president of this company into my office to object to a competition which McDonnell Douglas had held, and his company had lost. The British company, Martin-Baker, had won the contract for the F-18 ejection seat.

I called our legal officer, the general counsel for NavAir, when I saw Admiral Connolly on the schedule and asked him about Connolly coming to see me in connection with this competition. He told me that it was illegal for Connolly to come in and argue for this company getting the contract. So when Admiral Connolly got in, got to my office, I asked him if he was representing Stencil in connection with this contract, and he said he was. I said, "In that case, I'll have to ask you to leave, because it's illegal for you to do so." I said, "It's all right for the president of your company to come, but I won't talk to you about it, because I'm breaking the law if I do."

So Admiral Connolly stormed out. He was retired

then.* So my relations with Connolly were never good. From the time I said to him that I couldn't follow Admiral Baldwin's order about giving the company a piece of the action, that if they want somebody to do that, they'd have to get another man, my relations went downhill with Connolly, from then on. The man was a crook. No question about it. Jerry Miller won't agree with me, but he really was. It's not something I discuss with Jerry.

Q: Since Admiral Connolly probably knew how you felt already, it was kind of a futile trip on his part, wasn't it?

Admiral Lee: He has a lot of brass, that guy.

I should have handled it differently. I handled that poorly, because the news was around town in 30 minutes, that I'd thrown Connolly out of my office. That wasn't good. What I should have done was not be available. The retired community thought I was unfair to Connolly. I think they were right in a sense. If I had it to do again, I just wouldn't be available, and not put him in that position.

Q: Didn't they think that he was putting you in an unfair

---

*Vice Admiral Connolly had retired from active duty in September 1971, upon completion of his tenure as Deputy Chief of Naval Operations (Air).

position?

Admiral Lee: Yes, I'm sure of that. But I shouldn't have let it happen in the first place. That would have been a better way to handle it. We always tried to treat retired types very gently, and I didn't treat him very gently. So I could have handled it much better, and I should have.

Q: On the other hand, on the positive side, what you did sent a very effective message.

Admiral Lee: It sent a highly effective message. Didn't have any more problems like that. It was like firing that squadron commander in Air Wing Six—no more problems.

Q: In a happier context, you mentioned a name in passing before, Stansfield Turner. I wonder if you have any further to say about him.

Admiral Lee: Not really. Stansfield Turner is a very able man. I believe Stan Turner persuaded John Chafee to make Elmo Zumwalt Chief of Naval Operations. I believe that.

Q: That's what you said.

Admiral Lee: I think that happened. I think Chafee was

willing to listen, because he hadn't had the best relations with Moorer. He wanted somebody that would be agreeable to his agenda.

Although Stan Turner's a very able man, I think he has an ego to match. Very big ego. He thinks a great deal of Stan Turner. But he's a very capable man, very personable. Loves to be on TV. I got to know him pretty well. We loaned him our cabin for a week up in Deep Creek Lake in Garrett County, western Maryland. But Stan Turner is--I'd say more than most men, he's more interested in Stan--as John Chafee would say, "He's full of himself." As opposed to some other people I know like Jerry Miller who's, you know, very generous with his time, and whatever, with other people. Stan Turner would not be. That would be my description of him. But he's a damned able man.

Q: There are some people who are full of themselves that don't have the ability to match.

Admiral Lee: He has the ability to match, I think.

Q: Also before--and I'd appreciate it if you could amplify this--you said that your didn't think that Secretary Chafee reined in Admiral Zumwalt when he had the chance. What do you mean by that?

Admiral Lee: I think Chafee got more than he bargained for with Zumwalt. I think Chafee's ideas for the Navy were rather modest. He's interested in people, and his ideas were good. He didn't want a revolution; my idea of Chafee was that he just wanted the process of evolution to be speeded up a little bit.

But Zumwalt came in, and he wanted revolution. And Chafee didn't really know how to turn him off. He's damned hard to turn off. Not only that, I thought Zumwalt sort of turned on Chafee, and I was very sorry that Chafee caved into him.

Let me tell you what I mean. Chafee was Secretary of the Navy; he hoped to run for Senate from Rhode Island. After Zumwalt had been there about a year, he announced that he was going to close the Naval Air Station Quonset Point, the NARF at Quonset Point, and phase out basing destroyers in Narragansett Bay. I thought Zumwalt had a lot of chutzpah to do that to Chafee when Chafee wanted to go up there and run for the Senate. Zumwalt put it in such a fashion that Chafee had a very difficult time saying no. So he acquiesced. That may have been the reason he didn't make it to the Senate the first time around. So I thought Zumwalt treated Chafee very unfairly, and I thought Chafee early on had a chance to let Zumwalt know who was boss. But he didn't. He gave Zumwalt his head. I think it cost Chafee dearly in the end. This is my assessment.

Q: Did you hear from Chafee himself that he felt Zumwalt had gone too far?

Admiral Lee: No, I didn't. I really never discussed Zumwalt with Chafee. As I said to you earlier in this oral history, I had two tours of duty in the secretariat. I learned that you only discuss the things with the secretaries that they bring up. This is the best advice I can give an aide to civilian secretaries. You must be very circumspect, and don't ever be pushy. If you want influence with these secretaries, only discuss the items that they bring up. Don't have your own agenda, pushing this program and that program.

I would have liked to discuss Zumwalt with Chafee, but I never had the opportunity, because he never brought it up with me. He muttered a little bit from time to time about closing out naval operations in Rhode Island and a few other things. But it wasn't something that I ever discussed with him, for the reasons that I said. But I never, I never, I never brought up items or had my own agenda with those civilian secretaries because the aides that do are not very successful.

Q: Is it possible that he didn't turn Zumwalt off on the personnel things because he was comfortable with what

Zumwalt was doing?

Admiral Lee: I don't think he was uncomfortable. But I had the feeling that he thought Zumwalt was going a little far in many areas.

Q: What was your own view of the Zumwalt changes?

Admiral Lee: I thought Zumwalt went overboard in many ways.

The one thing that I liked about Zumwalt was his changing of the uniform, which Holloway changed back.* As you know, most of the personnel changes that Zumwalt put into effect disappeared without a trace under the two succeeding CNOs. I felt that those Z-grams took away the authority of the commanding officers.** I thought that Zumwalt almost caused a revolution in the Navy. He caused a lot of discontent among the blacks. He raised

---

*Until Admiral Zumwalt's tenure as CNO, enlisted men below the grade of chief petty officer wore traditional sailor uniforms with jumpers, white hats, and bell-bottom trousers. Zumwalt instituted a uniform essentially similar to a chief petty officer's for all Navy enlisted men. The traditional uniform has since been restored.

**Z-grams were consecutively numbered policy directives from Chief of Naval Operations Zumwalt that attempted to deal with such issues as enlisted rights and privileges, equal opportunity, and Navy families. Junior personnel viewed them much more favorably than did their seniors. See U.S. Naval Institute Proceedings, May 1971, pages 291-298.

expectations which couldn't be fulfilled, because we had to follow our standard promotion system for officers and enlisted men. It had stood the test of time. He alienated an awful lot of senior officers. He booted four-stars out and three-stars out right and left. Good people. So I think Zumwalt went too far in a lot of ways.

The absolute worst thing he did was erode the authority of the commanding officer. And he did that. We had riots on some of our carriers, which had never happened before. I think Zumwalt deserves full credit for those. So I think Zumwalt went much too far in many ways.

Some of the things he did or started I think were good. Changing the uniform I liked, because I had been a sailor myself. How can a first class petty officer with a family of three be dignified wearing that little white hat? So I liked that. I think Army uniforms and Air Force uniforms for first class petty officer pay grades are much better. But I think Zumwalt got carried away, went much too far.

Q: One thing you mentioned when we were having lunch is that you thought that Zumwalt picked good aviators for the four-star slots that he had the opportunity on.

Admiral Lee: Yes, he did. I thought Ralph Cousins was the best. I thought Ralph Cousins should have been the CNO in place of Zumwalt. He would have been a great CNO. Certainly Mickey Weisner was a good man. I've forgotten the other aviator four-star, or others that he picked. But the ones he picked were not cronies, because he didn't have any in aviation. I don't think anybody would fault those picks. They were generally applauded in naval aviation.

Q: Did you have a view on why Jerry Miller wasn't included in that number?

Admiral Lee: Yes. Jerry Miller and Zumwalt had known each other for years. They were aides together along the E-ring.* Zumwalt was aide to Nitze, and Miller was aide to the Vice Chief who was Rivero. I think they became very wary of each other in those years. I think through the years Jerry Miller became very pro-aviation. He had two tours of duty in OP-05 when, in my opinion, he should have branched out a little bit, gone to OP-06 or OP-03.** He became very close to Tom Connolly.

Zumwalt gave Jerry Miller Second Fleet and then Sixth Fleet--and while in Sixth Fleet Jerry put out an order or a message or a notice that there would be an operation shape-

---
*The concentric rings of the Pentagon are numbered from the center out. The most prestigious offices are in the outer E-ring.
**In the mid-1960s, the designations were as follows: OP-05--Deputy Chief of Naval Operations (Air); OP-06--Deputy Chief of Naval Operations (Plans and Policy); OP-03--Deputy Chief of Naval Operations (Fleet Operations and Readiness).

up, or something to that effect. All those men that were unsatisfactory performers in the commanding officers' eyes could be put ashore when they got to Sixth Fleet and, perhaps, sent back to the States. I think that infuriated Zumwalt. It was a challenge to his authority, and his management of the Navy and the ships he was sending over to the Sixth Fleet.

For the time being, Miller was immune to Zumwalt's wrath. But Zumwalt had the final word, because he had the power of promotion, the power of assigning jobs. I think with their complete split when Jerry had Sixth Fleet, Jerry was doomed. But even if that hadn't happened, I really don't believe Zumwalt would ever have promoted Jerry to four stars. It's just the luck of the draw. I think if Cousins had become CNO, Jerry probably would have made four stars. But that's the way the Navy is.

Q: On the other hand, Captain Kidd had been an aide during that same time that Zumwalt was, and he did make four stars. So that if there was an antagonism there, it didn't carry over.

Admiral Lee: Zumwalt was very high on Kidd. He thought Kidd was a "can-do" man. He sent Kidd to Sixth Fleet, and then gave Kidd four stars and brought him back to shape up Naval Material Command. Then Zumwalt and Kidd had a big falling out when Kidd was Chief of Naval Material over a number of items, which I won't go into here. By the time Zumwalt was ready to retire, he and Kidd were barely speaking. Kidd was not Zumwalt's nominee to succeed as CNO. As I understand it, Holloway was.

Q: His real choice was Worth Bagley.

Admiral Lee: I'm sure of that. That wouldn't sell, so he went with Holloway.

Q: You said before that Zumwalt had a way of putting a little twist on things he wanted. What did you mean by that?

Admiral Lee: I don't remember that expression, but Zumwalt is a very complex man. I suppose that's what I meant. My experience was that sometimes the obvious wasn't what Zumwalt had in mind. He was sometimes devious. If he wanted to go from point A to point B, he didn't necessarily go by a direct route. He would sometimes take detours. That's what I meant.

Q: There are a number of people like that.

Admiral Lee: Very complex man.

Lee #8 - 704

Q: You also mentioned before, just briefly in passing, the deliberations that Secretary Chafee went through on the Pueblo case. Do you remember any details on that?

Admiral Lee: No, I don't. I didn't have any role in it. I never discussed it with him. If I heard him discuss it, it was at lunch, or informally. But the legal aspects of it and what he should do and not do, he discussed with his legal counsel. He had a very good one who later made rear admiral. His name was Horace Robertson, and he was a first-rate Navy captain at the time.

Q: Did you think that he came to the conclusion on that that you would have?

Admiral Lee: I think so, I think so. I don't think any useful purpose would have been served by punishing the captain of the Pueblo further.

  I thought Chafee's action put an end to it and I thought that was important. It put that chapter behind us, which was his intention.

Q: You mentioned a name here, Admiral Weisner. What recollections do you have of him?

Admiral Lee: Admiral Weisner came in and relieved Admiral Connolly as OP-05, and I thought he did a fine job. I had known Mickey Weisner off and on over the years, and he went from the OP-05 job to be Vice Chief of Naval Operations and then out to CinCPacFlt. He's a very straightforward guy, very able, very hard-working.

I did have one unusual experience involving Weisner. Admiral Zumwalt wanted to see me one day when I was in OPA. He wanted to know what I thought of Weisner in OP-05, what kind of a job was he doing.

Q: Kind of an odd request, to ask a junior about a senior.

Admiral Lee: Zumwalt was like that. But he wanted to know because, as it later turned out, he was thinking of making Weisner the VCNO. I guess he wanted to know what an independent observer would think. I gave Weisner very high marks for his OP-05 work. Zumwalt thanked me, and away I went. That's the way Zumwalt worked.

Q: You said before the tape started that he was essentially doing a lot of the running of the Navy when he was the executive assistant in SecNav's office.

Admiral Lee: Yes, my impression was that Zumwalt had the confidence of Secretary of the Navy Nitze. Nitze believed that Zumwalt could do no wrong. Zumwalt was very loyal to Nitze and worked very hard. I believe Nitze asked Zumwalt's advice on almost every phase and every decision that he made. I think he wanted to hear what Bud would think about it or say about it. So I think Zumwalt had tremendous influence with Nitze and tremendous influence in the running of the Navy during those Nitze years. Probably more so than any four-striper in the history of the Navy.

Q: A name you mentioned before briefly was Captain Thor Hanson, later a flag officer. What qualities did you admire in him?

Admiral Lee: Thor Hanson relieved Stan Turner as naval aide to the Secretary of the Navy. Hanson was there the rest of the time I was in OPA. Hanson was a very personable man, Naval Academy graduate, Rhodes Scholar, and had worked down in McNamara's systems analysis group for a time. Thor Hanson was very able, very intelligent, very good man, big man, had a fine family. He was married to a Wellesley graduate, as was I. Had five children, and we became very good friends. I'm happy to report that I sat on the selection board in 1973 that picked Thor Hanson to be a rear admiral. Very fine officer.

Q: When we met a few months ago in Suitland, Maryland, to

look at the USS Enterprise logs, you mentioned to me another selection board recollection, and that was when Lando Zech was picked for admiral.* What were the circumstances?

Admiral Lee: He came up in the selection board of 1973. Lando Zech was a submariner and a very good one. Naval Academy graduate. He had a very fine record. Most of us were amazed, when we saw the record, that he had not been selected for admiral earlier, because he had a record such that he should have been selected.

After finishing his command of submarine tour, Lando opted to take command of a cruiser.** With that decision, he apparently was read out of the submarine club. Because in these flag selection boards, the numbers are divided up. So many aviators are picked, so many surface officers are picked; so many submariners are picked. Lando Zech had a submarine designator, and then I came to realize and appreciate why he had not been selected for flag rank. The submariners didn't own him, and I became convinced that the submariners got together beforehand and made a list. If a particular submariner was not on the list, why, they didn't vote for the man. I believe this list was cleared with

---

*Captain Lando W. Zech, Jr., USN.
**Captain Zech was commanding officer of the guided missile light cruiser USS Springfield (CLG-7) from 1968 to 1970. During Zech's command tenure the Springfield served as flagship for Commander Second Fleet.

Rickover beforehand. But, anyway, Lando Zech had not been selected for admiral. He was up for about his last chance.

On this particular board, the 1100 community took Lando Zech in and promoted him as an 1100 rather than an 1120. In other words, gave him an 1100 number. That's how Admiral Zech got promoted to flag rank. He later, of course, was the Chief of Naval Personnel, three stars and, I believe, at present is head of the Nuclear Regulatory Commission. Very good man. Due to the closed nature of the submarine community and, perhaps, to Admiral Rickover's influence, if it had not been for the generosity of the 1100 community that particular year, he would never have made flag rank.

Q: Interesting story.

Did you have any dealings with Harry Train?*

Admiral Lee: Yes, as a matter of fact. I sat on a flag selection board with him one time and knew him through the years. Harry Train wasn't a personal friend, but I knew him to talk to and speak to. He was a Naval Academy class of '49, and I knew a number of his classmates. I always found Harry to be very personable, and I thought he did a good job on the selection board that I sat on with him.

---

*Captain Harry D. Train, USN. Train eventually reached the rank of four-star admiral and served as Commander in Chief Atlantic Fleet.

Good man all around. I didn't know him that well and I never served with him except on a selection board.

Q: Did you have any contact with him when he was with Admiral Moorer?

Admiral Lee: Yes, he was aide to Admiral Moorer, and I had some contact with him then at one time or another as the aides have contact with all flag officers.

I thought Harry did a good job wherever he was. He was very aware politically. A good 1100.

Q: What views do you have about Admiral Moorer himself?

Admiral Lee: I think Admiral Moorer was a great naval officer. As I've said earlier, I thought he could have handled Chafee a little better, maybe for the benefit of the Navy. I saw Admiral Moorer through the years many times. He visited Enterprise with the President. He was CNO when I came back to Washington. He became chairman of the Joint Chiefs when I was out in Omaha. I think he's certainly one of the most able naval officers that I personally knew--very fine man.

I'm a little astonished at his politics since he retired, but I won't comment on those.

Q: When we were talking before about the Grumman contract, you said that Grumman probably could have won the F-14 contract with their initial bid, but then they felt they had to lower it. Why did you have that idea, that they felt they had to lower it?

Admiral Lee: I don't have any firsthand facts on this. When I became Commander Naval Air Systems Command, I was very interested, and I sent to the archives and got the F-14 competition and looked at it.

I had George Spangenberg come in, and I went over the F-14 competition with him. George told me that Grumman would have won without lowering their bid because the competition was based on the R&D contract. Their R&D contract was in line with the other bidder, which happened to be McDonnell Douglas, and that they would have won without lowering their bid. I didn't have any reason to argue with that.

But rumor had it--strictly rumor, I don't have any facts--that Grumman was told that they had to sharpen their pencil in order to win. So they lowered their bid--this is a fact--in the best and final by $370 million dollars. That led to their near bankruptcy. I don't have any reason to disbelieve the rumor that they were told they had to sharpen their pencil.

Q: There must have been some reason for lowering it.

Admiral Lee: They did in fact lower it--that's a fact. That led to the great troubles for the F-14 and for Grumman and the Navy.

Q: You talked before about your role as an aide for Admiral Ruble. What role did an aide play for you when you were a flag officer? In what ways was he useful?

Admiral Lee: I had a number of aides, of course. Wherever I was a flag officer, I had an aide. I found them good company. I discussed everything with them. If they played squash, or badminton, or some other game, I played it with them. I would ask their opinions about things. I enjoyed my aides. I had a good time with them. I tried to be informal with them. I invited them to my place for dinner, and up to our place in Deep Creek Lake. I had some very good aides. We still have contact with some of them, get Christmas cards and the like. I used them for all the things that aides are used for: to write letters, handle social events, run errands, take messages, handle confidential matters. I always took my aides into my confidence 100%, and I was never disappointed.

Q: In this role that you had them as a sounding board, did

you use them to represent the junior officer constituency?

Admiral Lee: Yes, that. I would ask them what they thought of various people and companies. I treated them as mature naval officers. I think they enjoyed that. I had some very nice aides, fine young men.

Q: After you retired, you came here to Logon Farm, and you said before that you deliberately wanted to get away from the Washington environment. I'm wondering if the choice of a farm was sort of recapturing some of the pleasures you'd known growing up.

Admiral Lee: Yes, I suppose so. I like to grow things. I like to grow tomatoes, fruit trees, everything else. I wanted to remove myself from the temptations of Washington. A lot of loose money there. I thought this was a good compromise. I didn't know if we'd like living in the country and having a farm or not. But we thought we'd try it. I think it's worked out very well.

Q: I'd be interested, Admiral, if you could talk a little more about your life here on the farm. You told me some interesting stories in the past about the young man who works for you and the older family who lives in the area.

Admiral Lee: We decided that we wanted to get out of Washington, as I've stated earlier, and that I didn't want to stay around in the Washington area and be a consultant, and be calling on old friends to sell to the Navy. We decided to try buying a farm--not in the hopes of making our fortune farming, but as a way of life. After many months of looking, we bought Logon Farm, which is down in Albemarle County about 17 miles from Charlottesville.

The farm has 153 acres and three houses. We inherited the Snow family. When I bought the farm, Tom Snow was about in his early 60s and lived with two sisters, and had lived on the farm for more than 30 years with the previous owner. His hobby was hogs and with him came nine sows, one boar hog, and about 30 pigs. The Snows were with us for about two and a half years. He then had trouble with his eyesight and had to retire. Mrs. Watson, the previous owner, had given him a small piece of land on the back side of the property. Mrs. Watson's nephew built a house back there, and the Snows moved there.

When Mr. Snow left, I retired the hogs. What we have primarily is a beef cattle operation. I have 153 acres here, and at the moment we're leasing about another 300 acres. This year we have 58 cows which ought to calve. At any given time we have 100 to 150 cattle on the place. And I have a full-time farm manager. That gives us time for travel or visiting our daughters and grandchildren, or whatever. We can work as much or as little as we want around the farm.

In addition, Washington is not far away, about 90 miles, less than two hours. Charlottesville and the University of Virginia is only 20 minutes, 17 miles away, with football games, basketball games, and the cultural activities associated with the university.

So that we have had a very quiet country life here in Albemarle County. As it turns out, there are literally dozens of people just like us, same age, essentially the same circumstances, who have retired to Albemarle County and run a few beef cattle or have horses. We, of course, have them as friends.

That about describes our farming life in Albemarle County. It's been a very happy life, and the years have been rolling by ever more swiftly.

Q: What do you do for intellectual challenge and stimulation?

Admiral Lee: My great hobby all my life has been reading. I've been able to do more reading here than I ever had the time for in the Navy. And, of course, as I say, there are all the events that we would like to attend from concerts to foreign relations seminars in Charlottesville, UVA. We go down there occasionally to hear or see one event or another. And, in addition, as I say, we're not all that far from Washington. So the intellectual stimulation that I've enjoyed above all others has been the reading that I can do here, and the very fine libraries at UVA and in Charlottesville.

Q: You've also told me about a discussion group that you're part of.

Admiral Lee: I joined a Rotary Club in Orange, and after three or four years, I was president of that for a year. Orange is the closest town to us, about 12 miles away. I joined the Rotary Club just to see what a Rotary Club is like and also to meet the county leaders and business leaders. We met once a week, and I found that interesting. Since I left the Rotary Club, I've joined a discussion group. Seven of us meet for about two hours each Thursday, and we solve all the problems of the day. That's been good fun.

Q: What has become of your daughters since they moved off on to their own?

Admiral Lee: All three daughters married, and all three were married here at Logon Farm. We had the wedding reception, the entire works right here.

Daughter number one, Nancy Lee, is married to Randolph H. Perry, also a lawyer. She is a partner in Jones, Day, Reavis and Pogue in Washington, D.C., and practices labor law. Randy is a partner in the law firm of Goddard and West in Fairfax. They have a daughter, Sarah, five, and a son, Christopher, two.

Daughter number two, Barbara, is married to Michael R. Eisenson, a lawyer and MBA who is a partner in Harvard Investment Corporation, which invests Harvard's endowment. Barbara has taught English in high school and has worked for Heath Textbook Company in sales. They have two sons, David, four, and Matthew, two.

Daughter number three, Marion, is an elementary school teacher in Middlebury, Vermont. She is married to a fellow teacher, John N. Leonard, who works primarily with the special education students. They have a daughter, Emily, five, and a son, Matthew, two. Of course, they come down to Logon Farm and see the cows and calves, and ride the horse, and enjoy the countryside at Christmastime and at other times during the year.

So, all in all, our life has been quite a happy one on Logon Farm.

Q: Certainly, the big part of the rearing of those daughters fell to your wife because you were away a lot.

Admiral Lee: At least 95% of it. I give her all the credit for some very fine daughters. They were well trained enough that they picked good husbands, which is very important.

Q: You mentioned very early in this series a man who was down at Miami with you in the enlisted experience, Spence Matthews, and you told me he came back to your life later over the F-18. What was his input on that?

Admiral Lee: Spence Matthews and I were at Miami together in 1941-42 as aviation machinist's mates. We both became aviation cadets in 1942, and both graduated from flight training and have had reasonably successful careers in naval aviation--both having command of aircraft carriers and both being promoted to flag rank.

Spence retired while I was Commander Naval Air Systems Command, and he then went to work for a congressman from Florida.* His congressman, for one reason or another--I think largely because LTV was supplying the A-7 aircraft for Cecil Field, which was in the congressman's district-- this congressman opposed the F-18 program, which was going to put the A-7 out of business. Spence Matthews worked for him. So Spence spent several years trying to kill my

---

*H. Spencer Matthews served as executive assistant for Representative William V. Chappell, Jr., a Democrat from Florida's fourth congressional district.

favorite program, the F-18. Of course, I'd known Spence for close on to 40 years, but, nevertheless, Spence took his boss's position. Although Spence promised me that he was going to kill the F-18, he was not successful, because the F-18 is now in the fleet and doing very well.

Q: You've exhausted my list of catch-up questions. We can go to yours.

Admiral Lee: I have one item I'd like to cover. It's sort of a postscript to the F-18.

I retired on 1 November 1976, and was relieved by a good friend, Forrest Petersen, who was in the nuclear program with me, and had also relieved me as commanding officer of Enterprise. I thought the F-18 program was in good shape and in good hands when I left, because we had signed the contract, and McDonnell Douglas was in process of putting it together.

I went down south on vacation after retiring, back to Alexandria for Christmas. Then my wife and I took a two-month trip out west, automobile trip, planning to take a skiing vacation through the western mountains, and then back East. We arrived back home some time in March, and not long after getting home, I received a telephone call from George Graff, who was vice president of McDonnell

Douglas, the builders of the F-18.*

He asked me if I had been keeping up with the F-18 program. I said no, that I had not. I'd been away and had decided that the F-18 was not my responsibility anymore.

He told me that they thought the F-18 program was in jeopardy, that the Navy was trying to kill the program. I said that I couldn't believe it but that I would look into it. So I then called Forrest Petersen, who was Commander Naval Air Systems Command, and asked him about this. At his suggestion I had lunch with Petersen, and he told me that, yes, indeed, the F-18 program was in trouble.

Petersen was a great backer of the F-18, because he realized the potential for man-hour savings and the maintenance and reliability, and also the potential for having a dual-purpose airplane on limited carrier decks. But Fred Turner was now OP-05, and that Turner was an F-14/A-7 man, and he had put together the budget for the following year, which excluded the F-18.** Holloway and Turner, apparently, had decided that they had a budget squeeze and that something had to go, and that the easiest thing for them to do would be to kill the F-18 program.

I couldn't believe it, but that was what I heard. I also sounded out some other sources, and was told that, yes, indeed, that was in the works.

---
*George S. Graff.
**Vice Admiral Frederick C. Turner, USN, was Deputy Chief of Naval Operations (Air Warfare), from 6 October 1976 to 30 June 1979.

Q: Were you doing this on behalf of McDonnell Douglas or just for your own edification?

Admiral Lee: I was doing this for my own edification at this particular time. I couldn't believe what I was hearing.

After I'd learned that the F-18 program really was in jeopardy, I called George Graff back and described it to him. He then invited me to come out to St. Louis and consult with them on the F-18 program to see what we could do.

I flew to St. Louis and went through their presentations, and they asked my advice on how to salvage the F-18 program. They asked me, also, about becoming a consultant to McDonnell Douglas, which I did to see if we couldn't get the F-18 program through this problem period. My advice to them was that there really wasn't much that could be done in the Navy itself, because Forrest Petersen was all for the F-18 program, but that Fred Turner and, presumably, Holloway were trying to kill the program.

Q: You said before that Holloway was not enthusiastic for it.

Admiral Lee: Yes. Holloway, I don't think, was ever enthusiastic for the F-18, but because Clements and his bosses were for it, why, Holloway did not oppose it. Holloway being a political realist.

I advised McDonnell Douglas that I believed that it would be very difficult, even for Holloway, to kill the F-18 program because it had lots of friends at OSD, and it had lots of friends among the staffers and in the Congress. I suggested that they should put 90% of their effort on informing people at OSD who worked for the F-18 program what was going on, and informing their friends in Congress as to the danger the F-18 program was in. As it turned out, there was a big debate over the F-18 program that year, but the OSD crowd supported the F-18 program. The members of Congress who had a vote on it supported the F-18 program, so that even though Fred Turner, OP-05, and Holloway made a run on the F-18 program, it survived.

After surviving that additional year, it was almost impossible to stop it after that.

That is the appendage I wanted to make to the F-18 program that I have earlier commented on.

Q: Admiral, the first seven interviews constitute an outstanding oral history, and I think what we've done today is gild the lily. It's even better, so I thank you for the first seven, and thank you even more for adding this eighth one.

Admiral Lee: Well, thank you. It's been my pleasure.

Index to

Reminiscences of

Vice Admiral Kent L. Lee, USN (Ret.)

Volume II

A4D/A-4 Skyhawk
   Difficulty replacing the engine, 548, 602; foreign sales, 607; pilot A. B. Price killed himself in an A4D accident in the 1950s, 654; planned use for strikes on Cuba in 1962, 679; used for close air support during the Vietnam War, 689

A-5 Vigilante
   Vigilante squadron replaced by Skyhawks for deployment to Cuba in 1962, 679

A-6 Intruder
   Night operations during the Vietnam War, 415-416; improved survivability of A-6 missions from the Enterprise (CVAN-65) during her 1969 deployment to Vietnam, 475

A-7 Corsair II
   The Enterprise (CVAN-65) underwent modifications in the summer of 1968 to facilitate changing from the A-4 to the A-7, 452; Lee's assessment of this plane, 476, 554; difficulty replacing an engine, 548-549, 602; used for close air support during the Vietnam War, 689

AD Skyraider
   Second generation bomber designed to be flown without a rear seat gunner, 631; in Korean War, 650, 654-655, 657, 659-600

AV-8 Harrier
   This British-built vertical or short takeoff and landing aircraft is the only really successful plane of this type developed, 613-614; Lee's experience as a passenger and a pilot in this plane, 615-616

Aerial Reconnaissance
   See Reconnaissance

Aides
   Lee's relationship with his aides while serving as a flag officer in the 1970s, 711-712

Aircraft Carriers
   Lee commanded the nuclear-powered Enterprise (CVAN-65) from 1967 to 1969, during two Vietnam War deployments, the Pueblo (AGER-2) incident, a port visit to Japan, and a major flight deck fire, 371-495, 687-691; Lee had his first experience at sea in riding the escort carrier Midway (CVE-63) to Hawaii in 1944, 626; Lee enjoyed his service in the Philippine Sea (CV-47) during a Korean War cruise in 1951, 653; the Intrepid (CVA-11) had a good deployment to the Mediterranean in 1959, 666-672; the Enterprise first deployed in 1962 and then planned for a possible Cuban intervention, 672-683

Air Force, U.S.
Secretary of Defense Robert McNamara decreed in the mid-1960s that the Air Force and the Navy should both use the F-111, 358-360; relations improved considerably between Air Force and Navy members of the Joint Strategic Target Planning Staff in the early 1970s, 528-533; Congress ordered the Navy to choose one of two Air Force lightweight fighters under development in the mid-1970s, as a supplement to the Navy's F-14, 555-558; feasibility of making planes suitable for Navy and Air Force use, 561-562; hasn't had much luck with missiles despite the great expense invested, 591-592; called for too many weapons in strategic planning, 641

Air Group Six
Lee's duties as commander in the early 1960s, 672-677; planning for Cuban strikes in 1962, 677-683

Alamo, USS (LSD-33)
Ship handling characteristics, 392-393

Alcohol
Cocktails and wine were served in the flag mess of the Enterprise (CVAN-65) when President Lyndon Johnson visited the ship in November 1967, 385

Alvis, Rear Admiral John H., USN (USNA, 1949)
As executive officer in the Enterprise (CVAN-65) in the late 1960s, 433-434; Lee brought Alvis to the Naval Air Systems Command in the mid-1970s, where he served as program manager for the F-14; advised Lee of some irregularities concerning the Iranian liaison officer overseeing the purchase of F-14s, 609

Atomic Bombs
See Nuclear Weapons

Attack Squadron 46
Deployment to the Mediterranean in the USS Intrepid (CVA-11) in 1959, 669-672

Attack Squadron 115
Lee's duties as operations officer in the early 1950s, 653-656; safety record during the Korean War, 656, 658; operations during the Korean War, 649, 656-660

Ault, Captain Frank W., USN (USNA, 1943)
Effective operationally as chief of staff to Commander Carrier Division One in 1968, 407-408, 472, 479-480

Aviation Maintenance
Frequent maintenance needs on board the Enterprise (CVAN-65) during a Vietnam deployment in 1969, 476-477; Lee was not able to do anything to improve airplane maintainability or dependability while serving in Naval Air Systems Command in 1969-70 because this wasn't a

priority with his boss, 498, 545; civilian companies were charging substantially more to do overhauls on helicopters than Navy rework facilities in the late 1960s-early 1970s, 499-502; Lee made maintainability and reliability his top priority as Commander Naval Air Systems Command in 1973-74, 538, 545-549, 601-603; Lee worked as an enlisted mechanic in 1941-42, 621-626; baseball stitch used to repair fabric wings, 625-626

Badoeng Strait, USS (CVE-116)
Lee's recollections of duty as staff watch officer in this carrier during the Korean War, 634-636

Bagley, Rear Admiral Worth H., USN (USNA, 1947)
As director of the General Planning and Programming Division in the CNO's office in the early 1970s, coordinated with Lee to make sure upcoming programs would meet with the Secretary of the Navy's approval, 516-517; CNO Admiral Elmo Zumwalt's choice for his successor in 1974, 703

Baird, Charles
Under Secretary of the Navy Baird fired Commander Carrier Division Five, Rear Admiral Roger Mehle, in the fall of 1967, 373

Baldwin, Rear Admiral Robert B., USN (USNA, 1945)
As director of the Aviation Programs Division in the late 1960s-early 1970s, ordered Lee to make sure a certain company got some Navy business, even though the firm had lost out in bidding, 502-503

Baldwin, Robert H. B.
Navy Under Secretary gave Lee a luncheon in 1967, just before he was detached to command the Enterprise (CVAN-65), 363-364

Bardshar, Rear Admiral Frederick A., USN (USNA, 1938)
As Commander Carrier Division Seven in 1967, consulted on visit by Vice President Hubert Humphrey, 381; selected to head inquiry into a fire on board the Enterprise (CVAN-65) on 14 January 1969, 460-461, 478; assessed by Lee, 478, 482

Boeing Company
Lost contract to overhaul H-46 helicopters in the late 1960s-early 1970s because it was charging too much, 499-502

Bombing
A-6 attacks against North Vietnam in 1968, 415-416; A-6 and A-7 attacks against North Vietnam in 1969, 475-476; VA-115 attacks on North Korea in 1951, 656-660

Bombs
> Purchase of 250-pound bombs in the early 1970s used as an example of the illogical conclusions of systems analysis, 511-512; Lee attended a nuclear weapons employment course in the summer of 1953, 660-664

Bowsher, Charles A.
> As Assistant Secretary of the Navy in the early 1970s, sent with Lee to Grumman to check on the quality of the F-14 program, 513-514, 518

Bureau of Naval Personnel
> Vice Admiral Hyman Rickover tried unsuccessfully in the early 1970s to keep a junior officer from leaving the service early, 508-509

Bureau of Naval Weapons (BuWeps)
> Having been consolidated into BuWeps in 1959, Lee thought it was a mistake to separate the aeronautics and ordnance functions into their own systems commands in the mid-1960s, 355-358

Bureau of Ordnance
> Affected by various reorganizations, dissolved in 1959, and eventually reinstated briefly as Naval Ordnance Systems Command, 355-358

Bureau System
> In the mid-1960s, the Navy's research laboratories were separated from a direct working relationship with the material bureaus they supported, 352-354; as Secretary of Defense in the 1960s, Robert McNamara sought to abolish the various Navy bureaus and to assume the authority of the bureau chiefs, 354-355; realignment of bureau system in 1950s and 1960s, 355-358

Cagle, Rear Admiral Malcolm W., USN (USNA, 1941)
> Not a very good operational commander while running a carrier division in the late 1960s, 482

Carr, Commander Charles H., USN (USNA, 1941)
> As the commanding officer of Attack Squadron 115 in the early 1950s, supported operations officer Lee in the idea that some targets were not worth risking an aircraft, 654, 657

Carrier Air Group Six
> See Air Group Six

Carrier Division One
> Assistance given to the _Enterprise_ (CVAN-65) by the carrier division staff in the late 1960s, 480-482

Carrier Division 15
> Lee's watch-standing duties while serving on this staff during the early days of the Korean War, 634-636

Carrier Division 17
  Lee was in on the ground floor of setting up this division in San Diego in early 1951, 646-647

Central Intelligence Agency
  Lee was not very impressed by the CIA's Soviet surveillance capabilities in the early 1970s, 532

Chafee, John H.
  As Secretary of the Navy, interviewed Lee to be director of the Office of Program Appraisal in 1970, 504-505; Lee's assessment of Chafee, 505, 518-521; choice of Admiral Elmo Zumwalt as Chief of Naval Operations in 1970, 506-508, 695-696; relations with CNO Admiral Thomas Moorer, 507-508, 519, 696, 709; relationship with Vice Admiral Hyman Rickover, 508-509, 519; concerned about the possibility of Grumman going bankrupt in the early 1970s, 512-515, 518; criticized for not controlling CNO Zumwalt, 520-521, 697-699; Lee's relationship with Chafee, 521-522; recommended Lee for promotion to three stars and deputy director position with the Joint Strategic Target Planning Staff in 1972, 524-525; chose not to prosecute any Pueblo (AGER-2) crew members after their release in 1968, 704

Chaplains
  Lee's favorable assessment of the chaplains in the Enterprise (CVAN-65) in the late 1960s, 439-440

Chapman, Captain Leonard F., III, USMC
  Served as underway officer of the deck on board the carrier Enterprise (CVAN-65) in 1968 in addition to commanding the ship's Marine detachment, 427-428

China Lake, California
  See Naval Ordnance Test Station, China Lake

Clements, William P., Jr.
  As Deputy Secretary of Defense in the mid-1970s, allowed the Navy to put out bids on a dual-purpose aircraft, but Congress ordered the Navy to join forces with an Air Force project, 555-557, 564-565; changed the designation of F-17 to F-18, 560; role in selecting the CNO in the mid-1970s, 584-585

Communications
  Setup on board the carrier Enterprise (CVAN-65) in November 1967 when President Lyndon Johnson visited the ship, 389; President Johnson called Lee on board the Enterprise following the seizure of the USS Pueblo (AGER-2) in January 1968, 411-412; overall communication setup in the Enterprise in the late 1960s, 690

Congress
  As Commander Naval Air Systems Command in 1973-74, Lee testified before Congress to justify Navy loans to the Grumman Corporation, only to find out that he had been deceived by Grumman, 550-553, 565; ordered the Navy to join forces with an Air Force fighter project under development in the mid-1970s, 555-556, 558-559, 564-565; as head of the NASC, Lee testified before committees regarding budget matters, 566; New Jersey congressman put Lee on the spot in the mid-1970s to explain the move to stop building at Lakehurst Naval Air Engineer Center, 573-575; political pressures on military procurements, 610-611; support for the F-18 program, 717-718, 721

Connolly, Vice Admiral Thomas F., USN (USNA, 1933)
  As Deputy Chief of Naval Operations (Air) in the mid-1960s, role in fighting the F-111 project, 359-360; involved in an order to Lee to award a contract to other than the lowest bidder, 502-503; chastised Lee for giving his opinion of the F-14 to the Secretary of the Navy in the early 1970s, 514-515, 517-518; tried to run Naval Air Systems Command along with his own responsibilities, 598, 694; after retirement, Connolly tried to influence Lee on behalf of his defense contractor employer, but Lee cut him off, 693-695

Cousins, Admiral Ralph W., USN (USNA, 1937)
  As Commander Carrier Division Five in 1967, proved to be talented and low-key operator, 373-374; as Vice Chief of Naval Operations in the early 1970s, 527, 700-701

Cuba
  As Commander Air Group Six in the Enterprise (CVAN-65) in 1962, Lee received detailed photographs of Cuba for use in planning strikes, 677-683

Damage Control
  Difficulties in a carrier, 379-380; during the Enterprise (CVAN-65) fire in January 1969, 380, 456-460, 464-467

Davies, Rear Admiral Thomas D., USN (USNA, 1937)
  As Deputy Chief of Naval Material for Development in the early 1970s, sponsored the thrust-augmented wing airplane concept that was never developed, 612-613

Defense Intelligence Agency
  Lee was impressed by the thoroughness and quality of Soviet surveillance by the DIA in the early 1970s, 531-532

De Poix, Captain Vincent P., USN (USNA, 1939)
  Characterized as a martinet as commanding officer of the Enterprise (CVAN-65) in the early 1960s, 673

Deputy Chief of Naval Operations (Air Warfare)
    Vice Admiral Thomas F. Connolly's operation of OP-05 in the late 1960s and early 1970s, 359-360, 502-503, 514-515, 517-518, 564-565, 598, 694; differences of opinion with Naval Air Systems Command in the early 1970s over the development of the F/A-18, 564-565; good relationship with Naval Air Systems Command when Vice Admiral Forrest Petersen was OP-05 in the mid-1970s, 598-599; Vice Admiral Frederick C. Turner did not support the F-18 program while serving as OP-05 in the mid-1970s, 719-721

DiBona, Charles J. (USNA, 1956)
    Conducted studies for CNO Admiral Elmo Zumwalt in the early 1970s, 511

Dietrich, Captain Henry T., USN (USNA, 1926)
    As chief of staff to Commander Carrier Division 15 in the early 1950s, relationship with his boss, Rear Admiral Richard Ruble, 646-647

Discipline
    Lee's handling of discipline in the Enterprise (CVAN-65) in the late 1960s, 435-438

Dittmar, William
    Civilian chief assistant in the Naval Air Systems Command in the mid-1970s feuded with an admiral in that organization over a woman, 595-596

Dosé, Commander Robert G., USN
    Discussion of what made him such an outstanding pilot in the 1950s, 665-666

Doyle, Captain James H., Jr., USN (USNA, 1947)
    As commanding officer of the Bainbridge (DLGN-25), invited Lee to accompany him to Singapore in the summer of 1967, 372

Drug Abuse
    Lee didn't consider drugs a problem among the crew of the Enterprise (CVAN-65) in the late 1960s, 440-441

E-2C Hawkeye
    Lee's assessment of this plane from the mid-1970s, 605

EC-121 Warning Star
    The Enterprise (CVAN-65) was sent to the Sea of Japan as a show of force in April 1969 after the North Koreans shot down an EC-121, 474

Electronic Countermeasures (ECM)
    There weren't enough ECM planes available in the late 1960s during the Vietnam War to combat North Vietnam's effective use of surface-to-air missiles, 417; handled by the Electronic Systems Command in the mid-1970s, 603-604

Engen, Lieutenant Commander Donald D., USN
  Discussion of what made him such an outstanding pilot, 665-666

Engineering Duty Officers
  Aeronautical engineering duty officers (AEDO) were not given the opportunity to head the Naval Air Systems Command (NASC) in the 1970s, 541-543; value of AEDOs to the NASC, 542-543

Engineering Plants
  Value of nuclear power training for Lee in understanding the engineering plants of the two ships he commanded in the 1960s, 368; characteristics of the plant in the Enterprise (CVAN-65), 393; difficulty with high chlorine count in Enterprise reactor in January 1969, 453-454, 492-494

Enterprise, USS (CVAN-65)
  Lee took refresher nuclear training prior to assuming command in 1967, 361, 364, 368; Lee spent an indoctrination period on board in mid-1967 before taking command of the ship, 371-372, 375-376; went to Hunters Point Naval Shipyard for modifications and repair work in the summer of 1967, 376-377; refresher training off San Diego, 378-379; visited by Vice President Hubert Humphrey in October 1967, 380-383; President Lyndon Johnson's visit in November 1967, 383-392; ship handling characteristics, 392-393; air operations during the Vietnam War, 394, 415-422, 429-431; conducted covert speed test on a trailing Soviet submarine in 1967, 395-397; visit to Japan in early 1968, 398-406, 686-687; weathered a typhoon on the way to Japan, 400-402; picked up distress signal from the Pueblo (AGER-2) on 23 January 1968, 407-411; liberty for the crew in Hong Kong and the Philippines, 419, 422, 435; underway replenishments during the Vietnam War, 423-426; Lee instituted a program to train junior officers to be OODs, 426-429; discipline, 435-438; chaplains, 339-340; had a full-time public affairs officer, 442-446; kept sizable nuclear arsenal on board in the late 1960s, 448-449; carried dependents and cars from Alameda to Bremerton in July 1968, 450-452; dry docked at Bremerton, 452-453; minor trouble with high chlorine count in a steam generator, 453-454, 492-494; explosion and fire on board on 14 January 1969, 455-460, 462-467; inquest into fire, 461-464; fire repairs, 468; went around briefly off Ford Island in Pearl Harbor in early 1969, 468-471; sent to the Sea of Japan in April 1969 after the North Koreans shot down a reconnaissance plane, 474; relations between Lee and the carrier division staff, 479-482; relations between Lee and the air wing and squadron commanders, 482-485; Lee instituted a monthly newsletter, 488-489; Lee felt two wartime tours in command was too much, 490-492; captain's quarters,

494-495; first deployment in 1962 and planning for possible Cuban intervention, 672-683; gathered intelligence photos on Vietnam, 687-688; communications facilities, 690; radars, 690-691

Epes, Rear Admiral Horace H., USN
Qualities while serving as Commander Carrier Division One in early 1968, 407, 479; handling of the distress signal from the Pueblo (AGER-2) on 23 January 1968, 407-410; apprised after the fact of President Lyndon Johnson's call to Lee in the Sea of Japan to change the direction of the Enterprise (CVAN-65) in the wake of the Pueblo capture, 412-413

Erly, Captain Robert B., USN (USNA, 1937)
Lee's recollections of Erly as an instructor at the General Line School around 1950 and as chief of staff to Commander Amphibious Force Pacific Fleet in the mid-1960s, 632-634

Essex (CV-9)-class Carriers
Lee's favorable assessment of these World War II-era carriers, 652

F-4 Phantom II
Two F-4s were on standby on the deck of the Enterprise (CVAN-65) in January 1968 when the USS Pueblo (AGER-2) was seized, 408, 410; the accidental lighting of a rocket attached to an F-4 on the deck of the Enterprise started a terrible explosion and fire on 14 January 1969, 455-460, 462-463

F4U Corsair
Flown by Marine squadrons during the September 1950 Inchon landings, 636-638; operations during the Korean War, 649-650, 659; F4U-5Ns flew night missions during the Korean War, 649; Lee's assessment of this plane, 650-651

F6F Hellcat
Landing and overall characteristics, 628-630, 650-652

F-14 Tomcat
Discussion of its engine and overall quality, 514, 517-518, 554-555, 577; contract restructured in the early 1970s, 539-540, 549-550; difficulty replacing an engine, 548-549, 602; in the mid-1970s, the Navy was pushed to find an alternative to this plane by Congress and the Secretary of Defense, 555-556; sale of F-14s to Iran in the mid-1970s, 575-576, 580, 606-609

F-15 Eagle
This plane was considered as a replacement for the F-14 in the 1970s, 562

F-16
  Lee visited the Northrop facility building this plane in the early 1970s, 531, 554; this was one of two aircraft under development by the Air Force that the Navy was told to consider in the mid-1970s, 555-559; the Air Force chose this plane, 558

F-17
  Lee visited the Northrop facility building this plane in the early 1970s, 531, 554; this was one of two aircraft under development by the Air Force that the Navy was told to accept in the mid-1970s, 555-559; renamed the F-18 by Deputy Defense Secretary William Clements, 560

F-86 Fury
  An example of a plane that was made suitable for both Air Force and Navy use during the Korean War, 561

F-111
  Secretary of Defense Robert McNamara decreed in the mid-1960s that the Navy and Air Force would use this plane, 358-360, 562, 684-685; discussion of its engine, 517-518

F/A-18 Hornet
  Background to the development of this dual-purpose fighter in the early 1970s, 531, 553-560, 563-565, 601; built with an eye toward maintainability, 548-549, 601-603; Lee's evaluation of this plane, 560, 617-618; foreign sales, 607; Florida congressman tried to kill the F-18 program, 717-718; this program was in some danger of being dropped after Lee retired in 1976, 718-721

Families of Servicemen
  Seven hundred dependents of USS Enterprise (CVAN-65) crew members rode the ship from Alameda to Bremerton in the summer of 1968, 450-452; Lee was able to spend little time with his family during his many deployments, 496, 717

Feightner, Commander Edward L., USN
  Discussion of what made him such an outstanding aviator, 665-666

Fires
  Explosion and fire in the Enterprise (CVAN-65) on 14 January 1969, 455-460, 462-467; insufficient equipment was available to fight the Enterprise fire, 458-460, 465-467

FJ Fury
  Example of aircraft that was modified for both Air Force and Navy use, 561

Foreign Military Sales
  Sale of aircraft and missiles to Israel in the fall of 1973, 565, 606; sale of F-14s to Iran in the mid-1970s, 575-576, 580, 606-609; Lee's thoughts on this practice, 607-608

Foxgrover, Rear Admiral James H., USN
  Impressed by Foxgrover's file while sitting on a selection board, Lee brought him to the Naval Air Systems Command in the mid-1970s, 541

Frosch, Dr. Robert A.
  Assistant Secretary of the Navy Frosch was the point man on the F-111 issue in the mid-1960s, 684-685

Gasch, Welko
  As engineer on the scientific advisory group to the Joint Strategic Target Planning Staff in the early 1970s, discussed ideal Navy plane with Lee, 531

General Dynamics
  This company's F-16 competed with Northrop's F-17 for contracts with both the Air Force and the Navy in the mid-1970s, 557-560

General Line School
  Lee's recollections of instructor Commander Robert Erly in the late 1940s, 632-633; value of training to Lee's watch-standing duties during the Korean War, 635

Goldwater, Barry M.
  Senator Goldwater was incensed to learn in the mid-1970s that the Grumman Corporation was making a sizable profit on money borrowed at low interest from the Navy, 552

Graff, George S.
  As vice president of McDonnell Douglas in the mid-1970s, contacted Lee, who had recently retired from the Navy, when the F-18 program appeared to be in trouble, 718-721

Gray, Commander Paul N., USN (USNA, 1941)
  As a squadron commander during the Korean War, went after targets regardless of the cost, 657

Grumman Corporation
  The Navy's concerns that Grumman would go bankrupt in the middle of the F-14 program after lowering its bid in the early 1970s, 512-515, 710-711; F-14 contract restructured and Navy project manager replaced, 539-540, 549-550; made money off a loan from the Navy by buying high-interest overnight stocks, 550-553; angered the Shah of Iran during a transaction to sell F-14s by using an agent, 575-576, 580, 608-609; Grumman filed a claim against the Navy in regards to the F-14, which the Navy counter-claimed, 577-579; fought the F-18 because it took business away from them, 617

"Gun Club"
   Lee sees the various reorganizations of the Bureau of Ordnance and the Naval Ordnance Systems Command as the death of the elitist attitude so prevalent prior to World War II, 358

H-2 Seasprite
   In the late 1960s-early 1970s, Lee looked into the costs for overhauling these Kaman helicopters, 499-502

H-46 Sea Knight
   Lee looked into the costs for overhauling these Boeing helicopters in the late 1960s-early 1970s, 499-500

Hanson, Captain Carl T., USN (USNA, 1950)
   As aide to Secretary of the Navy John Chafee in 1972, was able to tell Lee how he was selected to go back to Omaha for duty with the Joint Strategic Target Planning Staff, 524; assessed by Lee, 706

Harnish, Commander William Max, USN (USNA, 1943)
   In competition with Lee to be commanding officer of the Enterprise (CVAN-65) in 1967, 361-363; characterized as a martinet as executive officer of the Enterprise in the early 1960s, 673

Harpoon
   Difficulties with this missile program in the mid-1970s, 592-594

Hawaii
   Lee's recollections of Oahu from 1944, 627-628

Hayward, Rear Admiral John T., USN (USNA, 1930)
   Characterized as a political admiral as Commander Carrier Division Two in the early 1960s, 674

Helicopters
   Lee brought down the price for overhauling H-2 and H-46 helicopters while serving in the Naval Air Systems Command in the early 1970s, 499-502; Lee and Rear Admiral Richard Ruble explored atomic bomb site at Nagasaki by helicopter in 1950, 638-639

Holloway, General Bruce K., USAF (USMA, 1937)
   As commander of the Strategic Air Command in the early 1970s, unconcerned with Navy charges that the SAC dominated the Joint Strategic Target Planning Staff, 528-529, 533

Holloway, Admiral James L., III, USN (USNA, 1943)
   Lee's relationship with Holloway when both were captains in the Enterprise (CVAN-65) in the summer of 1967, 375-376; as CNO in the mid-1970s, supported the F-14 program over the F-18, 564, 719-721; background to selection as

CNO, 583-585; backed V/STOL aircraft as a candidate for CNO, 584, 611, 614; Lee told Holloway that he wanted to retire in 1976, 586-587; Lee thinks Holloway should have let stand his predecessor's uniform changes for enlisted personnel, 699

Hong Kong
Allowed the Enterprise (CVAN-65) in for a liberty visit in 1968, 419, 435

Houser, Vice Admiral William D., USN (USNA, 1942)
As Deputy Chief of Naval Operations (Air Warfare) in the mid-1970s, opposed the F-18 program in favor of buying more F-14s and A-7s, 564, 597-599

Humphrey, Vice President Hubert H.
Visited the Enterprise (CVAN-65) off California in October 1967, 380-383

Hunters Point Naval Shipyard, San Francisco, California
The Enterprise (CVAN-65) went to this shipyard for seven weeks of modifications and repair work in the summer of 1967, 376-377

Hyland, Vice Admiral John J., Jr., USN (USNA, 1934)
As Commander Seventh Fleet, invited Lee to accompany him to various parts of Vietnam during the summer of 1967, 371-372

Ill, Charles L., III
As Assistant Secretary of the Navy (Installations and Logistics) in the early 1970s, had Lee transferred to Washington to become Naval Air Systems Command, 522, 538

Inchon, South Korea
Lee's recollections of the September 1950 Inchon landings from his vantage point as a carrier division staff officer on board the Badoeng Strait (CVE-116), 635-638

Intelligence
The Enterprise (CVAN-65) conducted a covert test in 1967 to determine how fast a Soviet submarine that was following her could go, 395-397; quality of intelligence available during the Vietnam War, 489-490; quality of results provided by various U.S. intelligence organizations in the early 1970s, 532; excellent intelligence provided to Carrier Air Group Six during the 1962 Cuban Missile Crisis, 677-683; Enterprise planes gathered intelligence photos during the Vietnam War, 687-688

Intrepid, USS (CVA-11)
Remembered as a good ship with great morale in the late 1950s, 670

Investigations
   A board of inquiry followed the January 1969 flight deck fire on board the carrier Enterprise (CVAN-65), 461-464

Iran
   Unhappy with purchase of F-14s from Grumman in the mid-1970s because Grumman used an agent, 575-576, 580, 606-609

Israel
   The United States sent aircraft and missiles to Israel in the fall of 1973 during the Yom Kippur War, 565

Jackson, Henry M. (Democrat-Washington)
   This Washington senator entered into the Congressional Record, at Vice Admiral Hyman Rickover's urging, a favorable article about Lee and the Enterprise (CVAN-65) in mid-1968, 445

James, Commander Jack M., USN (USNA, 1942)
   Did an excellent job as air group commander in the Intrepid (CVA-11) in the late 1950s, 668-669

Japan
   The Enterprise (CVAN-65) visited Sasebo in January 1968, 398-406; protesters during the Enterprise's visit, 402-405, 686-687

Jessen, Rear Admiral George E., USN (USNA, 1950)
   Brought to Washington in the mid-1960s to help fight the F-111 project, 359, 684-685; Lee feels this aeronautical engineering duty officer should have been made Commander Naval Air Systems Command, but the job always went to line officers, 542-543

Johnson, U. Alexis
   As U.S. ambassador to Japan, flew out to brief the Enterprise (CVAN-65) crew prior to the carrier's visit to Sasebo in January 1968, 399-400, 686

Johnson, President Lyndon B.
   Visited the Enterprise (CVAN-65) in November 1967, 383-392; Lee's assessment of the President, 386-388; called Lee in the Sea of Japan to change the Enterprise's direction after the capture of the Pueblo (AGER-2) in January 1968, 411-412

Joint Strategic Target Planning Staff (JSTPS)
   Lee made it his mission in 1972-73 to mediate Strategic Air Command domination of the JSTPS with increased Navy participation, 528-530, 533; scientific advisory group, 531-532

Kaman, Charles H.
  As chairman of the Kaman Corporation in the late 1960s-early 1970s, personally contacted Lee to plead for continued business overhauling H-2 helicopters, 500-502

Kaman Corporation
  Fought unsuccessfully to keep the contract to overhaul H-2 helicopters in the late 1960s-early 1970s, 499-502

Kane, Captain Joseph L., USN (USNA, 1923)
  Served as Commander Carrier Division 17 when it was established in early 1951, 646, 648

Kelln, Commander Albert L., USN (USNA, 1952)
  Dealings with Vice Admiral Hyman Rickover during the sea trials of Kelln's submarine, the Ray (SSN-653), in early 1967, 367

Kellogg, Commander Edward S., USN (USNA, 1954)
  As reactor officer in the Enterprise (CVAN-65) in January 1969, advised Lee of problem with high chlorine count in a nuclear reactor, 453-454, 492-494

Kidd, Admiral Isaac C., Jr., USN (USNA, 1942)
  As Chief of Naval Material in 1973, relationship with Rear Admiral Thomas McClellan, 539; assessed by Lee as overbearing and harsh, 544, 581-583; candidate to be CNO in the mid-1970s, 583-584; relationship with Admiral Elmo Zumwalt, 702-703

Korea, North
  The Enterprise (CVAN-65) steamed off Wonsan in the aftermath of the North Korean capture of the Pueblo (AGER-2) in January 1968, 410-411; the Enterprise steamed off the Korean coast after the North Koreans shot down a EC-121 in April 1969, 474; VA-115 attacks on North Korea in 1951, 656-660

Korea, South
  Lee's recollections of the September 1950 Inchon landings from his vantage point as a carrier division staff officer on board the Badoeng Strait (CVE-116), 635-638

Korean War
  Lee's recollections of standing watch in the Badoeng Strait (CVE-116) during the early days of the war, 634-636; the landings at Inchon in September 1950, 635-638; air operations, 636-638, 649-650, 653-660

Laboratories
  In the mid-1960s, the Navy's research laboratories were separated from a direct working relationship with the material bureaus they supported, 352-354

Lakehurst (New Jersey) Naval Air Engineer Center
When a committee set up by Commander Naval Air Systems Command Lee decided in the mid-1970s that the facilities at Lakehurst should be scaled down, a Congressman put Lee on the spot to explain that decision, 572-575

Leadership
Lee perceives the executive officer billet as the hardest job in the Navy, 432-433; Lee's leadership tools as commanding officer of the Enterprise (CVAN-65) in the late 1960s, 486-489; Lee patterned his style after the commanding officer of his first squadron, 655, 667; CNO Admiral Elmo Zumwalt faulted for eroding the authority of the commanding officer, 700

Lee, Vice Admiral Kent L., USN
Family, 495-496, 713, 715-717; aircraft machinist at Miami Naval Air Station, 1941-43, 620; pilot with Bombing Squadron 15 in 1944, 631-632; commanding officer, Attack Squadron 46, 483; student, General Line School, 1949-50, 632-633; operations officer, Attack Squadron 115, 1950-51, 648-660; commanding officer, Attack Squadron 46, 1958-59, 668-672; commanding officer, USS Alamo (LSD-33), 426-427, 488, 633-634; staff, Carrier Division 15, 1950-51, 634; commanding officer, Carrier Air Group Six, 1962-63, 672-684; executive assistant to the Assistant Secretary of the Navy (Research and Development), 1965-67, 352-360, 684-685; commanding officer, USS Enterprise (CVAN-65), 1967-69, 361-496, 686-692; assistant commander for logistics and fleet support, Naval Air Systems Command, 1969-70, 497-505; director of the Office of Program Appraisal, 1970-72, 504-527; deputy director, Joint Strategic Target Planning Staff, 1972-73, 524-533; Commander Naval Air Systems Command, 1973-76, 538-587, 589-618; retirement as a gentleman farmer in Albemarle County, Virginia, since 1976, 588-589, 712-715; consultant to McDonnell Douglas after retirement, 718-721

Leighton, David T. (USNA, 1946)
Visited the Enterprise (CVAN-65) with his boss, Vice Admiral Hyman Rickover, at Bremerton in 1968, 452; inspected the Enterprise after a minor incident with a steam generator in January 1969, 493

Liberty
For the Enterprise (CVAN-65) crew during a visit to Japan in early 1968, 403-406; the Enterprise used the Philippines and Hong Kong for liberty in 1968 during a Vietnam deployment, 419, 422, 435; opportunities for Navy men in Hawaii in 1944, 627-628

Linder, Commander Isham W., USN (USNA, 1947)
Talented executive officer in the Enterprise (CVAN-65) in 1967, 377-378, 433-434

Ling Temco Vought (LTV)
   Filed protest with the General Accounting Office in the mid-1970s after a fighter plane they were developing along with General Dynamics was rejected by the Navy, 557, 559

Locke, Captain Walter M., USN (USNA, 1952)
   Outstanding as program manager of the Harpoon missile project in the mid-1970s, 593

Logistics
   The carrier Enterprise (CVAN-65) frequently replenished at night during the Vietnam War, 423-426

Los Angeles (SSN-688)-class Submarines
   Vice Admiral Hyman Rickover used information gained on the potential speed of Soviet submarines as justification for funding this class of subs in the late 1960s, 395-397

Maintenance
   See Aviation Maintenance

Maintenance and Material Management (3M)
   Lee feels this computerized report was underutilized in improving maintainability and reliability of aircraft in the mid-1970s, 545-547, 600-601

Marine Corps, U.S.
   The head of the Marine detachment in the Enterprise (CVAN-65) in 1968 became one of the carrier's best officers of the deck, 427-428; discussion of the Enterprise's Marines, 446-448; Marine air squadrons participated in the September 1950 Inchon landings, 636-638

Martell, Vice Admiral Charles B., USN (Ret.) (USNA, 1930)
   Wrote warm letter to Lee in the spring of 1968 after he was selected for flag rank, 472-473

Masterton, Captain Paul, USN (USNA, 1933)
   As commanding officer of the Intrepid (CVA-11) in the late 1950s, praised for his relationship with squadron commanders, 483, 666-667, 670

Matthews, Rear Admiral H. Spencer, USN (Ret.)
   Started his naval career with Lee as an aviation mechanic in the early 1940s, 624, 717; after retirement, worked for a Florida congressman who wanted to kill Lee's favorite aircraft program, the F-18, 717-718

McClellan, Rear Admiral Thomas R., USN (USNA, 1943)
   Lee was a strong supporter of McClellan's becoming Commander Naval Air Systems Command in the early 1970s, 522-523; relationship with Chief of Naval Material, Admiral Isaac Kidd, 539; did great job of turning over NASC to Lee in 1973, 539-540

McDonnell Douglas
   Along with Northrop, successfully competed for the F-17, which became the F-18, contract in the mid-1970s, 557-560; Lee worked as a consultant for a short time after retiring from the Navy in 1976 after he learned that the F-18 program was in trouble, 718-721

McNamara, Robert S.
   As Secretary of Defense in the 1960s, sought to abolish the various Navy bureaus and to assume the authority of the bureau chiefs, 354-355; role in the F-111 debacle in the 1960s, 358-360; visited the Enterprise (CVAN-65) with President Lyndon Johnson in November 1967, 384, 389; assessed by Lee, 389, 391-392; dispelled myth of a missile gap with the Soviet Union, 642

Mediterranean Sea
   Attack Squadron 46 did low-level atomic weapons missions in the Mediterranean region during a 1959 deployment, 669-670

Mehle, Rear Admiral Roger W., USN   (USNA, 1937)
   Fired as Commander Task Force 77/Commander Carrier Division Five in 1967, 373

Meyer, General John C., USAF
   As Commander in the Chief of the Strategic Air Command in the early 1970s, sympathetic to the Navy's concern over its limited role in the Joint Strategic Target Planning Staff, 529-530, 533

Miami (Florida) Naval Air Station
   Lee's fond recollections of duty as an aviation mechanic in Miami in the early 1940s, 620-626

Michaelis, Admiral Frederick H., USN   (USNA, 1940)
   Assessed as Chief of Naval Material in the mid-1970s, 583

Midway, USS (CVE-63)
   Lee's first experience at sea was in this jeep carrier on his way out to Hawaii in 1944, 626

Miller, Vice Admiral Gerald E., USN   (USNA, 1942)
   Loyalty to Vice Admiral Thomas Connolly, 360, 503, 694, 701; relationship with CNO Admiral Elmo Zumwalt, 526, 539, 701-702; considered for CNO in the mid-1970s, 584; assessed by Lee, 685

Mini, Lieutenant Commander James H., USN   (USNA, 1935)
   Lee modeled his leadership style on Mini, commander of Bombing Squadron 15 during World War II, 655, 667

Missiles
   Sidewinder invented by the technical director of the Naval Ordnance Test Station, Inyokern, in the early 1950s, 353; North Vietnam's effective use of surface-to-air missiles during the Vietnam War, 417; Sidewinder sent to Israel in the fall of 1973 during the Yom Kippur War, 565, 607; Lee feels that missile programs are among the most difficult to bring to a successful conclusion, 591-592; difficulties with the Harpoon program in the mid-1970s, 592-594; development of the long-range Tomahawk cruise missile in the mid-1970s, 593-594

Mobley, Commander Joseph S., USN (USNA, 1966)
   Enterprise (CVAN-65) A-6 pilot, shot down in June 1968 and taken prisoner by the Vietnamese, met Lee 18 years later as executive officer of the America (CV-66), 415-416

Moorer, Admiral Thomas H., USN (USNA, 1933)
   As Chairman of the Joint Chiefs of Staff in the early 1970s, chose not to promote Vice Admiral Thomas Connolly to full admiral, 360; as CNO in November 1967, involvement in President Lyndon Johnson's visit to the Enterprise (CVAN-65), 383-385, 389, 709; as CNO, sometimes circumvented the legal chain of command, 397-399; relations with Navy Secretary John Chafee, 507-508, 519, 696, 709; as JCS chairman, didn't give Lee much support in his effort to beef up the Navy's role in strategic target planning, 529

Morse, Dr. Robert W.
   Served as Assistant Secretary of the Navy (Research and Development) in the 1960s, 352-354, 359

Myers, Charles E., Jr.
   High-ranking Defense Department official who opposed the Navy's desire for a dual-purpose aircraft in the mid-1970s, 556-557

Nagasaki, Japan
   Commander Carrier Division 15 Rear Admiral Richard Ruble and Lee toured Nagasaki by air in 1950 to view damage wrought by the atomic bomb, 638-640

Naval Air Stations
   Lee's fond recollections of duty as an aviation mechanic at Miami, Florida, NAS in the early 1940s, 620-626; closing of Quonset Point, Rhode Island, NAS in the early 1970s, 610, 697-698

Naval Air Systems Command
   Lee thought it was a mistake to reorganize and separate the aeronautics and ordnance functions of the Bureau of Naval Weapons in the mid-1960s, 355-358; Lee served as assistant commander for logistics and fleet support, 1969-70, 497-505; Lee supported Rear Admiral Thomas

McClellan to head this organization in the early 1970s, 522-523; McClellan's turnover to Lee in 1973, 539-540; general discussion of organization and personnel, 540-543, 605-606; Lee's duties as commander, 543-553, 565-566, 586, 589-591, 598; commander's billet upgraded to three-star rank in 1973, 568; project manager signed a large, unjustified contract with a Florida university to study large-scale integrated circuits, 569-572; success with missile programs, 591-594; did its own electronics work, 603-604; Vice Admiral Thomas Connolly tried to run Naval Air Systems Command along with his own responsibilities as OP-05 in the late 1960s and early 1970s, 598, 694; after retirement, Connolly tried to influence Lee on behalf of his defense contractor employer, but Lee cut him off, 693-695

Naval Aviation
The Navy resisted adapting the F-111 for aircraft carrier use in the 1960s, 358-360; Lee commanded the nuclear-powered *Enterprise* (CVAN-65) from 1967 to 1969, during two Vietnam War deployments, the *Pueblo* (AGER-2) incident, a port visit to Japan, and a major flight deck fire, 371-495, 687-691; A-6 attacks against North Vietnam in 1968, 415-416; importance of a pilot learning to live with the inevitable danger and loss of life, 430-432; competition in the early 1970s that led eventually to the F/A-18 Hornet, 531, 553-560, 563-565, 601; Lee's impetus to become a pilot in the early 1940s, 624-625, 710-711

Naval Electronic Systems Command
Mission in the mid-1970s, 603-604

Naval Forces Japan
Commander Naval Forces Japan, Rear Admiral Frank Johnson, was in charge of the *Pueblo* (AGER-2) at the time of her capture in January 1968, 409-410

Naval Material Command
Lee doesn't think this organization did anything in the mid-1970s to contribute to the mission of the Naval Air Systems Command and should have been abolished, 544, 580-581, 583

Naval Ordnance Systems Command
Lee thought it was a mistake to reorganize and separate the ordnance and aeronautics functions of the Bureau of Naval Weapons in the mid-1960s, 355-358

Naval Ordnance Test Station, China Lake, California
The director of China Lake in the mid-1960s fought hard to have the research laboratories taken away from individual bureaus and centralized, 353-354

Naval Weapons, Bureau of (BuWeps)
See Bureau of Naval Weapons

Navigation
> High-level versus low-level navigation aircraft froma the USS Intrepid (CVA-11) in the late 1950s, 671-672

Navy Department
> Material bureaus were divested of their research laboratories in the mid-1960s, 352-354; discussion of key department officials in the early 1970s, 505-506

Newport News Shipbuilding and Dry Dock
> Rude treatment of this company's representative by Vice Admiral Hyman Rickover during the sea trials of the Ray (SSN-653) in early 1967, 366-367

News Media
> Coverage of President Lyndon Johnson's November 1967 visit to the Enterprise (CVAN-65), 386-387; Japanese coverage of the visit of the Enterprise to Sasebo in January 1968, 402-404; the Enterprise had a full-time public affairs officer to deal with the media, 442-446; covered Enterprise's difficulties with clogged condensers off Ford Island in March 1969, 471; called by a New Jersey congressman in the mid-1970s to question Lee's proposal to cut back Navy use of the Lakehurst Naval Air Engineer Center, 574

Nitze, Paul H.
> As Secretary of the Navy in the mid-1960s, put much faith in his executive assistant, Captain Elmo Zumwalt, 705-706

North Korea
> See Korea, North

North Vietnam
> See Vietnam, North

Northrop Aircraft
> Won contract along with McDonnell Douglas for a dual-purpose plane that started out as the F-17, but was later designated F-18 by the Navy, 531, 554-560

Nuclear Power
> Lee took refresher nuclear training prior to assuming command of the Enterprise (CVAN-65) in 1967, 361, 364, 368; the Enterprise encountered nuclear protesters during visit to Japan in early 1968, 402-405, 686-687; the Enterprise's generators were tested while she was dry-docked at Bremerton in the summer of 1968, 453; Enterprise had a problem with a high chlorine count in a steam generator, 454, 492-494

Nuclear Weapons
> The Enterprise (CVAN-65) kept on board a sizable group of nuclear weapons in the late 1960s, 447-449; Rear Admiral Richard Ruble and Lee toured the Nagasaki area by air in 1950 to view the bomb damage, 638-640; Lee attended a

weapons employment course in the summer of 1953, 660-664; most planes that could carry atomic weapons were given that mission in the late 1950s, 669

OP-05
See Deputy Chief of Naval Operations (Air Warfare)

Office of Program Appraisal
Duty as director of OPA in the early 1970s gave Lee an insider's view of what was going on in the Navy, 506; handled the program objectives memorandum, 510; makeup of staff, 510; advised the Secretary of the Navy of the quality of the F-14 program, 512-515, 517-518; coordinated with the CNO's office to troubleshoot conflicts, 516

Onstott, Commander Jacob, USN
Assessed as air group commander in the early 1950s, 648-649

Ordnance, Bureau of
See Bureau of Ordnance

P-3 Orion
When it was discovered in the mid-1970s that defective O-rings caused frequent fuel controls changes, the rings were inexpensively fixed, 547-548; Lee's assessment of this plane, 605

Packard, David
As Deputy Secretary of Defense in the early 1970s, advised Secretary John Chafee to settle with the Grumman Corporation before they went bankrupt with the F-14 program, 513, 518

Pahlavi, Mohammed Reza
The Shah of Iran was angered during a transaction with Grumman to buy F-14s in the mid-1970s when he learned that an agent had been used (even though the agent was his brother-in-law), 575-576, 580

Patuxent River (Maryland) Naval Air Test Center
Naval Air Systems Command study group came to the conclusion in the mid-1970s that test facilities should be consolidated at Patuxent, 572-575

Pearl Harbor Naval Shipyard
Repairs to the Enterprise (CVAN-65) after a January 1969 fire were completed in six weeks by working around the clock, 468; the Enterprise ran aground off Ford Island in early 1969, 468-471

Pearson, Drew
    Column mentioning President Lyndon Johnson's November 1967 visit to the Enterprise (CVAN-65) took liberties with actual events, 386

Peck, Commander Paul A., USN
    As air wing commander on the Enterprise (CVAN-65) in the late 1960s, 394, 483-484, 686

Peet, Vice Admiral Raymond E., USN (USNA, 1943)
    As Deputy Assistant Secretary of Defense (Security Affairs) in the mid-1970s, relations with CNO Elmo Zumwalt, 597

Personnel
    High quality of personnel in the carrier Enterprise (CVAN-65) and her air wing in the late 1960s, 485-486; Vice Admiral Hyman Rickover tried unsuccessfully in the early 1970s to keep a junior officer from leaving the service early, 508-509

Petersen, Vice Admiral Forrest S., USN (USNA, 1945)
    Lee's turnover of the Enterprise (CVAN-65) to Petersen in 1969, 375, 477; as Deputy Chief of Naval Operations (Air) in the mid-1970s, 587, 598-599; supported Lee's position that the thrust-augmented wing airplane was not practical, 612-613; supported the F-18 program, 718-720

Philippines
    The Enterprise (CVAN-65) used Olongapo and Subic Bay for liberty ports in 1968, 419, 422, 435

Philippine Sea, USS (CV-47)
    Lee's favorable recollections of this carrier during the Korean War, 653

PIRAZ
    See Positive Identification Radar Advisory Zone

Planning
    Role of aerial reconnaissance photos in helping Air Group Six plan for possible strikes against Cuba in late 1962, 677-683

Plucking Boards
    See Selection Boards

Positive Identification Radar Advisory Zone
    Enterprise (CVAN-65) air group worked with the PIRAZ ships during raids on North Vietnam in the late 1960s, 691

Potter, David S.
  As Under Secretary of the Navy in the mid-1970s, called Commander Sea Systems Command Lee to find out about an unauthorized contract with a Florida university to do research on integrated circuits, 569-572; called Lee in on a weekend to put together paperwork for a congressional appearance, 581-582

Pratt & Whitney
  Lee sat in on the procurement selection board in 1969 that chose this company to build F-14 and F-15

Price, Ensign Allen B., USN
  Brash young pilot in Attack Squadron 115 in the early 1950s eventually was killed while showing off in a plane, 654-655

Program Appraisal, Office of
  See Office of Program Appraisal

Promotion of Officers
  Lee selected for rear admiral in the spring of 1968, 471-472; Lee feels the Navy's selection process is as good as it can be in a large organization, 534-537; parochialism of submariners on selection board in the early 1970s, 707-708

Pueblo, USS (AGER-2)
  The Enterprise (CVAN-65) received the Pueblo's distress signal on 23 January 1968, but was not in immediate position to lend assistance, 407-411; Secretary of the Navy John Chafee's decision in 1969 not to impose further discipline on the crew, 520, 704

Puget Sound Naval Shipyard, Bremerton, Washington
  Did overhaul and repair work on the carrier Enterprise (CVAN-65) in the summer of 1968, 452-453

Quonset Point (Rhode Island) Naval Air Station
  Closed in the mid-1970s, 610; CNO Elmo Zumwalt's decision to close this facility put Navy Secretary John Chafee in an awkward position within his home state, 697-698

RA-5C Vigilante
  Unfavorable assessment of this plane from the late 1960s, 476, 688; used for reconnaissance during the Vietnam War, 687-688

RF-8 Crusader
  Provided excellent photographic intelligence on Cuba in 1962, 677, 682

Radar
  Various systems on board the carrier Enterprise (CVAN-65) in the late 1960s included phased-array antennas, 690-691

Ray, USS (SSN-653)
   Lee had an uncomfortable time accompanying Vice Admiral Hyman Rickover on the sea trials of this submarine in early 1967, 365-367

Readdy, Captain Francis J., USN (USNA, 1947)
   Capable aeronautical engineering duty officer who served in Naval Air Systems Command in the early 1970s but did not make flag rank because of a family problem, 546

Readiness Improvement Status Evaluation (RISE)
   Using data compiled on maintenance of aircraft, the Naval Air Systems Command developed this system in the mid-1970s that was invaluable in judging reliability, 546-548, 601

Reconnaissance
   Excellent photographic intelligence provided to Carrier Air Group Six during the 1962 Cuban Missile Crisis, 677-683; Enterprise (CVAN-65) planes gathered intelligence photos during the Vietnam War, 687-688

Religion
   Chaplains made an important contribution in the carrier Enterprise (CVAN-65) in the late 1960s, 439-440

Replenishment at Sea
   The carrier Enterprise (CVAN-65) frequently replenished at night during the Vietnam War, 423-426

Research and Development
   In the mid-1960s, the Navy's research laboratories were separated from a direct working relationship with the material bureaus they supported, 352-353; in the mid-1970s, a Naval Air Systems Command project manager signed a large, unjustified contract with a Florida university to study large-scale integrated circuits, 569-572; the Strategic Defense Initiative of the 1980s calls for a formidable R&D effort

Rickover, Vice Admiral Hyman G., USN (USNA, 1922)
   Personality traits, 362-363, 366-367, 434; invited Lee to join him on the sea trials of the Ray (SSN-653) in March of 1967, 364-367; discussion of his interview style, 369-370; miffed that Lee didn't spend his entire two months as the prospective skipper of the Enterprise (CVAN-65) on board the carrier, 371-372; used information on the speed of Soviet submarines to justify funding a new class of U.S. subs in the late 1960s, 395-397; had a senator put into the Congressional Record a favorable article about Lee and the Enterprise in mid-1968, 445; rift with Lee over minor problem with a steam generator in the Enterprise in January 1969, 453-454, 492-494; inflexible in the case of a lieutenant who wanted out of the nuclear program two months early so he could attend graduate school, 508-509

RISE
   See Readiness Improvement Status Evaluation

Robertson, Captain Horace B., Jr., USN (USNA, 1946)
   As legal counsel to the Chief of Naval Operations in the early 1970s, 596; as counsel to Secretary of the Navy John Chafee in 1969, 704

Rockets
   The accidental lighting of a Zuni rocket attached to a plane on deck was the cause of a terrible explosion and fire in the Enterprise (CVAN-65) in January 1969, 455-460, 462-463

Ruble, Rear Admiral Richard W., USN (USNA, 1923)
   Relations with the news media as Commander Carrier Division 15 in the early 1950s, 444; reaction to Inchon landings in 1950, 637; toured Nagasaki by air in 1950 to view atomic bomb damage, 638-639; relationship with his chief of staff, Captain Henry Dietrich, 646-647

S-3 Viking
   Lee's evaluation of this plane from the mid-1970s, 605-606

SBC Helldiver
   Lee repaired these planes at Miami in 1941-42, 621-623

SB2C Helldiver
   Landing characteristics, 628-630; rear seat gunners, 630-632

Safety
   During the Korean War, Ensign A. B. Price was flathatting in an AD Skyraider and should have been grounded, because he later killed himself in an aircraft accident, 654-655

Sands, Lieutenant Commander Jack, USN
   Lee's recollections of Sands as executive officer of Attack Squadron 115 in the early 1950s, 654

Sasebo, Japan
   The Enterprise (CVAN-65) visited this city in January 1968, 398-406; protesters during the Enterprise's visit, 402-405, 686-687

Schlesinger, James R.
   Defense Secretary Schlesinger allowed the Air Force to reveal the winner in a contract competition while the Navy was considering the same two planes, 558, 564; role in choosing the CNO in the mid-1970s, 584-585; support for Vice Admiral Ray Peet, 597

Sea Control Ship
  Lee's assessment of this concept espoused by CNO Admiral Elmo Zumwalt in the early 1970s, 614

Secret Service
  Precautions in connection with President Lyndon Johnson's visit to the carrier Enterprise (CVAN-65) in November 1967, 389-390

Selection Boards
  Lee selected for rear admiral in the spring of 1968, 471-472; Lee feels the Navy's selection process is as good as it can be in a large organization, 534-537; Lee requested two flag officers for duty in the Naval Air Systems Command after he sat on their selection boards, 541; plucking boards were necessary to thin out flag quotas, 534, 566-568; parochialism of submariners on selection board in the early 1970s, 707-708

Seventh Fleet
  Rear Admiral Roger Mehle was replaced by Rear Admiral Ralph Cousins as Commander Task Force 77 in 1967, 373-374; a Seventh Fleet task force gathered off North Korea following the seizure of the USS Pueblo in January 1968, 410-411; the Seventh Fleet put on a show of force off Korea following the shooting down of an intelligence plane in April 1969, 474; relationship of fleet commander to aircraft carriers during Vietnam air war, 480; Seventh Fleet liaison officer coordinated with the Air Force on air strikes against South Vietnam in the late 1960s, 689-690

Seymour, Vice Admiral Ernest R., USN (USNA, 1953)
  As executive officer of an A-4 squadron in the Enterprise (CVAN-65) in the late 1960s, moved up to be commanding officer when his predecessor was shot down, 493-494; as Commander Naval Air Systems Command in the late 1970s, supported Lee's suggestions about firefighting improvements, 484

Shah of Iran
  See Pahlavi, Mohammed Reza

Shear, Admiral Harold E., USN (USNA, 1942)
  VCNO Shear tried unsuccessfully to convince Lee to remain another year as Commander Naval Air Systems Command in 1976, 586-587

Shinn, Rear Admiral Allen M., USN (Ret.) (USNA, 1932)
  Headed study group gathered by Commander Naval Air Systems Command Lee in the mid-1970s that decided that naval air test facilities should be consolidated at Patuxent River Naval Air Test Center in Maryland, 572-575

Ship Handling
Characteristics of the Alamo (LSD-33), 392; characteristics of the Enterprise (CVAN-65), 392-393; methods used when the Enterprise encountered a storm en route to Japan in January 1968, 400-402; during underway replenishments by the Enterprise, 424-426

Shipyards
A Newport News Shipbuilding and Dry Dock representative was treated rudely by Vice Admiral Hyman Rickover during the sea trials of the submarine Ray (SSN-653) in early 1967, 366-367; the Enterprise (CVAN-65) went to Hunters Point Naval Shipyard for seven weeks of modifications and repair work in the summer of 1967, 376-377; Puget Sound Naval Shipyard did overhaul and repair work on the carrier Enterprise (CVAN-65) in the summer of 1968, 452-453; the Pearl Harbor Naval Shipyard worked quickly to repair the Enterprise (CVAN-65) following her flight deck fire in 1969, 468; the Enterprise ran aground off Ford Island in early 1969, 468-471

Sidewinder Missile
Invented by the technical director of the Naval Ordnance Test Station, Inyokern, in the early 1950s, 353; sent to Israel in the fall of 1973 during the Yom Kippur War, 565, 607

Single Integrated Operational Plan (SIOP)
Lee was critical that this plan continued to ignore the need for reserves, 641

Smith, Captain Allen, Jr., USN (USNA, 1927)
Low-key, capable commanding officer of the carrier Philippine Sea (CV-47) during the Korean War, 653

Snead, Rear Admiral Leonard A., USN (USNA, 1947)
Replaced as project manager for the F-14 in the mid-1970s after feuding with a civilian chief assistant over a woman, 540, 595-596; vetoed for position in Iran in the mid-1970s, 597

South Korea
See Korea, South

South Vietnam
See Vietnam, South

Soviet Navy
Monitoring communications off the coast of San Francisco in late 1960s, 395; when it was established that a Soviet submarine was tailing the Enterprise (CVAN-65) off the West Coast in 1967, the carrier was directed to speed up to get an idea of how fast the sub could go, 395-397; Soviet vessels in the Sea of Japan immediately following

the capture of the Pueblo (AGER-2) in January 1968, 411; Soviet vessels in the Sea of Japan after the North Koreans shot down a U.S. EC-121 in April 1969, 474

Soviet Union
Lee was impressed by U.S. capabilities at Soviet surveillance in the early 1970s, 531-532; Lee thinks the Soviets built up so many weapons in response to an irrational buildup by the United States, 641-643; Lee's thoughts on the feasibility of the Strategic Defense Initiative for combating Soviet missiles, 643-645; U.S. Navy attack squadron in the Mediterranean in the late 1950s had targets in the Soviet Union, 669

Spangenberg, George
Used as a consultant by the Naval Air Systems Command in the mid-1970s, 616-617, 710

Stewart, Lieutenant Commander Marlar E., USN
Discussion of what made him such an outstanding aviator, 665-666

Strategic Air Command (SAC)
Continued to dominate the Joint Strategic Target Planning Staff until the early 1970s, 528-530, 640; called for too many weapons in strategic planning, 641

Strategic Defense Initiative (SDI)
Lee's view of this 1980s program advanced by the Reagan administration, 643-645

Submarines
Lee had an uncomfortable time accompanying Vice Admiral Hyman Rickover on the sea trials of the Ray (SSN-653) in early 1967, 365-367; the Enterprise (CVAN-65) conducted a covert test in 1968 to determine how fast a Soviet submarine that was following her could go, 395-397; Vice Admiral Hyman Rickover used information gained on the projected speed of Soviet submarines as justification for funding the Los Angeles (SSN-688) class, 396-397; Lee's attitude about the submarine threat to the Enterprise during the Vietnam War, 429-430

Symington, Stuart
Senator Symington was furious to learn in the mid-1970s that the Grumman Corporation was using money borrowed from the Navy to make a big profit in the overnight market, 552

Systems Analysis
The Navy's reluctance to accept this discipline in the early 1970s, 510-512

Tactics
    Patterns varied for sending A-6 strikes against North Vietnam in 1968, 415-416; plan for possible carrier air strikes against Cuba in late 1962, 679-680

Task Force 77
    Rear Admiral Roger Mehle was replaced by Rear Admiral Ralph Cousins as CTF 77 in 1967, 373-374; relationship of task force commander to aircraft carriers during Vietnam air war, 480-481

Thach, Admiral John S., USN (USNA, 1927)
    Relations with the media while commanding an aircraft carrier during the Korean War, 444

Tierney, Rear Admiral John M., USN (USNA, 1946)
    As director of the General Planning and Programming Division in the CNO's office in the early 1970s, coordinated with Lee to make sure upcoming programs would meet with the Secretary of the Navy's approval, 516-517

Tomahawk
    Development of this long-range cruise missile in the mid-1970s, 593-594

Townsend, Vice Admiral Robert L., USN (Ret.) (USNA, 1934)
    Credited with never trading on his status as a retired flag officer when he went to work for Grumman in the 1970s, 579

Train, Captain Harry D., USN (USNA, 1949)
    Lee's assessment of Train from brief service together, 708-709

Training
    Refresher course in nuclear power for Lee before taking command of the Enterprise (CVAN-65) in 1967, 364, 368; refresher training at San Diego for the crew of the Enterprise (CVAN-65) in 1967, 378-380; Lee instituted a program to train Enterprise junior officers to be OODs, 426-429; value of General Line School in the late 1940s, 632-633, 635; Lee attended a nuclear weapons employment course in the summer of 1953, 660-664

Turner, Vice Admiral Frederick C., USN
    As Deputy Chief of Naval Operations (Air Warfare) in the mid-1970s, did not support the F-18 program, 719-721

Turner, Captain Stansfield, USN (USNA, 1947)
    Turner's probable role in getting Vice Admiral Elmo Zumwalt selected as Chief of Naval Operations in 1970, 506-507, 695-696; Turner has a large ego, 696

Tyler, Patrick
    Lee cooperated with Tyler on his 1986 book that mentions an incident when the Enterprise (CVAN-65) engaged a Soviet submarine in an unofficial race to see how fast she could go, 396-397, 443-444, 446

Typhoons
    The Enterprise (CVAN-65) weathered a typhoon on the way to Japan in early 1968, 400-402

U-2
    Reconnaissance plane that provided excellent photographic intelligence on Cuba in 1962, 677, 683

Underway Replenishment
    The carrier Enterprise (CVAN-65) frequently replenished at night during the Vietnam War, 423-426

Uniforms--Naval
    Lee approved of CNO Admiral Elmo Zumwalt's changes to Navy enlisted uniforms in the early 1970s, which were rescinded under his successor, 699-700

VFAX
    The Navy wanted to build an aircraft that could be used for both attack and fighter roles in the mid-1970s, 554-557, 563-564

Vertical or Short Takeoff and Landing Aircraft
    CNO candidate Admiral James Holloway incorporated V/STOL into a paper he wrote in the mid-1970s outlining his vision of the Navy of the future, 584, 611, 614; thrust-augmented wing airplane, a popular concept in early 1970s, was not practical, 611-613; the British built the only really successful V/STOL plane, the Harrier, 613-614; difficulties with concept, 614-615

Vietnam, North
    Tactics used for air strikes against Hanoi in 1968, 415-416

Vietnam, South
    The U.S. Navy provided air support of friendly ground troops in South Vietnam in the late 1960s, 688-690

Vietnam War
    Defense Secretary Robert McNamara and President Lyndon Johnson's positions on the war in the late 1960s, 391-392; Commander Carrier Division One, Rear Admiral John Weinel, kept Enterprise (CVAN-65) skipper Lee apprised of what was going on in the war in the late 1960s, 414; air operations in the late 1960s, 415-422, 429-431, 688-689; anti-war protest in the San Francisco area, 441; quality of Navy pilots during the war, 485-486; available

intelligence, 489-490, 687-688; input from Washington dictating air strikes, 678-679; the U.S. Navy provided air support of friendly ground troops in South Vietnam in the late 1960s, 688-690

Virginia
   Discussion of Logon Farm, the Lees' home in Albemarle County, 588-589, 712-715

V/STOL
   See Vertical or Short Takeoff and Landing Aircraft

Walker, Rear Admiral Thomas J., III, USN (USNA, 1939)
   As Commander Naval Air Systems Command from 1969 to 1971, not interested in Lee's ideas of improving maintainability and reliability of airplanes, 498, 524

Warner, John
   Concerned with speech making as Under Secretary and Secretary of the Navy in the early 1970s, 505; CNO Admiral Elmo Zumwalt asked Lee for his opinion of Warner, 525; choice for CNO in the mid-1970s, 583-584; offhand way of letting Lee know he had been considered as a candidate for CNO, 584-586

Weather
   Methods of ship handling used when the carrier Enterprise (CVAN-65) encountered a storm en route to Japan in January 1968, 400-401

Weinel, Rear Admiral John P., USN (USNA, 1939)
   As Commander Carrier Division One in the late 1960s, Weinel was an unusually effective tactical commander, 413-415, 430, 482

Weisner, Admiral Maurice F., USN (USNA, 1941)
   CNO Admiral Elmo Zumwalt asked Lee's opinion of Weisner as Deputy Chief of Naval Operations (Air) in the early 1970s, 525, 705; Lee's assessment of Weisner, 701, 705

Wilcox, Harvey
   Favorable assessment as head lawyer in the procurement office of Naval Air Systems Command in the mid-1970s, 541, 582, 589

Wilson, George C.
   Assessment of Lee by Wilson, a newsman with The Washington Post, 443-444

Yom Kippur War
   The United States sent aircraft and missiles to Israel in the fall of 1973, 565

Zech, Captain Lando W., Jr., USN (USNA, 1945)
   Circumstances surrounding his selection for flag rank in the early 1970s, 707-708

Zumwalt, Admiral Elmo R., Jr., USN (USNA, 1943)
   As CNO in the early 1970s, chose not to promote Vice Admiral Thomas Connolly to full admiral, 360; Lee feels there were worse discipline problems during the Zumwalt years than before, 437; speculation on his selection as CNO, 506-508, 695-696; Lee feels Navy Secretary John Chafee should have kept greater control over Zumwalt, 520-521, 697-699; Lee's relationship with Zumwalt, 525-526; relationship with Vice Admiral Gerald Miller, 526, 539, 701-702; decided to make the air and ship systems commands three-star posts, 568; relations with Vice Admiral Ray Peet, 597; spent a small fortune on the initial development of an aircraft concept that was impractical, 611-613; Lee's assessment of Zumwalt's sea control ship concept, 614; Lee's thoughts on Zumwalt changes, 699-701; relationship with Admiral Isaac Kidd, 702-703; assessed by Lee, 703; given free rein as executive assistant to Navy Secretary Paul Nitze, 705-706

Zuni
   The accidental lighting of a Zuni rocket attached to a plane on deck was the cause of a terrible explosion and fire in the *Enterprise* (CVAN-65) in January 1969, 455-460, 462-463

www.ingramcontent.com/pod-product-compliance
Lightning Source LLC
Chambersburg PA
CBHW082149070526
44585CB00020B/2139